# Team Depot

# Team Depot

## A Warehouse of Over 585 Tools to Reassess, Rejuvenate, and Rehabilitate Your Team

**GLENN PARKER**

JOSSEY-BASS/PFEIFFER
A Wiley Company
www.pfeiffer.com

# JOSSEY-BASS/PFEIFFER

A Wiley Company
989 Market Street
San Francisco, CA 94103-1741
415.433.1740; Fax 415.433.0499
800.274.4434; Fax 800.569.0443

www.pfeiffer.com

Jossey-Bass/Pfeiffer is a registered trademark of John Wiley & Sons, Inc.

ISBN:0-7879-6218-X

Library of Congress Cataloging-in-Publication Data
Parker, Glenn M.
  Team depot: a warehouse of over 585 tools to reassess,
rejuvenate, and rehabilitate your team / Glenn Parker.
       p. cm.
Includes bibliographical references and index.
  ISBN 0-7879-6218-X (alk. paper)
  1. Teams in the workplace. 2. Reengineering (Management)
I. Title.
  HD66 .P3455 2002
  658.4'02—dc21

2001006625

Copyright page continued on page 460.

Printed in the United States of America

We at Jossey-Bass strive to use the most environmentally sensitive paper stocks available to us. Our publications are printed on acid-free recycled stock whenever possible, and our paper always meets or exceeds minimum GPO and EPA requirements.

Acquiring Editor: Josh Blatter
Director of Development: Kathleen Dolan Davies
Senior Production Editor: Dawn Kilgore
Editor: Rebecca Taff

Manufacturing Manager: Becky Carreño
Interior Design: Bruce Lundquist
Cover Design: Bruce Lundquist and Chris Wallace

Printing 10  9  8  7  6  5  4  3  2  1

# CONTENTS

# Contents of the CD-ROM: TEAM TOOL SHED

Being Accountable

Choice Role: A Role-Clarification Activity

Communicating About Conflict: Learning Ways to Resolve Conflict

Criteria Grid

Cross-Functional Teams Conflict Survey

Escape from Gilligan's Island: A Consensus-Building Exercise

Free Cash: A Cash Game to Explore Trust

Got Culture? A Team Assessment Tool

How Do You Like Your Recognition? A Self-Assessment

Long and Sweet Norms

Team Culture Survey

Team Development: A Grid Perspective

Team Leader Assessment

Team Meeting Assessment

Team Member Listening Profile

Three-Way Teamwork

 **PREFACE**

**DURING THE PAST YEAR** I both sold an old house and bought a new home. It is not an experience that I recommend for anyone unless you enjoy months of arguing with builders, tough sales negotiations, and living out of boxes. Now, as I reflect on the past months, I see that I learned a great deal about my personal ability to deal with the process of change as well as practical aspects of negotiating my way around my new favorite store, The Home Depot®. This so-called "super" store has become both my second home and the one resource that I can depend on to solve just about any household problem. In case you are reading this book in a part of the world as yet not reached by Home Depot, I should mention that it is a chain of very large retail stores that sell everything for the construction and maintenance of a home—from tiny nails to floor tile to plants and shrubs. While they have neither endorsed the book nor had anything to do with its creation, the concept of a "warehouse" did provide some inspiration for me.

By now you are saying to yourself, "Why should I care about Parker's love affair with a superstore?" I agree. However, spending all that time wandering around those long and tall aisles, I concluded that what team leaders, managers, coaches, and others who are trying to mend a broken team—or at least get it back on track—could use is their own *Team Depot,* a warehouse with a multiplicity of tools designed to help rejuvenate a derailed team.

I wanted to pull together in one place a wide variety of resources on a wide variety of issues that create barriers to successful teamwork. As I created this warehouse, I had in mind the goal of providing a place that has everything you need and many things you don't even know you need, coupled with the personal service of your favorite neighborhood hardware store. Consequently, at the heart of *Team Depot* is a comprehensive service effort that directs you to the aisle that contains the tools you need to fix your team. As in any warehouse, there is the danger that you will spend time wandering around without direction trying to find your way to the needed solutions. To address this legitimate concern, I have provided a brief assessment to help you find your way to the aisles of the *Depot* that contain the solutions that will get your team back on track.

So now you understand how this book came to pass, but then you wonder: "Do we really need another book on teams?" There are already so many books, facilitator guides, videos, and surveys about teamwork. This book is different in two ways:

1. Rather than a concept book or a handbook of team-building exercises, this is a "warehouse" of concepts, exercises, surveys, advice, cases, quotations, and examples. *Team Depot* has it all!

2. Rather than focus on the general aspects of team effectiveness or provide tips to kick off a new team, *Team Depot* provides practical tools for reviving a sick team and sustaining a troubled team through difficult times.

And yes, there are some good books on this subject. Specifically, my colleague, Deborah Harrington-Mackin (1996) and Moran, Musselwhite, and Zenger (1996) have produced quality works on ways to sustain the team process. However, *Team Depot* covers different subjects and provides many more examples and resources for getting teams back on track.

## PURPOSE OF THE BOOK

*Team Depot* provides specific advice and practical tools for people in organizations who are struggling with the frustrations of teams who are facing barriers to success and need help getting back on the road to high performance. This book comes out of and draws on my work with teams across a variety of industries who have "hit the wall" and come to me for assistance to help them refocus and move in the proper direction again.

I call the book a warehouse, but I sometimes use the metaphor of a smorgasbord to describe the concept. As in a smorgasbord, where you have many different types of foods (hot, cold, fish, meat, salads) from which to choose, *Team Depot* provides a variety of solutions from which to select the ones that respond to the needs of your team. And, just as with a smorgasbord where there are foods you never select because they do not appeal to you, there will be *Team Depot* tools that you will not select because they are just not necessary or appropriate for your team. If I have learned anything, it is that one size does not fit all—whether it is one survey, one concept, one exercise, one sample, or one case. There are many ways to rebuild a team, and in this book you will find nearly six hundred ways to rebuild your team. A few of these tools will be just what your team needs.

I wrote the book to serve as a resource for team leaders, coaches, managers, facilitators, and trainers who are looking for tools to help refocus and refresh their:

- Direction and goals;
- Membership mix;
- Role expectations;
- Empowerment dimensions;
- Talent bank;
- Style differences;
- Norms;
- Climate;
- Work plan;
- Accountability;
- Meetings;
- External networks;
- Conflict resolution skills;
- Trust level;
- Communications skills;

- Level of commitment;

- Consensus skills;

- Rewards program;

- Assessment process; and/or

- Celebrations.

## AUDIENCE

*Team Depot* provides tools for a varied audience of practitioners:

- *Team leaders* and *team members* who are looking for ways to understand why their teams have stumbled and how they can lead their teams back to success will find numerous assessment instruments, practical advice, and tips that will target the issues that have created barriers;

- *Trainers* will find a wide variety of team-building activities, games, and videos they can use to design and implement programs that target the specific needs of their teams;

- *Managers* and *coaches* who want to know more about the issues that have caused teams in their area to falter will find references to books and articles, explanations of fundamental team concepts, and advice to add to their repertoire of consulting skills; and

- *Facilitators* who are looking for ideas and tools to redirect their teams will find quotations to stimulate a lively discussion, exercises to build team competencies, and scenarios that serve as learning vehicles.

## OVERVIEW OF THE CONTENTS

*Team Depot* begins with a stop at "customer service" for an orientation to the warehouse. The orientation consists of a directional assessment, "Lost in Team Depot: Finding Your Way to the Right Aisle." This one-hundred-item survey covers the twenty areas in the warehouse. Completing the survey and scoring the results will help guide you to the aisles that contain solutions to the problems faced by your team.

From there we enter the warehouse, where you will find twenty aisles containing twelve different types of tools for getting your team back on track.

## TEAM DEPOT AISLES

Each of the twenty aisles represents a key area for team effectiveness and, more specifically, for getting a derailed team back on the right track again.

*Aisle 1: Revisit Your Team Goals.* Usually the best place to start with an effort to get your team back on track is with vision, mission, goals, and objectives.

*Aisle 2: Refresh the People Mix.* Sometimes you just have to change the people. Here you will find ways to get the right mix of people on your team, how to change the mix, and how to deal with the inevitable churn of team membership.

*Aisle 3: Redefine Everyone's Role.* Role ambiguity, role conflict, and just plain confusion are addressed in this section. Here you will find tools to clarify expectations as a means of reducing conflict, increasing productivity, and eliminating role disputes that can bring a team down.

*Aisle 4: Reexamine the Team's Empowerment Charter.* Authority is a tricky issue for a team. In this area you can locate tools for clarifying the authority of the sponsor, manager, team leader, and the team.

*Aisle 5: Refurbish the Team's Talent Bank.* Your mission may have changed and, therefore, you may need different competencies to do the job. Go to this section of the warehouse to find ways to ensure the talent on your team is ready for the challenges you face.

*Aisle 6: Reconsider Style Differences.* In this aisle you will find tools to nurture and exploit the value of style differences and ensure your team is making best use of the style strengths of the members.

*Aisle 7: Reestablish Ground Rules.* Get your norms updated to address the current realities with exercises, samples, and other tools found in this area of the *Depot*.

*Aisle 8: Re-Create a Relaxed Climate.* Assessment tools, examples, and ideas on how to reestablish and maintain an informal, relaxed environment are the focal points of this section.

*Aisle 9: Reconstitute the Work Plan.* Various tools for preparing a project plan, tracking results, and getting back on plan are located in this aisle.

*Aisle 10: Refocus on Accountability.* One reason your team may be underperforming is that members do not feel accountable for results. Here you will find ways to track results and get the team back on plan and emphasizing performance.

*Aisle 11: Rejuvenate Team Meetings.* Meetings, the necessary evil. One clear indicator of a derailed team is a poor quality meeting. Go to this aisle for many ideas for making your team meetings satisfying and productive.

*Aisle 12: Rehabilitate External Networks.* This aisle focuses on the importance of and techniques for rebuilding relationships with key stakeholders inside and outside of the organization.

*Aisle 13: Reduce Conflict Successfully.* Many exercises and other tools to help team members resolve interpersonal conflicts that are impeding progress are available in this area of the warehouse.

*Aisle 14: Rebuild a Climate of Trust.* If you find that lack of trust is stalling your team, go to this aisle for ways to reconstitute trusting relationships among members and between your team and others in the organization.

*Aisle 15: Resuscitate Failing Communications.* In this area you can locate tools to redevelop effective communication among members and techniques to improve the quality of communication with stakeholders.

*Aisle 16: Regain Member Commitment.* This aisle offers many ideas and tools for reestablishing the commitment of members to the goals of the team through a process of involvement.

*Aisle 17: Restore Consensus Decision Making.* In this section you will find lots of information about team decision making in general and how to achieve consensus decisions specifically.

*Aisle 18: Reassess Team Performance.* If you want to go beyond the "Lost in Team Depot" Survey go to this aisle, where you will find various methods and examples of team evaluations and how to use the results to put your team back on track.

*Aisle 19: Revamp Team Rewards.* Here you can locate examples and tools to create project team awards and member recognition programs that encourage collaboration and motivate team members to high performance.

*Aisle 20: Revive Team Celebrations.* Ready to have some fun? Go to this aisle for a variety of options for breathing some life back into celebrations of team successes.

## TEAM DEPOT TOOLS

Among the twenty aisles are twelve different types of tools:

1. *Quotes.* More than forty quotations from such diverse sources as Tom Peters, Katherine Hepburn, and Euripides will help you kick off a discussion or focus on a specific team issue. For each quote, I have provided a list of suggested questions designed to stimulate a discussion.

2. *Fundamentals.* Here you will find over one hundred concepts, definitions, and well-established ideas about the essentials of teamwork that provide the underpinning for changing the nature of your team.

3. *Examples and Samples.* Learn from some fifty examples of how other teams and organizations have solved the same issues you are facing.

4. *Scenarios and Cases.* I've shared over fifty actual stories drawn from my experience working with teams and organizations that may help you address some of the same situations.

5. *Exercises, Activities, and Games.* In almost every aisle, you will find several team-building or training exercises that you can put to use with your team. In all, more than one hundred activities are available to you.

6. *Assessments.* Not sure if you have a real problem in one of the areas? Use one of the more than fifty assessment tools from quick "pulse-taking" readings to comprehensive diagnostic surveys.

7. *Advice.* In almost every section, I provide opinions and thoughts that have grown out of my experience or the experiences of other team-building experts.

8. *Quick Hits.* I also provide more specific "how-to" ideas to solve team problems or establish good teamwork practices.

9. *Books and Articles.* There are many excellent books and articles that can help your team redirect its efforts. I reference more than thirty of them across most of the areas in the warehouse.

10. *Videos.* I also mention a few good videos that you can use to educate or motivate your team to address key barriers that are standing in the way of success.

11. *Implements.* More than fifty different tools to help you solve some key team problems in a number of important areas are included.

12. *Web Resources.* In the course of my work, I have come across and used resources from a number of excellent websites. The web continues to be a useful source for ideas on increasing team effectiveness.

## MAXIMIZING THE VALUE OF TEAM DEPOT

Follow these suggestions to maximize the value of *Team Depot*:

1. *Complete Lost in Team Depot.* To minimize your frustration and time spent wondering through the aisles, I suggest you begin your journey with *Lost in Team Depot*. While it takes some time to complete and score the one-hundred-item survey, the results will lead you to the aisles that contain the resources to address the specific issues that will help get your team back on track.

2. *Go Directly to a Specific Aisle.* If you have done an assessment and know the problems faced by your team, go directly to the aisle that contains the tools to address those issues. For example, if you know that your team is experiencing difficulty gaining support for its project from key stakeholders, go to Aisle 12 for tools on how to rehabilitate external networks. However, keep in mind that there is overlap among team issues and that you may find help in other aisles that contain resources designed to rebuild trust, reduce conflict, and improve communication.

3. *Review Your Guide to Team Depot Tool Types.* Here you will find all of the tools in the warehouse categorized by type, such as quotes, exercises, advice, or tips. You may find it easier to locate just the right tool by using this index. For example, let's say you sense that your team needs to reestablish a climate of trust but you are not sure. You want to collect some data using an assessment survey. I suggest that you go to the Assessments section in the Guide and look at the assessment instruments in the trust aisle as well as those in related aisles, such as empowerment, style differences, and climate.

4. *Use the Tips and Questions.* Many of the tools in Team Depot include tips or questions:

 Tips are suggestions for making effective use of the tool or creating a variation to extend the value of the tool. Look for the icons in all of the aisles.

**QUESTION**

Questions—Here I have provided questions to encourage you to explore the tool in greater depth, apply it to your team, or to guide a discussion with team members. Look for these icons throughout the Depot.

5. *Browse the Resource Desk.* I find it helpful to look at a list of books, articles, and other resources. I often find a new (or new to me) resource that will address an issue I am facing. The Team Depot Resource Desk may include the item that will contain the answers you need to get your team moving ahead again.

6. *Wander Around the Tool Shed.* Back in the Shed you will find a CD containing exercises, assessments, and other tools that are "good to go." Spending time in the Shed, you may locate just the right tool for your team that is in just the right format so that you can print and use it tomorrow.

7. *Adapt, Tailor, Customize.* Team Depot tools can be tailored to your work environment with minimal changes, for example, changing "manager" to "director." Other tools may need more extensive customization to bring them in line with your organization, for example, increasing the difficulty of the problems. In any event, the CD-ROM in the back of the book allows you to easily adapt the items in the Tool Shed, and I encourage you to do it.

# TIPS FOR TEAM MECHANICS

In many of the aisles you will find quotes, assessments, cases, and other tools that include questions and general directions for using the tool. These tools, unlike the exercises and activities found in the aisles and the Tool Shed, require some preparation prior to use and facilitation to ensure their successful implementation. Here are some suggestions for turning those general directions and questions into a successful experience.

Some of the team tools, specifically the quotes, examples, scenarios, advice, tips, and some assessments, do not include specific directions for using the tool with your team. While many of you are experienced team mechanics capable of designing ways to effectively use the tool with your team, new mechanics may need some guidance. Therefore, some tips for effective facilitation follow:

1. *Start with a Problem.* Before you start wandering up and down the aisles, make sure you are clear about the problem or issue that is blocking team progress. And make sure the team agrees with your assessment. Never simply use a tool because it looks interesting or fun. You could get hurt, and the team could regress.

2. *Be Clear About Your Purpose.* Decide on the goal or outcome of the session. Your objective should be to get your team back on track.

3. *Develop a Plan.* Take some time to design a session or meeting that incorporates the tool and accomplishes your goal. Make sure you are comfortable with the tool and know how to use it.

4. *Communicate the Goal and Format.* Open the team meeting with a clear statement of the purpose and how you plan to get there. For example, "As you know, the assessment revealed that we do not have a clear vision of the future. Our goal today is to develop a clear statement of purpose for our team. We'll use this quote to kick off our discussion and then move into the development of a draft vision statement."

5. *Keep Focused on the Outcome.* As the discussion proceeds, always keep your end result in mind. Intervene when you see things getting off track. For example, "We're making some good points here, but we need to get back to our goal of coming up with a vision statement."

6. *Use Open-Ended Questions.* Open-ended questions—ones that cannot be answered with a simple "yes" or "no"—are most effective in obtaining the maximum amount of participation. For example, you might try something like, "What do you think this quote means?" or "How does this quote apply to our team?"

7. *Watch the Time.* Make sure you leave enough time to conclude the session effectively. Leave sufficient time to summarize and prepare action items. Try this: "I know we all feel strongly about these issues, but we need to spend some time now summarizing our agreements and deciding on a plan of action."

8. *Summarize.* Always summarize what was learned or decided. Never have a meeting simply end because time was up. You can ask the team to come up with a summary or you can take the lead by saying something like, "It looks like we have agreed to focus our energies on two goals, one, increasing customer satisfaction and two, speeding up the development process."

9. *Next Steps.* Try to leave the session with a look to the future. Help the team identify next steps or ways to use the new learning in the future. As appropriate, obtain commitments from team members to complete action items or implement personal change plans.

10. *Review.* Ask yourself: "How did it go? Was it successful?" You may incorporate feedback from team members in the review process. You can take a few minutes at the end of the meeting to ask two quick questions: (1) "How do you feel about what we accomplished at this meeting?" and (2) "In what ways can we improve our meetings in the future?"

# LOST IN TEAM DEPOT

## Finding Your Way to the Right Aisle

*Process*: Please read each of the following statements in the context of your own team. If you feel that a statement is broadly true about your team, place a check in the checkbox to the left of the statement. If you feel the statement is not broadly true, simply move on to the next statement.

☐  1. We do not have a clear vision of where we are heading as a team.

☐  2. We do not have a current team mission statement or team charter.

☐  3. Our team goals are not always SMART (specific, measurable, attainable, relevant, and time-bound).

☐  4. Our team goals are not related to the organization's goals.

☐  5. We do not know how to prepare an effective problem statement.

☐  6. The membership of our team has not changed much, despite a change in our mission and/or business conditions.

☐  7. We lack a real team spirit.

☐  8. We need a change in our team membership, but it is just not possible to move people onto and off our team.

☐  9. We have some members who are just not happy being on our team.

☐ 10. We don't have a good process for adding new members or saying farewell to old members.

☐ 11. We do not understand the importance of role clarification for team success.

☐ 12. We have not engaged in a role clarification exercise in more than one year.

☐ 13. Many members are unclear about just what is expected of them as members of this team.

☐ 14. We do not effectively employ basic team roles, such as facilitator, scribe, and parking lot attendant.

☐ 15. We have a number of people playing dysfunctional roles (such as dominator or blocker) on our team.

☐ 16. Our team does not clearly understand the meaning of empowerment.

☐ 17. We have not clarified our level of empowerment.

☐ 18. Our management does not provide us with their expectations of the areas in which we have the authority to act.

☐ 19. Most of us just don't feel empowered.

☐ 20. We probably have more authority than we choose to exercise.

☐ 21. We do not have the right mix of technical expertise on our team.

☐ 22. We have not completed a team talent inventory in more than one year.

☐ 23. We do not have the right mix of teamwork skills on our team.

☐ 24. Our mission and/or customers have changed, but our competencies have remained the same.

☐ 25. We do not send people on a regular basis to courses to upgrade their technical and/or teamwork skills.

☐ 26. We are not especially aware of style differences among members of our team.

☐ 27. We do not understand the strengths and weaknesses of various team player styles.

☐ 28. Most of us pretty much have the same team player style.

☐ 29. We have not identified and analyzed our team player styles in more than one year.

☐ 30. We do not appreciate the different style strengths that each team member brings to the team.

☐ 31. We do not have a written set of team norms.

☐ 32. We have team norms, but many of them are counterproductive.

☐ 33. We have norms, but members do not follow them.

☐ 34. Our norms were established by management and/or with little member involvement.

☐ 35. Most of us do not understand or appreciate the value of norms for a team.

☐ 36. The climate on our team is not conducive to successful teamwork.

☐ 37. We do not do anything to improve the overall climate on our team.

☐ 38. We do not recognize the importance of an informal, relaxed climate.

☐ 39. Sometimes our climate is not supportive of open communication and trust.

☐ 40. We have not assessed the climate on our team for more than a year.

☐ 41. We do not have an effective planning process.

☐ 42. Members of our team do not value planning.

☐ 43. We do not know how to prepare a project plan.

☐ 44. We rarely review projects upon their completion.

☐ 45. Members of our team do not feel especially accountable for tasks and projects.

☐ 46. We get a lot of work done, but it may not be the right work.

☐ 47. We have too many project reviews that are a waste of time.

☐ 48. We often re-do work because of lack of clarity about task assignments.

☐ 49. Our team is not sufficiently focused on task completion.

☐ 50. Leadership on our team does not provide support for task completion.

☐ 51. Our meetings are poorly planned.

☐ 52. We rarely have a meeting agenda that is more than just a list of topics.

☐ 53. We do not make effective use of electronic/computer support tools for meetings.

☐ 54. Member behavior at team meetings does not contribute to the success of our meetings.

☐ 55. Our meetings are usually too long.

☐ 56. Relationships with some of our external stakeholders are not effective.

☐ 57. We have not done an assessment of our external relationships in more than a year.

☐ 58. Relationship building with external stakeholders is haphazard at best.

☐ 59. Many members of our team believe building external relationships is not necessary or is a waste of time.

☐ 60. We need help from some key stakeholders, and we're not getting it.

☐ 61. Our typical approach to conflict on our team is to simply deny it or attempt to smooth it over.

☐ 62. We do not have a healthy respect for the value of differences of opinion.

☐ 63. When a conflict arises on our team, we rarely see it as a positive opportunity to engage in serious problem solving.

☐ 64. We do not have norms for dealing with conflict on our team.

☐ 65. We do not have sufficient tools for conflict resolution.

☐ 66. Members do not trust one another to do the right thing in the right way.

☐ 67. Members of our team do not honor their commitments.

☐ 68. Members of our team do not feel free to express their feelings openly because they fear possible negative consequences.

☐ 69. There are hidden agendas and/or "secret plan Bs" on our team.

☐ 70. Other teams do not trust our team.

☐ 71. Members of our team do not effectively share information with each other.

☐ 72. Interpersonal communication among team members is not as effective as it should be.

☐ 73. We are not especially effective at using the tools of active listening.

☐ 74. Our norms concerning communication are ineffective or nonexistent.

☐ 75. Our communication to/from management needs improvement.

☐ 76. Members are no longer truly committed to the goals of the team.

☐ 77. Members do not seem to be committed to each other.

☐ 78. Members are not committed to our team because they are not involved in key decisions.

☐ 79. Members no longer seem committed to meeting the needs of our customers.

☐ 80. Members of the team complain about the team to each other and, at times, to outsiders.

☐ 81. The key decisions on our team are made by the leader with minimal member involvement.

☐ 82. We are not very effective at using the consensus method of making decisions.

☐ 83. We are not clear about when to use or not to use the consensus method for decision making.

☐ 84. We often assume we have a consensus decision just because members do not voice an opinion on the subject.

☐ 85. We do not have a clear set of norms that deal with how we will make team decisions.

☐ 86. We have not completed an assessment of our team in more than a year.

☐ 87. We rarely ask ourselves: "How are we doing?"

☐ 88. We do not have solid measures for assessing our progress.

☐ 89. We do not have the expertise to conduct a team self-assessment.

☐ 90. We do not regularly ask stakeholders, such as management, customers, and support groups, to assess our performance.

☐ 91. We are still using "winner take all" awards such as "employee of the month."

☐ 92. Our team awards do not really encourage collaboration among team members.

☐ 93. We do not make enough use of noncash awards to recognize team members.

☐ 94. We do not do a good job of communicating why a person or a team received an award.

☐ 95. We don't tailor our awards to the person but rather assume "one size fits all."

☐ 96. We do not have lots of little celebrations of team successes.

☐ 97. When we do have a celebratory event, most members are not involved in the planning.

☐ 98. Celebrations are considered a "waste of time and money."

☐ 99. Team events such as a picnic or party are designed to acknowledge a holiday, rather than celebrate a team success.

☐ 100 We don't have fun anymore.

# INTERPRETATION

*Instructions:* The survey has been divided into twenty "aisles," below, each representing a specific topic. If you placed a check next to an item, also check the number on the line after it here. Then total the items in each aisle. Begin your improvement project in the Team Depot aisle with the most checked items. However, do not ignore any aisle with a checked item. As with remodeling a house, refurbishing a team takes some time and effort.

| 1. Goals | 2. People | 3. Roles | 4. Empowerment | 5. Talent |
|----------|-----------|----------|----------------|-----------|
| 1.___ | 6.___ | 11.___ | 16.___ | 21.___ |
| 2.___ | 7.___ | 12.___ | 17.___ | 22.___ |
| 3.___ | 8.___ | 13.___ | 18.___ | 23.___ |
| 4.___ | 9.___ | 14.___ | 19.___ | 24.___ |
| 5.___ | 10.___ | 15.___ | 20.___ | 25.___ |
| TOTALS: ___ | ___ | ___ | ___ | ___ |

| 6. Styles | 7. Norms | 8. Climate | 9. Work Plan | 10. Accountability |
|-----------|----------|------------|--------------|--------------------|
| 26.___ | 31.___ | 36.___ | 41.___ | 46.___ |
| 27.___ | 32.___ | 37.___ | 42.___ | 47.___ |
| 28.___ | 33.___ | 38.___ | 43.___ | 48.___ |
| 29.___ | 34.___ | 39.___ | 44.___ | 49.___ |
| 30.___ | 35.___ | 40.___ | 45.___ | 50.___ |
| TOTALS: ___ | ___ | ___ | ___ | ___ |

| 11. Meetings | 12. External | 13. Conflict | 14. Trust | 15. Communication |
|--------------|--------------|--------------|-----------|-------------------|
| 51.___ | 56.___ | 61.___ | 66.___ | 71.___ |
| 52.___ | 57.___ | 62.___ | 67.___ | 72.___ |
| 53.___ | 58.___ | 63.___ | 68.___ | 73.___ |
| 54.___ | 59.___ | 64.___ | 69.___ | 74.___ |
| 55.___ | 60.___ | 65.___ | 70.___ | 75.___ |
| TOTALS: ___ | ___ | ___ | ___ | ___ |

| 16. Commitment | 17. Decisions | 18. Assessment | 19. Rewards | 20. Celebrations |
|---|---|---|---|---|
| 76.___ | 81.___ | 86.___ | 91.___ | 96.___ |
| 77.___ | 82.___ | 87.___ | 92.___ | 97.___ |
| 78.___ | 83.___ | 88.___ | 93.___ | 98.___ |
| 79.___ | 84.___ | 89.___ | 94.___ | 99.___ |
| 80.___ | 85.___ | 90.___ | 95.___ | 100.___ |
| **TOTALS:** ___ | ___ | ___ | ___ | ___ |

# ACTION PLANNING GUIDE

**THE KEY ISSUES OR PROBLEMS** that seem to have led to the derailment or decreased effectiveness of our team are

1.

2.

3.

4.

5.

Team Depot Aisles that we should go to first include:

1.

2.

3.

4.

5.

Types of tools that will probably be needed include:

1.

2.

3.

4.

5.

Next steps for us include:

| **What** | **By When** |
| --- | --- |
| 1. | |
| 2. | |
| 3. | |
| 4. | |
| 5. | |

## AISLE 1

# REVISIT YOUR TEAM GOALS

## OVERVIEW

**THERE ARE ONLY A FEW SURE THINGS ABOUT TEAMS,** and one of them is that *successful teams have clear goals.* It's that simple. If you sense that your team is just not working, this is the first place to look. There are many ways to look at the issue of team goals, and where you begin depends on the nature of your team, including both its history and its current situation.

Senior management teams may start with vision, while a natural work group looks at problem definition. Some teams prefer to start with a mission or charter, while others begin with a specific problem statement. In the end, all teams need to examine the current direction of the team, refresh their purpose, and reset their goals to make them clear, specific, and relevant to today's world.

In this aisle you will find more than fifty tools from which to choose. You will probably need to implement only one or two to get your team back on track. The tools include:

- Ways to create a compelling vision;

- Methods for developing a new mission or charter;

- The mechanics of setting goals and objectives;

- How to prepare a clear problem statement;

- Help in ensuring that your team's goals are aligned with the organization's strategy and that team members are committed to your team's goals; and

- Suggestions for increasing team learning and stimulating thought-provoking consideration of the importance of resetting your team's direction.

## 1. WHAT'S A VISION?

Does your team have a *vision*? What, you ask, is a vision? It is not a religious experience, although it can have a somewhat spiritual quality.

*A vision is simply a statement of where you'd like to be or what you'd like to be. It's your "druthers," your hopes, your dreams . . . a place you've never been.*

## 2. ANOTHER VIEW OF VISION

Another way of describing a vision is

A statement of a team's *preferred* future, as opposed to its *predicted* future.

## 3. ARE YOU A VISIONARY?

"The best visionaries aren't necessarily those who can predict the shape of the 21st Century. Rather, they are people who can draw a conceptual road map from where the organization is now to some imagined future, who can say, 'This is how we get there.'"

—*David Campbell, Center for Creative Leadership.*

## 4. WHY A TEAM MUST HAVE A VISION

- It gives focus to the team's work.

- It serves as an anchor when the team tends to drift.

- It helps resolve conflicts about priorities.

- It serves to motivate and engage team members.

- It is a unifying force that brings and keeps team members together.

## 5. CHECKLIST: WHAT MAKES A VISION INSPIRING?

*Directions:* Assess your team's vision statement against this checklist of questions. How does it stack up?

☑ Is it a challenge?

☑ Is it big enough to be a little bit scary?

☑ Does it reflect some higher purpose?

☑ Does it go beyond the everyday goal of getting a good product out the door?

☑ Is it sufficiently future oriented?

☑ Will it require more than just the completion of a list of action items over the next six months?

☑ Is it something sufficiently different from what we're doing right now? In other words, it is more than just quality improvement?

 **T I P** Use this checklist as a quick assessment of your current vision or as a step in the process of creating a new vision for your team. If you are using this checklist with team members ( and I recommend this), give each person a copy of the list, along with a copy of the vision statement, and ask each person to answer the questions. Then facilitate a discussion based on their answers.

# 6. VISIONING A VISION: A TEAM-BUILDING ACTIVITY

Here's a proven exercise for developing a new vision for your team (Parker & Kropp, 1992).

## Process

- You'll need a flip chart, a full pad of chart paper, paper and pencils, lots of felt-tipped markers, and plenty of masking tape or push pins for this activity.

- After you have given the team a definition of a vision, explain that the purpose of this exercise is to create a vision statement for the team.

- Ask the members to relax, perhaps close their eyes, and put themselves in this scene: "It is five years from now [the year 20XX]. You are in a helicopter hovering over [this location]. What would you like to see? What would please you? What are we doing? How are we working? Think in terms of our work processes, our customers, our work environment, and our relationships."

- Then: "Once you have some images in mind, write them down. Feel free to draw a picture, a cartoon, a chart, or a list."

- Finally: "Take a sheet of chart paper, a marker, and some tape (or pins). Transcribe your vision to the paper and post it on the wall. Don't forget to sign it."

- Encourage team members to walk around the room and view the "vision exhibit." Ask them to look for common themes, surprises, good ideas, and other things that should be included in a shared vision for the team.

- Facilitate a discussion on elements of a vision statement for the team. Post the responses on the flip chart. Probe for understanding of the items. Push for commitment to the items. Conclude the discussion when there appears to be a consensus around the elements of a vision.

- Conclude the session by restating the purpose of a vision statement. Ask each team member to come up to the flip chart and sign the statement as a gesture symbolizing his or her commitment to and support of the vision.

## 7. ONE TEAM'S VISION

A team's vision might be "to manage a hassle-free order-entry process that exceeds customer expectations with a team of trained professionals who care about each other and have fun every day at work."

## 8. WORLD-CLASS TEAM VISION STATEMENT

Some years ago, the executive management team of a telecommunications organization created this statement:

"We are a world-class team of inspired professionals committed to creating a challenging and rewarding environment. Openness, integrity, and the willingness to resolve tough issues characterize our culture. Quality and attention to the needs of our customers are paramount."

## 9. NEXT STEPS

Now that you have some information and have completed some exercises about your team's vision, it will help to answer some basic questions.

### Does Your Team Have a Vision Statement?

| Yes | No |
|---|---|
| Does the current vision still make sense? | Do you need one? |
| What needs to be done to bring it up-to-date? | If it will help your team to have a vision, how and when will you prepare it? |

## 10. MISSION POSSIBLE

You have a vision statement, or perhaps the nature of your team does not require a vision. But does your team have a mission statement? Perhaps you call it a charter or a statement of purpose. Many teams now use the term charter to convey the same idea because "mission" sounds like something reserved for senior management teams.

Whatever it is called, it is extremely important that your team have a clear sense of purpose. Why does your team exist? What are you trying to accomplish? Who are your customers? What are your fundamental beliefs? Teams that have been in existence for some time often lose their way or their purpose becomes cloudy—they forget why they came into being in the first place or their original purpose has changed over time and their charter has not been updated.

 **T I P**   One important way to revitalize your team is to either revisit your existing charter or create a new one from scratch.

## 11. YOUR MISSION . . .

A mission, purpose, or charter should accomplish a few basic things for a team. It should state the team's overall purpose or its reason for being (raison d'être). It should indicate why the team is needed and how it fits into the overall organizational goals. It should specify the team customers or clients—the groups for whom they are doing the work. It may also say something about the team's values or philosophy.

## 12. WHERE DOES A TEAM'S MISSION COME FROM?

The direction that forms the basis for a team's mission or charter should come from management. Management should provide the overarching goal that provides the framework for the charter. No team should exist that is not somehow related to an overall organization goal or directive from above. It is management's role to set out its expectations for the team. The team, in turn, translates those expectations into a statement of purpose. For example, one company had a strategic objective of increasing cash flow. A team in that organization stated its mission as "to reduce the cycle time for XYZ products by 20 percent." They understood that reducing cycle time increases cash flow.

 **QUESTION**   Is your team's mission statement still aligned with a corporate goal?

## 13. HOW A CLEAR MISSION HELPS A TEAM

It's pretty clear that a solid team charter helps management ensure that all teams are focused on issues that support the company's strategic objectives. But what does a clear statement of purpose do for a team?

### The Role of a Team Mission

- It fosters collaborative behavior among members;
- It establishes responsibility and accountability for certain outcomes;
- It serves as a guide to addressing issues, making decisions, and taking risks by team members; and
- It helps resolve conflicts among team members.

**QUESTION**  How many of these results are important for your team?

## 14. A TEAM MISSION IS A LIVING DOCUMENT

The world of work, your world, changes rapidly . . . your mission should change, too. To keep your team vital, periodically—at least once a year—pull out the statement and give it a thorough review. Make the creation of a team charter more than just an exercise.

**T I P**  A careful assessment will revitalize your team.

**QUESTION**  Have you reviewed your team charter recently?

# 15. A DESIGN FOR CREATING A TEAM MISSION

## Process

- Prior to the team meeting, send each member some background information on a team charter (you can use some of the above material). Ask them to think about what should be included in your team charter.

- Have a flip chart, markers, and some tape or push pins available at the meeting. You can also use an overhead projector, LCD projector, or electronic tool if members are not face-to-face.

- After reviewing the purpose of the exercise, ask the team to brainstorm words or phrases that describe the team's mission. Record the responses on the flip chart or screen.

- Eliminate duplicates ("clients" and "customers") and combine words that naturally go together ("honesty" and "openness").

- Discuss any words that need to be clarified. Seek a consensus on words that should be deleted.

- Ask each member to draft a team mission statement that includes the ideas on the flip chart or screen. Indicate that (a) the statement should include one or two sentences at the most and (b) the goal is not to use all of the words but to incorporate the gist of the ideas.

- Post one of the examples on the flip chart or screen. Facilitate a discussion that incorporates other ideas and results in an edited mission statement.

- Seek volunteers to edit the draft statement and send it to the members.

- Discuss the revised statement at the next meeting and seek a consensus decision on a final version.

- Distribute high-quality printed versions to all members for posting at their work stations. Display the statement in prominent locations around the work area.

## 16. A CLEAR, ELEVATING GOAL

"Two insights about teams emerged early, consistently, and very emphatically from our interviews. First, high performance teams have both a clear understanding of the goal to be achieved and a belief that the goal embodies a worthwhile or important result. Second, whenever an ineffectively functioning team was identified and described, the explanation for the team's ineffectiveness involved, in one sense or another, the goal."
— *Larson & LaFasto (1989, p. 27)*

## 17. GOALS MAKE THE DIFFERENCE

The results are in, and they are clear. Research supports it. Experts agree. The one factor, above all others, that distinguishes high performing teams are clear performance objectives.

## 18. GOALS PROVIDE AN INCENTIVE

Goals spur the team to action. Whether it's forging a river in a team-building exercise, putting a man on the moon, or beating the competitors to market with a new product, a compelling goal motivates team members to give their best efforts.

## 19. GOALS RESOLVE CONFLICTS AND FACILITATE COMMUNICATION

Clear goals help team members discuss differences, evaluate alternatives, resolve conflicts, and decide the best course of action. Mushy goals, on the other hand, encourage, well, mushy thinking and little productive action.

## 20. GOALS ESTABLISH A SCOREBOARD

Goals tell a team how they're doing, what they've achieved, how much farther they have to go—all of this keeps them focused on outcomes.

**QUESTION** What do you need to make goals an effective scoreboard? (*answer:* objective measures).

 **T I P** Brainstorm measures for your goals.

## 21. GOALS BUILD PARTNERSHIPS

Goals provide the basis for positive relationships between the team and its key stakeholders. Teams often turn to other teams, support groups, functional departments, and senior management for help with such things as resources, ideas, budgets, and information. When stakeholders are included in the team's goal-setting process, they see themselves as partners strategically linked with the team.

**QUESTION** What stakeholders should be involved in your goal-setting process?

## 22. GOALS EMERGE FROM THE TEAM'S MISSION

This is a critical step. It is essential that your team translate the statement of purpose into one or more specific performance objectives. All team goals should be in support of the mission of the team.

> The mission of the A Team is to provide quality service to all customers as the Northeast Region migrates to a goal of "respond to all customer requests within twenty-four hours by the end of the third quarter with no customer complaints."

## 23. GOALS MUST BE SPECIFIC

A goal can be as lofty as "put a man on the moon by the end of this decade" or as down to earth as "develop a tracking system by the end of this year that follows each copier through the distribution process." In any case, it must have a tangible or observable result.

## 24. GOALS MUST BE COMPELLING

Goals must be worthwhile. Members should see the goal as challenging and the results useful. It will make a difference. While not every team goal can be as momentous as landing a person on the surface of the moon, pharmaceutical company scientists can find decreasing the time to market of a new cure for cancer personally satisfying.

## 25. GOALS MUST BE SMART

Check your goals against these criteria. Are your goals SMART?

*Specific:* The outcome or end result is very clear to everyone.

*Measurable:* You can tell if you have achieved your objective because you can count it or see it.

*Attainable:* While achieving the outcome may be a challenge, it is possible with the current team and its resources.

*Relevant:* The objective is in line with the direction provided by senior management and is aligned with the strategy of the business.

*Time-Bound:* All objectives must be achieved within a particular time period, such as by the end of the quarter, or by a specific date.

## 26. WHY TEAMS DON'T SET GOALS

If it is agreed that setting goals is a good thing to do, why don't more teams set clear goals? Here are some of the responses we've heard:

- We don't have time; we have a lot of work to do.
- This place is always in a state of crisis, so why bother?
- I heard there's a big reorganization coming soon; let's wait until after that.
- We might look bad if we don't achieve the goals.
- Nobody looks at those things anyway.
- Nobody follows those things anyway.
- Our boss should set the goals; our job is to carry them out.
- The last team that did it is not here anymore.

 **QUESTION** Do any of those comments sound familiar?

 **T I P** Distribute a copy of this list to the team. Ask the members to check all that apply to the team. Facilitate a discussion that analyzes the results and develops ways to overcome these barriers.

## 27. SOME TYPICAL TEAM GOALS

- Develop a plan to reduce cycle time for XYZ product from 89 days to 35 days by June 30.
- Reduce the December reject rate by 25 percent with no increase in basic costs.
- Increase the customer satisfaction rating for the year by 10 percent.

- Produce a new product with the following specifications by the end of the third quarter.

- Reduce the average waiting time for patients in the emergency room to 10 minutes for the first six months of 2003.

- Respond to all customer requests within 24 hours by October 1.

# 28. GOAL-SETTING: A CRITICAL STEP IN THE TEAM-DEVELOPMENT PROCESS

More than thirty years ago, a psychologist, Bruce Tuckman (1965), said there are four stages of group development:

1. Forming
2. Storming
3. Norming
4. Performing

During the forming stage, there is a lack of clarity about the team's purpose and the roles of the members. In order for the team to progress beyond the forming stage, these issues need to be addressed. The most critical question for teams in the forming stage: *What is our purpose?*

Teams that do not answer this question effectively will never mature into a high-performing, successful team. Just as we refer to a person who lacks direction as immature, teams that do not develop a mission statement and clear goals will remain floundering in the forming stage.

**QUESTION**  What stage are you in?

**TIP**  Some so-called "mature" teams need to revisit the forming stage to see whether their original purpose and goals are still relevant.

## 29. GO TO THE SOURCE

Most people, even many team-building consultants, have only read summaries of Tuckman's ideas in other books or articles. Read the original, go to the source. It's a great article and a classic. Here's the full citation:

Bruce W. Tuckman. Developmental Sequence in Small Groups. *Psychological Bulletin*, 1965, *63*(6), 384–399.

## 30. TIE TEAM GOALS TO ORGANIZATIONAL GOALS

At the best companies, teams select goals that help the business get where it needs to go. Does your team know where the business is headed? And how well do your team's goals match the company's? Will both your goals take you in the same direction?

Here is a chart prepared by a customer service team:

| Company Goals | Team Goals |
| --- | --- |
| Meet or exceed customer expectations | Personally follow-up on customer needs after every sale |
| | Ask customers what we do well and what could be done better |
| Improve in all areas of our business | Measure customer satisfaction quarterly |
| Develop dedicated and highly knowledgeable workers | Provide each person with a minimum of twenty hours of training annually |
| Develop long-term customers | Contact major customers at least once each quarter |
| Explore new markets and develop new products | Brainstorm new product ideas based on customer feedback at every monthly staff meeting |

# 31. COMPANY GOALS + TEAM GOALS = SUCCESS

If your team is stuck, try this exercise.

- Facilitate a discussion around this question: "Why is it important that we match our team goals with company goals?"

- Discuss and post the responses on a flip chart.

- Post the four or five key company goals on the board.

- Create an equal number of subgroups and assign one goal to each group. Allow members to select a goal and join that subgroup.

- Post this subgroup task on the flip chart: "Prepare a team goal that supports your company goal." Encourage the members to make their goal clear, specific, and measurable.

- After each subgroup presents its team goal, facilitate a discussion using such questions as:

  - How does it support the company goal?

  - Is it specific?

  - Is it clear?

  - Is it measurable?

  - Is it realistic?

  - Are you willing to add this goal to our team's charter? (In other words, are you ready to embrace it and work toward its achievement?)

- Conclude this exercise by asking one person to collect the goals and distribute them to team members and stakeholders.

## 32. A GOOD EXAMPLE

ADC Kentrox Corporation, a division of ADC that manufactures telecommunications equipment, provides a good example (Hitchcock & Willard, 1995). The company measures and reports to workers on a quarterly basis what it calls its "Six Ups." These are six key measures of profitability and customer service:

- Customer request date versus ship date;
- Customer returns versus sales;
- First contact to resolve customer issues;
- Revenue growth over prior period;
- Return on sales; and
- New product revenues as a percentage of goal.

These six measures keep the company focused on what it has determined to be its few critical success factors. Every team organization aligns its measures to support the Six Ups. To make sure the teams are continuously measuring the variables most relevant to their success, these measures are reviewed annually against the organization's strategic goals and issues.

## 33. BASE GOALS ON DEFINED PROBLEMS

Goals seem to be most effective when they are based on some prior definition of the problem or exploration of an issue. Sometimes the exploration and analysis are done by the team, but often another group does them. In the pharmaceutical industry, discovery teams conduct preliminary research on the feasibility of a potential compound. If potential exists, the product is turned over to a project team to carry the ball from there. In other industries, the senior management team or key leader develops ideas or identifies problems that are, in turn, handed off to a product development or process improvement team.

## 34. REVITALIZE YOUR TEAM WITH PROBLEM IDENTIFICATION

Natural work group teams usually do their own problem identification. One way to rejuvenate your team is to conduct a no-holds-barred, free-flowing, brainstorming session that focuses on "Problems in Our Work Area."

Once you have a list of potential problems, assess each problem against these criteria:

☑ Is this problem something we can ignore?

☑ What would happen if the problem disappeared tomorrow?

☑ Is the problem creating an obstacle for one or more of the company's strategic goals?

☑ What are the consequences of not solving the problem?

☑ Is another team better equipped to handle this problem?

☑ Does another problem need to be addressed before this one can be solved?

## 35. PRIORITIZE PROBLEMS ACCORDING TO ORGANIZATIONAL GOALS

This activity can be very effective, but it requires careful pre-meeting planning.

### Process

- Prior to the meeting, find a copy of the company's goals and edit the survey below to reflect those goals. Make copies of the survey for everyone.

# PRIORITY SURVEY

*Instructions:* Use the following scale to judge how the solution to each problem will support the company's current goals (the goals listed here are hypothetical; substitute your corporate goals).

1 = Not at All     2 = Somewhat     3 = To a Moderate Extent     4 = To a Great Extent     5 = To a Very Great Extent

**Problem:** _____

| Goals | Circle One Number |
|-------|-------------------|
| 1.  Number 1 in market share | 1   2   3   4   5 |
| 2.  90 percent customer satisfaction rate | 1   2   3   4   5 |
| 3.  4.0 mean on employee attitude survey | 1   2   3   4   5 |
| 4.  20 percent of revenue from products >5 years old | 1   2   3   4   5 |

## Process

- Distribute sufficient copies of the survey for each team member. You will need one copy for each problem identified.

- Ask each team member to complete the survey for each problem.

- At this point, you can collect the surveys, summarize them, and distribute a report at the next meeting. At the next meeting, facilitate a discussion on the results with the goal of arriving at a consensus ranking of the problems. You could also discuss the results at the meeting at which the surveys were completed by tallying the results on a flip chart and then going on with the discussion.

 **T I P** Go to Aisle 17 for help in reaching a consensus.

## 36. START WITH A SOLID PROBLEM STATEMENT

A team can't fix a problem that it hasn't identified well. Coming up with an accurate problem statement is the first step in solving any problem and achieving a meaningful goal. In fact, an accurate problem statement will usually suggest a possible solution.

A problem is the gap between what *should* happen and what actually *does* happen because something gets in the way. Good problem solving begins with looking for how to get around what got in the way.

## 37. GUIDELINES FOR A GOOD PROBLEM STATEMENT

A good problem statement should:

- State the problem narrowly enough so that the team can handle it;

- Be a declarative statement not a question;

- Be detailed rather than general;

- Avoid mentioning blame, causes, or solutions; and

- Use measurable quantities when possible.

# 38. WRITE A GOOD PROBLEM STATEMENT 1

Here are some sample problem statements. Follow the guidelines to improve the statements. Write your improved problem statement in the space provided. Then match your statement with the recommended answers below.

a. *Make It Narrow:* "Shipping is getting all kinds of sloppy paperwork."

b. *Make a Declarative Sentence:* "Why can't the right paperwork get to the shipping department on time?"

c. *Be Detailed Rather Than General:* "The shipping department is getting the wrong color copies of paperwork."

d. *Avoid Mentioning Blame, Causes, or Solutions:* "If the traffic department would start processing paperwork correctly, shipping services would improve."

e. *Use Measurable Quantities When Possible:* "Shipping is getting too much incorrect paperwork."

*Sample Answers:* (a) "Shipping received incorrectly prepared bills of lading to the shipping department late, delaying deliveries"; (b) "People are sending bills of lading"; (c) "Shipping is receiving yellow copies of bills of lading when it should be getting blue copies"; (d) "Paperwork procedures between the traffic and shipping departments should be reviewed to improve work flow"; (e) "In the past twelve months, the shipping department received twenty-two incorrectly submitted bills of lading."

# 39. WRITE A GOOD PROBLEM STATEMENT 2

Here's another useful exercise.

## Preparation

Prior to your meeting, prepare a handout of the "Problem Statements" below. You could also prepare a transparency and display it on an overhead projector. You will need a copy of the guidelines for problem statements from number 37 above.

## Process

- Distribute a copy of the problem statements and the guidelines for problem statements to each team member.

- If the team is small, you can conduct the exercise as a total group discussion. If there are more than eight members, divide into subgroups of three to four each.

- Explain that the task is to decide which statements meet the guidelines. If any of the statements need revision, ask the team members to make the changes.

- Facilitate a discussion based on the answers and come to a consensus on the best responses, including revisions of the statements.

---

**Problem Statements**

1. The total number of errors is .06 per 100 produced.

2. We don't have enough meeting rooms for all the quality action teams.

3. Productivity would increase if lighting and ventilation were better.

4. Customers complain that telephones in the department are not answered during the noon to 1 p.m. time period.

---

**Answers**

1. This statement is good, although it could be more specific by adding the time period and the type of errors. A better way to state it would be "The number of errors in the claims reports is six per 100 reports processed during the second quarter of the year."

2. This statement is too general and is not measurable. Here's a more specific statement: "During the month of January, six team meetings were cancelled because a meeting room was not available."

3. This statement includes solutions. Here's a better way: "Productivity decreased 5.7 percent during the six-month period ending June 30."

4. This statement is specific, narrow, and does not mention solutions. However, it does not specify how many customers and/or how many calls. An improved problem statement looks like this: "During the second quarter, three of our five largest customers reported being unable to speak directly to a service representative on two or more occasions when they called during the noon to 1 p.m. time period."

# 40. WHAT'S THE PROBLEM?

Here's a quick and fun way to revisit the idea of getting down to the basics of a problem. First, remind the team about the elements of a good problem statement (see numbers 37 and 38). Then distribute the "What's the Real Problem" case and ask team members to discuss it and to come up with a concise problem statement.

(Our definition of the problem: The Car Won't Start.)

# 41. QUESTION THOSE ASSUMPTIONS

We want team members to take a hard look at some of our assumptions about goals and problems. Experienced team members should be able to take a critical look at these "rules." Mature teams, in the course of revitalizing their goal-setting and problem-definition process, should be pushed to a deeper understanding of these guidelines. Here are some questions to guide the facilitation of a discussion of the guidelines outlined in number 37 above. Possible responses are provided, but do not use them until you have brought out the opinions of the team members.

- *Why narrow the problem statement?* Doesn't making it broad give us more flexibility? (Not really. Broadening its scope may make the problem too big, preventing the team from ever completely resolving it. Not only that, but a large-scale problem may extend beyond the scope of your work area or your team's control.)

- *What's wrong with making it a question?* Doesn't that open up more possibilities? (No, questions don't state problems; they search for information.)

- *How does being specific help?* (It helps the team focus clearly on a single problem and not on a larger, fuzzier problem area.)

- *Why not include causes?* Isn't that what we want to know . . . the causes of a problem? (You don't want to look for causes or blame. The problem can come from a number of causes. You want to keep your mind open, not become locked in to any single cause before you've collected enough information and data on the problem.)

- *Why does it have to be measurable?* Some things just can't be measured very easily. (Even though some things aren't easily measurable, we can still be pretty specific about them. The better you can measure a problem, the more likely you'll know when you've actually solved it. For example, "All emergency room patients will be seen by a health care professional within thirty minutes of arrival" is a clearer goal to measure against than "Reduce waiting time for emergency room patients.")

## 42. TEAM OR INDIVIDUAL GOALS OR BOTH?

When the tasks to be accomplished are highly interdependent, team goals are appropriate. This is the conclusion of Edwin Locke and Gary Latham (1984), two researchers who studied the motivational impact of goal setting extensively. However, they believe that, when team goals are set, provisions must be made to measure the contributions of each member as well. Otherwise, members will put forth less effort than if they were working alone on the same task. There is a kind of "Let George do it" mentality that develops. Therefore, Locke and Latham (p. 38) point out that "the optimal strategy is to set goals for the group as well as for each individual within the group. This is often what occurs in effective team building and quality circle sessions. The group decides on a common objective and action steps are then set showing who will do what, when."

## 43. ALIGN INDIVIDUAL AND TEAM GOALS

One of the key success factors is the meshing of team member goals with the goals of the team. The inability of members to adopt a mind shift that includes a willingness to set aside personal position and power in favor of a collaborative orientation is one of the most important barriers to team success. When mature teams go astray, it is often a result of members being more concerned about their own welfare than the success of the team. Equally important, members do not see their success being directly related to the success of the team. In sports, for example, the award for Most Valuable Player rarely goes to a player on the last-place team. Smart team players see their success as being intertwined with the success of the team.

## 44. ORGANIZATIONAL SUPPORT FOR GOAL ALIGNMENT

Your organization can help ensure individual and team goal alignment by insisting that the performance management processes measure individual contributions to the team. One reason your team may have gotten off track is the lack of organizational support for the team's goals.

**QUESTIONS**

- Does your performance management form include behaviors that focus on effective contributions to the work of the team?

- Are managers and executives measured on their role as supporters of team goals?

# 45. TEAM GOAL ALIGNMENT

Just as team and individual goals must be aligned, all team members need to agree on the purpose and the goals of the team. In addition, success is conditioned on a clear understanding of these shared goals. Of course, we're not saying we want a team of robots who march in lock step behind the leader toward the goals. We want a diversity of opinion during the debate over the mission and goals; but once a consensus has emerged, success requires a commitment to those outcomes.

A useful exercise for a team in need of reenergizing is to assess the degree of commitment to the existing purpose and goals of the team. This exercise is adapted from Eggelton and Rice (1996) who, in turn, borrowed the parameters of commitment from Senge (1990). Here's how it works.

## Preparation

Provide each member with a copy of the Team Goal Alignment Survey along with a copy of the team's mission (charter or purpose) statement and goals. Please note that, if you have more than three goals, you will need to add more lines to the survey.

# TEAM GOAL ALIGNMENT SURVEY

*Instructions:* Please assess the degree of commitment exhibited by you and your teammates toward the team's purpose (mission or charter) and its goals according to the following scale:

1. *Apathy.* Neither for nor against it. No interest. No energy.

2. *Noncompliance.* Do not see the benefits of it and will not do what's expected to accomplish it.

3. *Grudging Compliance.* Do not see the benefits. But also do not want to lose their job. Will do enough of what's expected because it is required, but let it be known that they are not "on board."

4. *Formal Compliance.* On the whole, see the benefits. Will do what's expected and no more. "Good soldier."

5. *Genuine Compliance.* See the benefits. Will do everything expected and then some. Follow the letter of the law. A better soldier, but still a soldier.

6. *Enrollment.* Wants it. Will do whatever can be done within the "spirit of the law."

7. *Commitment.* Wants it. Will make it happen. Go the extra mile. Create whatever "laws" are needed.

Please circle the appropriate number for each of the items below.

| | | | | | | | |
|---|---|---|---|---|---|---|---|
| 1. Team Mission: My Commitment | 1 | 2 | 3 | 4 | 5 | 6 | 7 |
| 2. Team Mission: My Teammates' Commitment | 1 | 2 | 3 | 4 | 5 | 6 | 7 |
| 3. Team Goal 1: My Commitment | 1 | 2 | 3 | 4 | 5 | 6 | 7 |
| 4. Team Goal 1: My Teammates' Commitment | 1 | 2 | 3 | 4 | 5 | 6 | 7 |
| 5. Team Goal 2: My Commitment | 1 | 2 | 3 | 4 | 5 | 6 | 7 |
| 6. Team Goal 2: My Teammates' Commitment | 1 | 2 | 3 | 4 | 5 | 6 | 7 |
| 7. Team Goal 3: My Commitment | 1 | 2 | 3 | 4 | 5 | 6 | 7 |
| 8. Team Goal 3: My Teammates' Commitment | 1 | 2 | 3 | 4 | 5 | 6 | 7 |

## Process

- Collect and summarize the surveys. Prepare a report of the results.

- Distribute the report. Facilitate a discussion on the results using some of the following questions:

  - What are your overall impressions of the results?

  - What does it say about our team?

  - How do you feel about the differences in perception between your individual commitment and your teammates' commitment?

  - What are the differences in commitment toward our various goals?

  - What do we need to do to reenergize our team based on these results?

- Prepare an action plan based on the discussion.

# 46. ANOTHER VIEW OF ALIGNMENT

Another way to look at alignment is to assess the overall state of the team's alignment around the goals. Use this Team Alignment Assessment tool. Follow the same Preparation and Process steps as in the previous Team Goal Alignment tool.

# TEAM ALIGNMENT ASSESSMENT

*Instructions:* Please assess the degree to which the team demonstrates the characteristics listed in the left column according to the following scale:

1 = Not at All     2 =Somewhat     3 = To a Moderate Extent     4 = To a Great Extent     5 = To a Very Great Extent

Circle one number for each item below.

| Team Characteristics | Rating | | | | |
|---|---|---|---|---|---|
| 1. We have a common purpose/mission | 1 | 2 | 3 | 4 | 5 |
| 2. We have shared goals | 1 | 2 | 3 | 4 | 5 |
| 3. Individual goals are aligned with team goals | 1 | 2 | 3 | 4 | 5 |
| 4. There is a high level of trust among members | 1 | 2 | 3 | 4 | 5 |
| 5. There are no hidden agendas/no secret plan Bs | 1 | 2 | 3 | 4 | 5 |
| 6. There is a high level of collaboration among members | 1 | 2 | 3 | 4 | 5 |
| 7. Members' energies are focused on achieving the goals | 1 | 2 | 3 | 4 | 5 |
| 8. Team rewards are shared among members | 1 | 2 | 3 | 4 | 5 |

**Total Alignment Score:**

## Interpreting Your Results

32 to 40   Alignment

17 to 31   Compliance

08 to 16   Misalignment

# 47. THE ROAD TO . . . ?

Use this quote to stimulate a discussion:

"If you don't know where you're going, any road will take you there."
(Attributed to the Cheshire Cat in *Alice Through the Looking Glass*)

**QUESTIONS**

- What is the meaning of this quote?
- Do we know where we're going?
- To what extent does it describe our team?
- In what ways is it not a good description of our team?
- What are we currently doing (or not doing) that makes this quote an apt description of us?
- How would you revise this quote to make it a more accurate description of our team?
- What can we do to address the issues implied by this quote?

# 48. WISDOM FOR THE AGES

"When you get to a fork in the road, take it."
—*Yogi Berra*

**QUESTIONS**

- Beyond the humor, what's the meaning of this quote?
- In what ways does it apply to our team?
- What does it say about the goals of our team?
- What does it say about the clarity of our direction?
- What happens when we come to a fork in the road?
- What do we need to do to address these issues?

## 49. TEAM WISDOM

"Teams develop direction, momentum and commitment by working to shape a meaningful purpose. . . . Most teams shape their purposes in response to a demand or opportunity put in their path, usually by management. . . . The best teams invest a tremendous amount of time and effort exploring, shaping and agreeing on a purpose that belongs to them both collectively and individually. In fact, real teams never stop this 'purposing' activity because of its value in clarifying implications for members."
—*Jon Katzenbach & Douglas Smith,* The Wisdom of Teams, *pp. 49–50.*

## 50. GOOD NEWS AND BAD NEWS

The pilot on a corporate jet walked back to the cabin and announced to the executive team on board: "I've got good news and I've got bad news. Which do you want first?" "Let's start with the good news," the team leader said. "Well," said the pilot, "the good news is that we're making good time . . . but the bad news is: We're lost!" "Sounds just like us," came a voice from the rear of the cabin.

**QUESTIONS**

- Do you sometimes feel that you are "making good time" but don't have a clear idea of where you're going?

- What causes a team to work "fast" but not "smart"?

## 51. ONE STORY IS WORTH A THOUSAND DEFINITIONS

When my daughter, Ellen, was in the fourth grade, the teacher began an art lesson by asking the students to simply draw a picture of anything. As the children were working, the teacher walked around the class looking over the students' work. When she came to Ellen she asked, "What are you drawing?" Ellen replied, "It's a picture of God." "But, honey," the teacher said, "we don't know what God looks like." Ellen looked up at her and said, "Well, you will when I'm done." She had a vision.

## 52. A GOAL IS . . .

A goal is a dream taken seriously.

## 53. GOALS ONLINE

There is a website that provides a good format for reestablishing your team goals and then helping you track them as well. Individual team members may also find it useful for preparing and tracking their goals. The site is at www.goalsontime.com.

**IN THIS AISLE** various ways of refocusing your team's direction have been presented, from vision to mission to goals to problems. However, the direction-setting process should not be isolated from related issues such as empowerment, commitment, and performance management—found in other Team Depot aisles. In your case, your direction may be clear but your team membership may need to be refreshed. Check out Aisle 2 for tools in this area.

**AISLE 2**

# REFRESH
# THE PEOPLE MIX

## OVERVIEW

**OFTEN TEAMS GET STALE BECAUSE THE PEOPLE GET STALE**. Your current members may be good people—but not good for this team . . . at this time.

The same members who helped create and build the team during the early stages of the team's development may not the right people now. Your team may need people to sustain and maintain a process or system—and that requires members with a different skill set, and more importantly, a different style. Or your team may need an injection of folks who can shake things up a bit, breathe some new life into the team with fresh ideas honed in the trenches with other teams and in different organizations.

The mission of your team may have changed and you simply need a different mix of people who more closely match the new focus of the team. Perhaps you now need members who work in the field, who come from other cultures, who have different training, or who have had different experiences.

While you do not want to move team members around too often because that works against building a positive team climate, moving some new people in and some current members to other teams can keep your team vital. If your team has stagnated, refreshing the people mix can revitalize it.

Keep in mind that simply bringing in new members may not be sufficient. New members with new ideas need to be supported so their ideas will be heard and seriously considered by other team members. Therefore, it also may be necessary to revisit your team norms dealing with open communication and listening.

By the way, team members often want to move to another assignment because a change can be good for them, too. Moving to another team can provide a member with an opportunity to share his or her expertise, learn new skills, and add a different experience to their resume.

What? You say you can't easily change the composition of your team. It's true. Many teams are permanent, intact teams that do not have the luxury of moving people around. Teams in this category have to find ways to refresh the mission and rekindle the fire that once got the team going. It's a challenge to revitalize an intact team, but it can be done.

We have provided a variety of different ways of refreshing the people component of your team. In this aisle are several tools for assessing the current people mix on your team, as well as ideas for changing the composition of your team, what to do when a person leaves or joins your team, how to deal with problem people on your team, and ways to refresh the team when you cannot or do not want to change the membership.

## 54. CHANGE FOR CHANGE'S SAKE

One team leader in a telecommunications company tries to change the people mix on a regular basis. He believes that "inbreeding" leads to "groupthink," which in turn results in a decrease in creativity and innovation. With this philosophy in mind, he brings in new people with fresh ideas and different styles but maintains the core culture of the team. He is careful to bring in only one or two new people at a time but then keep the team intact for at least eighteen months to fully integrate them. He always carefully considers his twin goals of revitalizing the team while sustaining the fundamental culture of the group.

**T I P** Think about this case . . . and perhaps use it to facilitate a discussion with your team.

- Would our team benefit from the addition of some new people with fresh ideas?
- What type of person could help us?
- What can we do to add some new people to our team?
- Are some current members interested in moving to another team assignment?
- What are some current aspects of our team culture we want to preserve?
- How do we change the people mix and yet maintain the positive aspects of our culture?

## 55. TEAMWORK REQUIRES TEAM PLAYERS

In a team-based organization, effective teamwork requires more than just people with the right education, training, and experience. Teamwork requires team players.

- If subject-matter experts are unable or unwilling to share their knowledge, teamwork fails.
- If team members have lots of good ideas but are not open to the ideas of others, teamwork fails.
- If team members have good presentation skills, but poor listening skills, teamwork fails.

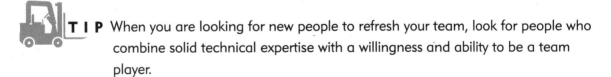 **T I P** When you are looking for new people to refresh your team, look for people who combine solid technical expertise with a willingness and ability to be a team player.

## 56. FACILITATE A DISCUSSION ON THE NEED TO REFRESH THE TEAM

If you sense that the team is stagnating, initiate a discussion on ways to refresh the team. Here are some possible discussion questions:

- How satisfied are you with our progress?

- How satisfied are you with the way we are working as a team?

- What's happened to our team spirit? How would you describe our team spirit?

- How would you characterize the level of enthusiasm on our team? Do we still have the same spark that marked our early history? How can we get that spark back?

- Comparing our team today with the way it was functioning a year ago, in what ways have things changed? Are you pleased with the changes?

- In what ways do we need to change now in order to help the team move forward?

- What can we do to refresh the team? Rekindle the old spirit? Find that old spark?

## 57. INITIATE A TEAM-BUILDING ACTIVITY

A solid team-building process can uncover the issues associated with the people mix on the team. The process should begin with a careful data collection phase that includes interviews with team members, a diagnostic survey, and observation of the team (on the job or in meetings). These data should then be shared with the team and form the basis for problem solving and development of plans for change.

 **T I P** For more on this see Dyer (1977).

# 58. START WITH AN INDIVIDUAL ASSESSMENT

A good way to begin the process of refreshing your team is to engage in a team player assessment. Members may use the results to alter their behavior to bring it more in line with the desired team-oriented culture. Others may decide that the current team is not a good "fit" for them and opt to move on to another assignment.

## Preparation

Provide each team member with a copy of the Team Member Assessment.

## Process

Ask each team member to complete the assessment. Then encourage each person to meet with you to discuss his or her answers. At that meeting, use open-ended questions (for example, "What are some of the ways you have shared your expertise with the team in the last year?") to help the person analyze the results and come up with ways to be a more effective team member.

# TEAM MEMBER ASSESSMENT

*Instructions:* Just as you go to your doctor for an annual physical examination, consider an annual assessment of your participation on this team. This simple, easy-to-complete survey will provide you with the data to prepare your own diagnosis. You might consider asking your teammates to provide their assessments of your performance by responding to the same questions.

Please review each behavior and then indicate the extent to which you do it by circling one number on the following scale.

1 = Not at All    2 = To Some Extent    3 = To a Moderate Extent    4 = To a Great Extent    5 = To a Very Great Extent

Circle the number that applies for each item.

| Behavior | Rating | | | | |
|---|---|---|---|---|---|
| 1. I do my fair share of the work | 1 | 2 | 3 | 4 | 5 |
| 2. I pitch in and help my teammates | 1 | 2 | 3 | 4 | 5 |
| 3. I share my knowledge and expertise | 1 | 2 | 3 | 4 | 5 |
| 4. I support the team's objectives | 1 | 2 | 3 | 4 | 5 |
| 5. I show up on time to all meetings | 1 | 2 | 3 | 4 | 5 |
| 6. I encourage and support my teammates | 1 | 2 | 3 | 4 | 5 |
| 7. I use active listening skills | 1 | 2 | 3 | 4 | 5 |
| 8. I am open to new ideas | 1 | 2 | 3 | 4 | 5 |
| 9. I challenge old ideas | 1 | 2 | 3 | 4 | 5 |
| 10. I keep my promises | 1 | 2 | 3 | 4 | 5 |
| 11. I back off when a consensus has been reached | 1 | 2 | 3 | 4 | 5 |
| 12. I am positive and enthusiastic | 1 | 2 | 3 | 4 | 5 |

**Total Score:**

| Your Score | Interpretation |
|---|---|
| 12 to 24 | *Go Back to Team School.* You need lots of help or an assignment that does not require lots of collaboration. |
| 25 to 42 | *Keep Going.* You are headed in the right direction. Keep doing the things that support and promote teamwork and address the areas that require improvement. |
| 43 to 60 | *Go to Team Player Hall of Fame.* You're doing great! Keep it up. Continue to engage in periodic self-assessment and development. |

# 59. SPIRIT SIGNALS

Teams often lose both the fire and the fun that characterized the forming and storming stages of the team's development. One signal that your team is effective is that the members enjoy being around one another. They look forward to team meetings, project reviews, and other get-togethers because they are enjoyable and productive. Positive team spirit and a relaxed, informal climate lead to creative idea generation, innovative problem solving, and responsible risk taking.

**QUESTION**   What's your team spirit quotient?

# 60. TEAM SPIRIT ASSESSMENT

Here's a quick, nonscientific assessment of the fun factor on your team.

## Preparation

Give each person a copy of the assessment and ask that they complete it and bring it to the next meeting.

## Process

Facilitate a discussion of the results. Review each statement, ask each person to share his or her answer, and probe for examples and reasons. Conclude the session by coming up with ways to increase team spirit.

# FUN FACTOR ASSESSMENT

*Directions:* Read each statement and write a number in the space next to the statement that represents your assessment of the current situation on your team according to the following scale:

1 = Almost Never    2 = Rarely    3 = Sometimes    4 = Often    5 = Almost Always

_____  1. Sounds of laughter are often heard during our team meetings.

_____  2. We are able to both have fun and get the work done.

_____  3. When team members get together, there is a lot of good natured kidding of each other.

_____  4. There is a positive, friendly manner to just about everything we do.

_____  5. We regularly get together for coffee, lunch, dinner, or other informal activities.

**Total Score:**

## Interpreting Your Results

19 to 25     *High Spirit.* Your team is just plain fun. Your meetings are never boring, always enjoyable, and usually productive. Other people want to know how they can sign up to work with you.

11 to 18     *Loosen Up a Little.* You are just sticking your big toes in the spirit waters. Let go, loosen up, and enjoy it. Your team will be more productive, creative, and enjoyable.

5 to 10      *Spirit Transplant Needed.* Enough said.

# 61. STAGNATION—THE NEXT STAGE AFTER PERFORMING?

One of the real dangers for a team that achieves some success is the tendency to lose interest once the problem has been solved, the product has been launched, the system is up and running, or performance meets expectations. The challenge for a mature team is to maintain interest and enthusiasm when the mission shifts to implementation, maintenance, or evaluation. Be on the alert for potential stagnation. At the first signs, it may be time to refresh the people mix, revise the mission, or both.

# 62. SIGNS OF STAGNATION

It may be time to refresh the people mix when you see certain indicators of team stagnation.

*Instructions:* Look at the following checklist. Then indicate the extent to which you see these signs according to the following scale:

1 = Not at All    2 = To a Little Extent    3 = To Some Extent    4 = To a Great Extent    5 = To a Very Great Extent

| Behavior | Rating | | | | |
|---|---|---|---|---|---|
| 1. Members are absent from meetings | 1 | 2 | 3 | 4 | 5 |
| 2. Members come late or leave early | 1 | 2 | 3 | 4 | 5 |
| 3. People send substitutes to the meeting | 1 | 2 | 3 | 4 | 5 |
| 4. There is a lot of chronic complaining | 1 | 2 | 3 | 4 | 5 |
| 5. Action items are not completed | 1 | 2 | 3 | 4 | 5 |
| 6. People drop out/space out during meetings | 1 | 2 | 3 | 4 | 5 |
| 7. Irrelevant conversations are common | 1 | 2 | 3 | 4 | 5 |
| 8. Side conversations are the norm | 1 | 2 | 3 | 4 | 5 |
| 9. Members often criticize the team to outsiders | 1 | 2 | 3 | 4 | 5 |
| 10. Members question previous decisions | 1 | 2 | 3 | 4 | 5 |

**Total Score:**

### Next Steps

If your score is over 30, probe deeper for the reasons behind the behavior. Develop a change strategy that includes changing the mission or the membership or both.

 **T I P** You may find it useful to get team members' responses to these signs of stagnation. Simply distribute the survey to members, ask them to complete it, and then facilitate a discussion of the results.

## 63. YOUR BLANK TEAM

### Preparation

Prepare a copy of Our Team for each team member.

### Process

Ask members of the team to complete the Our Team report by filling in the blanks with words that they think describe the team now.

## OUR TEAM

The members of our team are _____ committed to the team's mission. I believe that most of the members believe the current mission is very_____.

I would describe the team's climate as _____. Members of the team seem to _____ the interactions with their teammates. The discussions are very _____ and _____.

Interpersonal relationships among team members may be best described as _____. Members often _____ one another. Conflicts are resolved by _____.

Meetings often start _____. During our meetings members usually _____ and _____. Meetings are opportunities for members to _____. Discussions during our meetings are often _____. Decisions are made by _____ and members are usually very _____ with team decisions.

The future of our team is quite _____ and _____. At this point, we should _____. I am personally very _____ with my involvement on this team and hope to _____ in the future.

Frankly, we need to _____ the membership of our team. We also need to _____ the team's mission.

## Process

Facilitate a discussion among the members. Begin by asking one person to read his or her report. Ask others to join in by adding the words they used to fill in the blanks. Another approach is to review one paragraph at a time, obtaining everyone's responses and drawing some conclusions before moving on to the next paragraph. You can also give everyone a transparency of the sheet along with a transparency pen and ask team members to fill in the blanks. Then when you ask for their responses, each person can simply display his or her transparency.

### QUESTIONS

- How do you feel about the discussion?
- What does it say about the future of our team?
- What suggestions do you have for changing the people mix on our team?
- What changes are required in the team's mission?
- What other changes seem to be necessary?

## 64. ALIGN THE TEAM MISSION WITH YOUR PEOPLE MIX

Do this quick exercise.

*Instructions*: Make three lists: (1) the components of your team charter or mission statement, (2) the competencies required to accomplish the mission, and (3) team members and their expertise.

# TEAM ALIGNMENT CHART

| Mission/Charter | Required Competencies | Members' Expertise |
|---|---|---|
| | | |

**QUESTIONS**

- What does this exercise tell you?
- Is there alignment between your mission, the required competencies, and the expertise of your current membership?
- Do you need to change the mix?
- If you cannot change the membership of the team, what can you do to get the required alignment? Augment the team with ad hoc adjunct members? Send current members for training?

**T I P** Turn this chart into a team exercise. Post the chart or the wall, projector, or computer screen. Facilitate a discussion with the goal of filling in the chart. Then use the questions to discuss next steps.

# 65. THE BAD SEED

A small, start-up company was heavily dependent on the reputation of one member of the senior management team. He was a renowned scientist whose track record and name were synonymous with exemplary work. As a result, he was a critical player in the early stages of the company because of his ability to bring in business. He was, in the vernacular, "a rainmaker." As effective as he was on the outside with clients, he was just that ineffective on the inside in his daily interactions with other people in the company. He was a tyrant, universally disliked for his lack of patience, insensitive remarks to colleagues, failure to communicate basic business information to others, and generally "holier than thou" manner.

The management team was unsure about how to handle the situation. On one hand, they needed the business he was able to generate but they were very concerned about his negative impact on the remainder of the team as well as the rest of the organization.

**QUESTION** How would you handle this situation?

## 66. THE BAD SEED REVISITED OR WHAT TO DO WITH THE RAINMAKER?

The company decided that at this stage in its development they could not afford to lose the rainmaker. The management team reasoned that some customers would take their business elsewhere, investors would get nervous, and other employees might wonder whether the business could remain viable. As a result, it was decided to appoint him senior vice president for business development, where his duties involved bringing in the business and then turning it over to the operations area for implementation. He was happy with his elevated status (and additional stock), and the employees were pleased that he was still around but not where they would have to interact with him on a regular basis. Sometimes a role change is all that is necessary.

## 67. CHANGE THE HAND YOU'VE BEEN DEALT . . . NOT

Sometimes it's just not possible to change the composition of your team. Let's say you realize the need to "refresh the people mix," but it's not possible. What do you mean? How can that be true?

**QUESTIONS**

- What are some of the reasons or conditions that prevent a team from changing its membership?

- To what extent do these reasons or conditions apply to your team?

- What can be done to overcome these reasons or conditions?

# 68. CHANGING YOUR HAND: IS IT POSSIBLE?

If you realize the need to refresh your people mix, is it possible? What are the barriers you will face? What factors will facilitate the changes?

## Process

In the space below, under Restraining Forces, list the potential obstacles. Under Positive Forces, list the potential supports for changing the people mix on your team.

| Positive Forces | Restraining Forces |
|---|---|
|  |  |

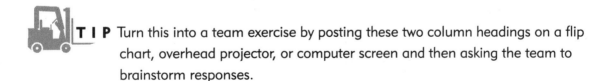 **T I P** Turn this into a team exercise by posting these two column headings on a flip chart, overhead projector, or computer screen and then asking the team to brainstorm responses.

## 69. WHEN YOU CANNOT CHANGE THE PEOPLE MIX

Here are some situations in which it is not possible or at least it is extremely difficult to change the composition of your team. Which situations apply to your team? Place a check in the box to the left of all situations that apply.

☐ The team works in a remote location.

☐ Team members do not want to change jobs or location.

☐ Your boss does not want to move people around.

☐ Team members have just completed a lengthy training program.

☐ Team membership requires a specialized skill or knowledge that few people possess.

☐ Team members are close to retirement age.

☐ Team members share a strong common bond, for example, race, gender, age, or location.

☐ Other.

**QUESTION**    Are the situations checked sufficiently compelling for you to forgo any attempt to change the people mix?

## 70. HOW TO REFRESH YOUR TEAM WHEN YOU CANNOT CHANGE THE MIX

- Change the mission or charter.
- Change the roles of team members.
- Appoint ad hoc or adjunct team members.
- Invite guests to attend your meetings.
- Facilitate a discussion on the need to refresh the team.
- Initiate a team building activity.
- Address specific team member problems.
- Revisit and revise your team norms.
- Do something fun together.

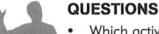

**QUESTIONS**

- Which activity is the easiest to implement?

- Which activity is the most difficult to implement?

- Which activity will have the most positive impact?

- Which activity would you start with?

# 71. CHANGING YOUR HAND: WHY?

Change is not easy, especially when it involves people—people who have been together for a while, shared experiences, worked through problems, known success, and established a comfort level. So even if there is a shared understanding that change is necessary and inevitable, moving people out and moving others in can be difficult. Why do it? The answer will vary with the team and its dynamics.

In the space below, brainstorm:

**Reasons for Changing the People Mix on This Team**

Once you have your list, reduce the list by eliminating duplicates and combining reasons that naturally go together (for example, our mission has changed and our customer base has changed).

**T I P** Take a hard look at the final list. Discuss it with your teammates.

**QUESTION** Are the reasons sufficiently compelling to come to the conclusion that a change in the people mix is required?

## 72. CHANGE THE MISSION OR CHARTER

When was the last time you took a hard look at your team's mission or statement of purpose? Most of us prepare a mission statement and then it just gathers dust. If your mission is dusty, maybe it's time to dust it off and turn it in for a new model. Your purpose then may not be your purpose now. Your team may have lost its zest because the members are still operating off an old, outdated mission that does not inspire anyone. Your customers' needs may have changed. Your technology may have changed. Your culture may have changed. But you are still playing those old "8-track" mission tapes.

 **T I P** Facilitate an open team discussion that focuses on WHAT YOU DO . . . your purpose, goals, and strategy . . . FOR WHOM YOU DO IT . . . your customers, suppliers, and stakeholders . . . to refresh the team by revitalizing the current team members as they see new challenges on the horizon.

## 73. CHANGE ROLES

You can't change the people but you can change their roles, and that can refresh the people mix. Move team members around. Give them new assignments within the same team structure. One leader of an intact team—actually a department head—believes that "musical chairs management" not only revitalizes a team but aids the professional development of team members. Team members like the change because every few years they get to take on a new challenge and yet stay within the comfort zone of the existing team. It takes some courage for an information technology manager to take over the marketing function, but it works.

**QUESTIONS**

- Can team members switch roles or assignments?
- Is there a different way of organizing the work?
- Are team members willing to move to another role?
- How will your customers react to such changes?

## 74. APPOINT AD HOC OR ADJUNCT TEAM MEMBERS

You can bring in new blood by involving other people on a part-time or temporary basis. Want to get some idea about how the field staff feel about a team proposal? Invite a representative to dial in on a teleconference line during your meeting. Need the expertise of a specialist periodically? Ask a person to join your team as an adjunct member with the understanding that occasionally he or she will be asked to attend a meeting or react to a proposal.

You can gain fresh ideas from many people both inside and outside the organization who are willing to share their insights but may not be interested in joining the team as full-time members. They enjoy using their expertise, and the team gains the benefit of their knowledge and experience.

In one organization where just about everyone was on a team, when a team went looking for help that was not available on its team, they could not persuade anyone to switch teams or become a member of a second team. Therefore, they simply asked a person to come to one meeting or agree to be interviewed by a team member.

## 75. INVITE A GUEST TO ATTEND YOUR MEETING

Ask someone from another organization or an outside expert to attend a team meeting. Speak with the person in advance about your situation or have the team generate a list of questions for the guest. Often another point of view, especially from someone who has lived through a similar situation, can spark a team to action.

## 76. THE CHRONIC COMPLAINER

The people mix on a team can be spoiled by the continued existence of a few "rotten apples." Their behavior can lower morale on the team and make it appear that everyone is unhappy. In one situation, the team leader thought that the entire team was dissatisfied when, in fact, one very loud team member was responsible for all the negative talk—much of it within earshot of the leader. The member was given some feedback and coaching that altered his behavior, and the team got back on track. In another situation, the team member, a contract employee, was dismissed. In yet another situation, the team member was transferred to another team where his complaints were redirected to a focus on ways to improve the project.

## 77. THE POOR PERFORMER

A team's spirit can be deflated by the unsatisfactory performance of one member. When members see that one of their teammates is not carrying his or her weight, it can be devastating. The problem should be addressed as soon as possible and in the fairest way possible. How does your organization handle performance issues? Is it the responsibility of the supervisor or manager? Some team-based organizations use a peer-review process where each member's performance is evaluated by other members of the team. No matter what the process, do it quickly. If there is no way of dealing with performance problems, create one for your team.

 **T I P** For more on peer review see McGee (1998).

## 78. HAVE SOME FUN TOGETHER

Give yourself permission to have some fun together. Call it team building . . . call it attitude adjustment . . . call it anything that is politically correct in your environment. Sometimes all you need to do to revive the people mix is to get out of the formal, corporate box. What might team members like to do? What would they like to do together? Here are some ideas that have been used by other teams:

- Go white-water rafting.
- Charter a fishing boat.
- Go to a ball game.
- Attend a course together.
- Cook a group meal.
- Have a barbecue or picnic.
- Spend an evening playing games at Dave & Buster's®, ESPN Zone®, or a similar place.
- Spend an evening bowling or playing billiards.

## 79. REVISE YOUR NORMS

Can't change the members? Change the way you work together. Take a look at your norms. Maybe they need some modernizing to be more aligned with the current mission and culture of the team. Sometimes a team that is stagnating is playing by the old rules that just don't apply anymore. You can refresh the people mix on your team by changing the way the people interact with each other. The enthusiasm that marked the forming days of the team may no longer be there. It may not even be appropriate at this point in the lifecycle of the team.

**QUESTION** When was the last time you looked at your team norms?

# 80. WHAT TO DO WHEN A MEMBER LEAVES THE TEAM

When a member leaves your team as part of your effort to refresh the people mix, it's important to deal with two issues:

1. The impact on the team and

2. The feelings of the person.

Let's begin with the second issue. When a person leaves your team, take the time to do the following:

☑ Acknowledge the person's contribution to the team. Take note of his or her work, special skills, and personality style (for example, "hard worker" or "great sense of humor").

☑ Thank the person at a team meeting, in a personal note, or both.

☑ Ask the person to talk about his or her personal experiences on the team and how he or she feels about leaving.

It is also necessary to discuss the impact of the departure on the team. For example:

• Will we be able to replace the person with another team member? What kind of a person will we look for?

• In the meantime, how will we continue to get the work done? Who will pick up the slack?

• How do we each feel about the loss of the person?

## 81. THINGS TO CONSIDER WHEN ADDING A NEW MEMBER TO YOUR TEAM

If you have some choice in the matter, look for someone who can bring something new and different in terms of expertise or team player style. If your mission has changed, your customer base is different, or the team's culture has shifted, seek out a person who will help the team respond to those changes. If your work now requires more direct customer interface, try to recruit someone who has good interpersonal skills. If the new culture emphasizes consensus building, look for a new person with a process-oriented style.

## 82. HOW TO ADD A NEW MEMBER TO YOUR TEAM

When a new person joins your team:

- ☑ Assign a mentor to help orient the person to the team.
- ☑ Provide him or her with a copy of the team mission, goals, and norms along with recent project reports and meeting minutes.
- ☑ Schedule a breakfast, lunch, or informal time prior to your next meeting to introduce the person to the other team members.
- ☑ Ask the mentor to introduce the new member, providing background on the person's work experience, team experience, skills, and personal life (hobbies, interests, family).
- ☑ As soon as possible, start the person working on a team project.*

*Adapted from Thiagarajan and Parker (2000).

# 83. FOCUS ON TEAM SKILLS

In 1995 New Zealand won the America's Cup Regatta by refreshing the people mix on their crew. In the past their team had the right technical skills but experienced serious communication breakdowns and antagonisms that resulted in poor performance. The team leader, Peter Blake, selected team members not purely for their skills and abilities but for how the members were likely to interact with one another. As a result, the 1995 Team New Zealand put all their emotion into winning "rather than conflicting secondary agendas."

For more on this story, see Maani and Benton (1999).

# 84. PEOPLE FIRST

Lipman-Bluemen and Leavitt (1999) coined the phase "hot groups" to describe high-energy, dedicated teams whose members are turned on by a challenging task. These groups have a sense of urgency and a can-do attitude. Organizations that spawn hot groups first spend lots of time selecting the team members and then get out of the way. Members of hot groups can generate challenging and useful work for themselves or respond to whatever task is presented to them. Keys to success are getting the right people together and then stepping aside, loosening controls, and providing challenges. But first get the right people on board.

# 85. "A GOOD HEART IS BETTER THAN ALL THE HEADS IN THE WORLD"

Sometimes a team can be too smart for its own good. The focus is solely on the team's ability to analyze the technical aspects of a problem to the exclusion of the human elements. When a team loses its spirit and fails to look at the soul of issues, it often misses the essential elements of a sustained solution.

**QUESTION**  Is your team "all head and no heart"?

**T I P** This quote by can be used as a discussion starter for a consideration of your team's orientation to problem solving and decision making. While you may not need or be able to change the composition of your team, the team's style can be refreshed.

## 86. PLAYERS WHO PLAY THE RIGHT WAY

My favorite basketball coach, Larry Brown, looks for "players who play the right way." He is never quite clear about what that means, but his teams always seem to be defined by a clear but flexible plan, a willingness to play hard at all times, members who know their strengths and limitations, mutual trust, and, above all, collaboration. Players who play the "right way" are often not the most skilled but they understand that basketball is a team game and "chemistry" can usually compensate for a shortage of skill and experience.

**QUESTION** Do the members of your team play the "right way"?

## 87. "I WANT TO BE ALONE"

A famous film star from the early days of Hollywood, Greta Garbo, became famous for this line . . . an expressed preference for being alone. She had no desire for teaming! In fact, there are many people in organizations with the same feeling. They prefer to work alone. The whole team thing is just not their thing. There is no need to force them to participate in the group activities of a team (such as meetings or team training), but they can contribute to the team in other ways. They can research a problem, analyze data, write a report, prepare slides, or make suggestions. So don't require loners to join group activities and infect the people mix on your team. Allow them to help the team in ways that are comfortable for them and useful for the team.

**QUESTION** Does your team include some "loners"?

**T I P** Have a private conversation with each "loner" to explore alternative ways to contribute to the team, such as providing research data or technical advice that do not require group interaction.

## 88. "THE POWER OF WE IS STRONGER THAN THE POWER OF ME"

**QUESTIONS**

- What is the meaning of the quote for your team?
- Is it true for your team? What examples do you have that support the statement?
- In what ways is the statement not true for your team?
- What are some team situations when the ME should be more powerful that the WE?
- How can both the WE and ME be strong at the same time?

## 89. THE FUTURE BELONGS TO . . .

Use this quote to stimulate a discussion about the future of your team:

**"The future belongs to those who believe in the beauty of their dreams."**
*—Eleanor Roosevelt*

**QUESTIONS**

- Do we still believe in our initial dream?
- Is it time to dream a new dream?
- Is it time to change the dreamers?
- How do you feel about our future as a team?
- If our dreams are reflected in our mission statement, are those dreams still valid?
- Is it time to change our dreams and our mission?
- Are our dreams still worthy, but do we need some players to make the dreams come true?

**IN THIS AISLE YOU HAVE FOUND IDEAS FOR REFRESHING THE PEOPLE MIX** on your team. However, do not limit yourself to tools in this aisle. Other helpful tools can be found in many other aisles that focus on climate, style differences, and meetings. Once you have your people mix set, stroll down Aisle 3 for ideas on how to redefine member roles.

 **AISLE 3**

# REDEFINE EVERYONE'S ROLES

## OVERVIEW

**ROLE IS ONE OF THE MOST MISUNDERSTOOD AND,** therefore, most underutilized concepts in team building. Lack of clarity about members' roles can lead to all sorts of team breakdowns, including:

- Conflict among members;
- Lack of productivity;
- Negative team climate; and
- Stagnation.

Role conflicts often surface as personality conflicts among team members. Members get mad at each other because, for example, a work assignment was not completed. The assignment was not completed because there were differing expectations about who was supposed to do the work and how it was to be done. Lack of communication leading to lack of clarity about expectations is at the heart of the need to redefine everyone's role.

After a team has been in existence for some time, roles may change, or at least some of the expectations may change. For example, as the mission and goals of the team change over time in response to customer needs, roles usually need to be realigned with the new mission.

In this section, you will update your understanding of the concept of role and its relationship to team effectiveness. You will find tools for role clarification and exercises for role negotiation. The aisle also includes information on process roles, task roles, and dysfunctional roles on teams. In addition, there are tools to help you make best use of team roles, such as facilitator, scribe, sponsor, and coach.

## 90. ROLE IS . . .

A set of activities or behaviors that a team member is expected to perform and constitutes a link between the person and the team or organization. Clarifying the expectations of each member can get a team back on track.

## 91. THE ROLE AND THE TEAM

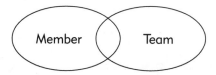

A role is created by the overlap of the member and the team. Each role is the sum of the conception of the member and the expectations of his or her teammates—and perhaps other stakeholders such as customers. In other words, role is both how I see what I am expected to do and how others see it. It's clear from that definition how and where problems can arise.

- What problems can arise?

- What problems has your team experienced?

## 92. ROLE ALIGNMENT

The process of working toward role clarity, acceptance, and efficacy must be in line with the team's goals and ultimately the organization's goals. In the above diagram, the team overlaps with the individual to create the role. The critical elements of the team are the vision, mission, and goals. Therefore, any role-clarification activity must be preceded by goal clarity, including a consensus on the part of team members to support the goals.

## 93. A ROLE IS NOT A POSITION

A *position* is the actual job a member holds in the organization, such as maintenance mechanic or systems analysis. A position description lists duties and responsibilities and is used for hiring, performance appraisal, and compensation. A *role* includes the activities and behaviors that a member is expected to demonstrate while holding the position.

## 94. ROLE IS NOT STYLE

Role is what you do, whereas style is how you carry out your role. For example, "My role is to provide a strategic vision for this team. I use a participative leadership style to involve team members in the process of creating a plan to implement the vision."

## 95. ROLE CLARIFICATION IS THE GOAL

Role clarification is the outcome of a process whereby all team members have a clear and congruent understanding of each other's roles. It can be a time-consuming and tedious process when the team is large and conflicts have developed over a long period of time. Each member's role has to be studied, discussed, and—often—renegotiated. Enter this process with your eyes wide open: It is not a quick fix!

 **T I P** See role clarification exercises in this aisle and the Choice Role activity in the Team Tool Shed.

## 96. ROLE EXPECTATIONS

These are what your teammates think you are expected to do. It is their perceptions, how they see your role, and often includes what they would like you to do and how they would like you to do it.

## 97. ROLE CONCEPTION

This is what *you* believe you are expected to do. This is what you perceive the role to require and often involves how you have been taught to do it.

## 98. ROLE CONFLICT

Conflict occurs when there is a discrepancy between role conception and role expectations. Open communication and renegotiation of the member's role is often called for at this point to get the person and the team back on track.

## 99. ROLE ACCEPTANCE

This is the end result of a role clarification exercise. Acceptance defines what you are willing to do, including the extent of your willingness to accept others' expectations of you.

## 100. ROLE BEHAVIOR

Role behavior is an expression of what you actually do in carrying out your role. It moves beyond the normative state of what you and others expect from you to your actual performance as a member of the team. In other words, it looks at the "rubber meeting the road."

## 101. ROLE EFFICACY

This is an evaluative process in which you and your teammates measure your performance (role behavior) against the role you have accepted. In the end, this is the goal of a role-clarification exercise—to increase your effectiveness as a member of the team.

## 102. ROLE AMBIGUITY AND TEAM EFFECTIVENESS

In an early classic study (Kahn, Wolfe, Quinn, & Snock, 1964), it was found that role ambiguity was highly linked with such factors as employee anxiety, job satisfaction, and team effectiveness.

**QUESTIONS**

- Why do you think role ambiguity was linked with anxiety, job satisfaction, and team effectiveness?
- In what ways are they linked on your team?
- If there is a link, what can be done to change the situation?

## 103. ROLE AMBIGUITY AND PROFESSIONAL SUICIDE

Don Cole, in his seminal work *Professional Suicide* (1981), reported that "the stress of ambiguous situations and not knowing" was one of the most important organizational characteristics that create and encourage professional suicide. Cole's ambiguous situations included such factors as lack of clarity about (1) goals and their relationship to me, (2) the plan and my role in the plan, (3) my responsibilities, (4) my authority, (5) how my performance will be evaluated, (6) how I'm doing and how I can improve, and (7) how I will be rewarded for my performance.

**QUESTION**   Do you see any ambiguous situations on your team?

## 104. ROLE CLARIFICATION ACTIVITY FOR A MATURE TEAM

Here's a simple but powerful exercise that can help a team redefine everyone's role, but don't start the process unless you have sufficient time to work through the issues with each team member.

### Pre-Work

Prepare the following questions in the form of a handout, allowing sufficient space between the questions for each person to write his or her answers. As an alternate, the questions can be posted and people can answer them individually on separate sheets of paper.

- What did I expect to contribute to this team?
- What do other team members not fully understand about my role?
- What type of help do I need from other team members in order to carry out my role successfully?

## Process

Start the meeting with one member providing his or her answers and then facilitate a discussion, with the goal of reaching a consensus on role acceptance. Continue the process until all members have had a turn.

# 105. FACE OFF: A ROLE COMMUNICATION ACTIVITY

This exercise is designed to both clarify team member roles and improve interpersonal relationships. An ancillary goal is to open the lines of communication on a team that has experienced some deterioration.

## Pre-Work

Prepare a copy of the handout, Face Off: Part A, and distribute to the members of the team. Ask that they bring the completed handout to the team-building meeting.

## Process

At the meeting, distribute a sufficient number of copies of the handout, Face Off: Part B, to each member of the team. Explain that the session will be composed of a series of one-on-one meetings between team members who need to spend some time clarifying their respective roles and improving communication. Allow approximately thirty to forty-five minutes for each of these meetings. At the end of the session, facilitate a discussion summarizing outcomes and benefits of the session for each person. If there is an odd number of team members, form one group of three people.

# FACE OFF: PART A

*Purpose:* Teams can easily incur uncertainty and confusion over working relationships when expectations are formed or changed in ways that team members do not understand or know about. Team members usually do not talk about these relationships, especially as they relate to their roles. Therefore, the purpose of this activity is to minimize any misunderstandings among members of the team around their respective roles and their impact on working relationships. The outcome should make it easier for you to carry out your role, make your work more enjoyable, and increase the quality of teamwork.

Your *role* includes those activities and behaviors that you are expected to demonstrate while holding your position in the organization.

*Pre-Work:* Prior to our team-building meeting, please answer the following questions. You may answer in bullet points now, as you will have an opportunity to elaborate on the items in a series of dialogues with your teammates during the session.

1. What is your role on this team? What are you expected to do?

2. Identify the people on the team with whom it is important that you clarify your role, understand their roles, and improve the quality of communication.

# FACE OFF: PART B

*Instructions:* Write your partner's name in the blank space. Your partner will provide answers to questions 1 through 4. Take notes. Ask questions to clarify points. At question 5, indicate what you can do to help. Complete question 6 at the end of your dialogue.

Name:

1.  What is your role on this team? What are you expected to do?

2.  What is the one thing you think I do not understand or fully appreciate about your role on this team?

3.  What do you need from me in order to carry out your role effectively? Be specific.

4.  Is there anything else I can start doing or stop doing that would be helpful?

5.  *My turn.* Here's what I can do to address your issues.

6.  When can we meet again to check on progress, further clarify roles, and discuss ways we can more effectively collaborate?
    Date:                Time:

## 106. FACE-OFF SCENARIO

The leadership team of a major health care facility went through this activity. An assessment revealed the need for role clarification because (1) it was a large team (twelve members); (2) more than half of the team was new to the organization; (3) they tended to have "polite" rather than open communication; and (4) they did not have many opportunities to interact outside of formal meetings. They met at an offsite location. After a brief orientation, they spent the remainder of the day having one-on-one conversations using the Face-Off protocol. They agreed to have follow-up sessions to review progress.

## 105. COMMON TEAM PROCESS ROLES

While everyone has a defined (and one hopes clear) role as a member of the team, all teams have certain common functions that need to be filled. Assignment to these roles does not need to be permanent and, in fact, many successful teams rotate these roles from time to time. In this section, we define each of these common team roles.

1. *Team Leader.* Elected or appointed, he or she ensures that the work gets done by coordinating task assignments, providing or obtaining resources, communicating information, and managing outside contacts, as well as being a contributing team member.

2. *Team Facilitator.* A person—sometimes the team leader, sometimes an outside expert, sometimes a team member—who manages the discussion and decision-making process of the team by involving everyone, keeping things on track, resolving conflicts, summarizing ideas, and identifying decisions and action items.

3. *Team Recorder.* Sometimes called the scribe, this team member captures the team's decisions, action items, and task assignments—often on a flip chart or screen. This information is used to summarize the meeting, serve as a permanent record, and simply be a reminder to all members of what was agreed to.

4. *Team Sponsor/Champion.* An outside person, usually a manager, who charters the team, provides the initial overarching goals, authorizes resources, removes barriers, monitors team progress, and, in general, supports the team.

5. *Team Coach.* As the name implies, this person is the team's mentor, advisor, and trainer who works with, but does not direct, the leader and team members.

6. *Parking Lot Attendant.* Usually a member of the team who takes responsibility for recording issues that come up during the meeting that the team does want to discuss at the time but wants to "park" for consideration at a later time.

**QUESTION**   Does your team have someone in these roles?

# 108. TEAM ROLES ASSESSMENT: HOW DOES YOUR TEAM STACK UP?

## Preparation

Prepare and distribute a copy of the assessment form to each team member.

## Process

After everyone has completed the survey (you can ask people to complete the survey prior to the meeting), facilitate a discussion of the responses with the goal of identifying strengths, improvement opportunities, and action items. Conclude the session by creating a list of action items designed to improve the effectiveness of team process roles. For example, action items might include clarifying the expectations of the team leader, assigning a recorder at every meeting, and making better use of the team's sponsor.

# TEAM ROLES ASSESSMENT

*Directions:* Please complete the following survey and be prepared to discuss your answers with your teammates. You may check more than one response in each category.

### Team Leader

- [ ] Primarily a subject-matter expert.
- [ ] Focuses primarily on completing the task assignments.
- [ ] Runs an effective meeting.
- [ ] Completed leadership and/or facilitation training.
- [ ] Additional leadership development needed.

### Team Facilitator

- [ ] Leader also serves as facilitator.
- [ ] Little process facilitation takes place.
- [ ] Facilitation is handled by someone other than the leader.
- [ ] Facilitator or leader handles the team's process issues effectively.
- [ ] Additional facilitation skills training needed.

### Team Recorder

- [ ] We have a permanent scribe.
- [ ] We rotate the role of scribe among the members.
- [ ] We don't record our actions.
- [ ] No one wants to be the scribe.
- [ ] We need additional help in effective recording of our actions.

### Team Sponsor/Champion

- [ ] We don't have a sponsor.
- [ ] Our sponsor is an active supporter of our team.
- [ ] Our sponsor is rarely involved in our work.
- [ ] Our sponsor tends to dominate our work.
- [ ] We need additional help in making effective use of the sponsor role.

### Team Coach

- [ ] We don't have a coach.
- [ ] Our coach is our supervisor.
- [ ] Our coach is someone from outside our area.
- [ ] Our coach serves as an effective mentor and trainer.
- [ ] We need additional help in making effective use of the coach role.

### Parking Lot Attendant

- [ ] We don't have a parking lot attendant.
- [ ] Our leader is our parking lot attendant.
- [ ] Our facilitator is our parking lot attendant.
- [ ] We consider all issues whenever they come up.
- [ ] We need additional help in making effective use of the parking lot attendant role.

## Process

After everyone has completed the survey individually, facilitate a discussion of the responses with the goal of identifying strengths, improvement opportunities, and action items.

# 109. ROLE CLARIFICATION FOR TEAM LEADERS

Here's an exercise devised by our colleague, Lynne Cannon of Lawrenceville, New Jersey. It's helps a team leader get back on the right role track.

## Preparation

Prepare a handout and slide of the following roles and questions.

| | |
|---|---|
| Champion | Strategic Thinker |
| Technical Expert | Ambassador |
| Process Facilitator | Negotiator |
| Knowledge Manager | People Manager |
| Boundary Manager | Task Manager |

### QUESTIONS

- Where are you spending most of your time?

- Where are you spending the least amount of time?

- Where should you be spending most of your time?

- Where should you be spending the least amount of time?

- What changes do you need to make in how you spend your time?

## Process

Ask the participants to answer the first two questions by circling the roles, the next two questions by boxing the roles, and the last question by making some notes.

Facilitate a discussion on the barriers—organizational, team, and personal—that inhibit the leader from focusing on the most important roles. Close with the development of actions necessary to shift to a focus on the most important roles, including those actions that can be initiated by the leader alone and those that require external support.

# 110. POSITIVE TEAM MEMBER ROLES

In effective teams, members take on various roles that help move the team forward in the achievement of its goals and maintenance of the team. Behavioral scientists refer to these roles as task and process roles. It is important to have a healthy balance between the task and process roles on your team as well as a minimal number of dysfunctional roles. Dysfunctional roles are those negative or anti-group behaviors that inhibit or block a team's success.

 **T I P** Look around at your team, especially at your team meetings, and see whether the necessary roles are being played. Most important, is there a healthy balance between task and process? If, for example, you observe an overemphasis on task roles, this may mean members are so focused on getting the job done that they are ignoring the interpersonal process that sustains a team over time. Getting the team back on track may mean rebalancing member roles.

# 111. POSITIVE TASK ROLES

Task roles "are actions that help the team reach its goal, accomplish an immediate task, make a decision, or solve a problem. Teams tend to be most effective in this area because, by training and temperament, people are more task-oriented. Most role models and most training in education and business settings focus on what to do to accomplish a task. Consider all the books and workshops on time management, meeting planning, and goal setting" (Parker, 1996, p. 51).

The following items describe various task roles.

*Initiator.*   Proposes team tasks, goals, or possible actions; defines group's problems or suggests a procedure. "I see our job today as. . . ." "Let's begin by making a list of. . . ."

*Information Giver.*   Provides data or other facts. Offers an interpretation or opinion on the facts. "Our research indicates. . . ." "My feeling is that this means. . . ."

*Information Seeker.*   Asks for data, other facts, and opinions. "Where's the data to support this conclusion?" "I'd like to hear how other people feel about. . . ."

*Clarifier.* Interprets information or elaborates on ideas; asks questions in an effort to understand or promote understanding. "Here's how I see the issue." "Help me understand how. . . ."

*Coordinator/Summarizer.* Pulls together related ideas; restates suggestions; offers a conclusion or possible decisions for consideration. "It looks like we all seem to agree that. . . ." "One possible way to go is. . . ."

*Evaluator/Reality Tester.* Makes a critical analysis of a recommendation; tests an idea against some data, constraint, or policy. " Let's take a hard look at. . . ." "We need to examine this approach in light of. . . ."

**QUESTIONS**

- Which ones do you observe on your team?
- Which ones are missing?
- What is the impact on your team?
- What can you do to fill in the blanks?

# 112. POSITIVE PROCESS ROLES

While task roles focus on what the team is doing, process roles emphasize how the team goes about accomplishing the task. It is the "interpersonal glue" that holds team members together and helps make best use of all their resources. "On the whole, teams tend to be less process oriented because traditional training stresses such axioms as "the end justifies the means" and "winning is everything." Effective teams, however, know that the quality of their decisions is impacted by the manner in which they make their judgments" (Parker, 1996, p. 51).

The following items describe various process roles.

*Harmonizer.* Reconciles differences and attempts to reduce conflicts; helps people explore differences and work toward resolution. "Let's take a look at both sides of this issue." "Rebecca is saying. . ., while Ira, you are saying that. . . ."

*Gatekeeper.* Helps others to participate; keeps lines of communication open; facilitates broad-based participation. "I'd like to hear from the folks in marketing about. . . ." "Sanji, you work in systems. How does this impact your clients?"

*Encourager.*   Responds to others in a friendly, warm, supportive manner; provides verbal and nonverbal interest in what others are saying. "Maria, that's a good point, tell us more about. . . ." "That's helpful, Raoul, . . ."

*Consensus Builder.*   Sends up a trial balloon to test a possible conclusion; tests to see whether the team is ready to move toward an agreement. "It looks like all agree that. . . ." "Are we ready to move forward on this issue?"

*Compromiser.*   Modifies his or her own position to help the team move forward; offers a revised version of the various proposals in the interests of group cohesion. "I'm willing to back off my position on. . . ." "Here's an alternative that seems to incorporate the essential elements of both sides."

### QUESTIONS

- Which ones do you observe on your team?

- Which ones are missing?

- What is the impact on your team?

- What can you do to fill in the blanks?

## 113. DYSFUNCTIONAL TEAM ROLES

Members sometimes attempt to satisfy some individual needs that are irrelevant and often counter-productive to the positive task and process roles of the team. These anti-team roles tend to work against the accomplishment of the team's task and the building of the internal team process. Allowing team members to continue to play out these dysfunctional roles can derail a team. Expert facilitation, effective norms, and training are all ways to overcome the existence of the roles and get the team back on track.

The following items describe various dysfunctional roles.

*Dominator.*    Tries to assert authority or superiority in manipulating the team or certain members to his or her own agenda. Domination usually takes the form of asserting higher status, giving directions authoritatively, using expert knowledge, or interrupting the contributions of others. "I know how to do this task because I have done it many times before." "In my position as vice president of. . . ."

*Recognition Seeker.*    Works in various ways to call attention to himself or herself through such things as boasting, reporting on personal achievements, acting in unusual ways (arriving late, leaving early), or volunteering for all presentations.

*Blocker.*    Tends to be negative and stubborn, resistant to all team actions, disagreeing and opposing without or beyond reason, and attempting to maintain or revive an issue after the team has rejected it.

*Aggressor.*    Works in many ways to bring down other team members—deflating the status of others; expressing disapproval of the values, actions, or feelings of others; attacking the team or the team's problem area; joking in a negative or sarcastic manner; or attempting to take credit for the work of others.

*Avoider.*    Tries to do the least amount of work possible by not becoming involved in team discussions, sitting quietly (or doing other work) during meetings, not volunteering for team assignments, presentations, or action items, and never accepting any leadership responsibilities.

*Jokester.*    Makes a display of his or her lack of involvement in the team's work by such things as making cynical remarks, adopting a nonchalant attitude, using an excessive amount of humor, or engaging in horseplay with other members.

### QUESTIONS

- Which ones do you observe on your team?
- What have you done to address the people involved?
- What can you do to address the people in the future?

## 114. ROLE CONFUSION CAN LEAD TO PERSONALITY CONFLICTS

A small product development team came to me with a team-building issue: "There are a lot of personality conflicts on our team." However, the data collection revealed that the real issue was not personality or style differences, but real confusion over roles. Members simply had different expectations of each other. For example, one member of the team saw his weekly update report as critically important for the success of the team because it was their main communication vehicle to the stakeholders, who could "make or break" the team. Other team members saw the report as a routine, administrative task and, therefore, treated his requests for timely, quality information as a low priority. He was furious with his teammates and characterized them in very negative terms that resulted in many so-called "personality conflicts." A role-clarification exercise, similar to ones found in this aisle, cleared up the confusion and got the team back on track.

## 115. ROLE NEGOTIATION

The concept of role negotiation and most role-clarification exercises owe an intellectual debt to Roger Harrison (1973), who pioneered the idea. Harrison's role negotiation process includes four steps:

1. *Contract Setting.* Each member prepares a list for each other member with three headings: (a) things to do more, (b) things to do less, and (c) things to do the same.

2. *Issue Diagnosis.* Each member writes out a master list combining the lists written about him or her. This list is posted on the wall. Members are then asked to clarify any items that need explanation.

3. *Role Negotiation.* After the clarification, members decide which items they want most and sit down in pairs to negotiate, usually with a third party to assist in the process.

4. *Written Role Negotiation Agreements.* The outcome of the role negotiation is a set of written agreements that spell out the agreements and concessions each party finds satisfactory.

## 116. ROLE PLAYERS

Sports teams, especially basketball teams, refer to certain team members as "role players." Role players are usually people who are willing to help the team by performing certain specific roles that are necessary for the team to be successful. A role player is usually not the star of the team, but rather an average performer who is willing to sacrifice him- or herself for the good of the team. A role player on a basketball team is typically someone who specializes in rebounding, tight defense, or three-point shooting. Successful teams combine designated role players with star performers and all-around players.

**TIP** Successful business teams need the same talent mix. They need role players who are willing to do such things as conduct statistical research, take the meeting minutes, and prepare handouts for presentations. They also need star performers who have high-level technical expertise, years of experience, and excellent presentation skills. They need the all-around players who can perform a wide variety of team functions.

## 117. ROLE OF THE STAKEHOLDER

Role clarification should extent beyond the borders of the team to include key stakeholders. Functional department managers who provide resources to cross-functional teams need to understand what's expected of them and the people in their unit who are members of the team. Sometimes department heads see the work of their departments as the number one priority and communicate that to the folks in the department. However, it may be that the work of the cross-functional team (for example, a product development team working on a hot product) may be even more important to the overall organization.

 **T I P** If members of your cross-functional team are not actively participating, consider talking to their managers with the goal of clarifying their role as team members vis-à-vis their roles as members of the department. At the same time, you can clarify expectations of the managers' role as stakeholders in your team and your role as team leader. In other words, what can you both do to help each other be successful.

## 118. ROLE DIFFERENTIATION

Role clarification can sometimes lead to a useful differentiation among expectations of the contributions of team members. Large teams can increase their effectiveness by creating two classes of team members:

1. *Core Members.* Core members comprise a small leadership group responsible for active involvement in all team planning, problem solving, and decision making.

2. *Adjunct Members.* Adjunct members provide the team with specific advice, resources, and work products as required and requested by the core team members.

## 119. CORE TEAM MEMBERS

Some large teams create a small leadership cadre representing the key functions necessary for completion of the project. For example, an information technology team might include a core group composed of one person each from hardware, software, marketing, sales/service, testing and evaluation, and operations. The core group develops the team's mission and project plan and then tracks progress. The core group decides what tasks need to be done and then ensures the items are completed by working with their functional work groups. They also coordinate the participation of the adjunct members, deciding how and when the adjuncts can help the team.

# 120. ADJUNCT TEAM MEMBERS

In many organizations, there are just too few people in certain functional areas to have the luxury of having them actively participate in teams on a continuing basis. In addition, the expertise of these functional specialists is only required at certain times and for a specific task. Therefore, these functional experts serve as adjunct team members—available to assist the team on an as-needed basis. It's a win-win for everyone. The team does not have a lot of people attending meetings who are unable to contribute and may be unhappy about being there. The adjuncts are allowed to use their expertise in a variety of places and make efficient use of their time and effort.

# 121. THE WORLD IS NOT INTERESTED . . .

**"The world is not interested in how many storms you encountered, but whether you brought in the ship."**
—*Anonymous.*

### QUESTIONS

- What's the meaning of this quote?
- How does this quote help us understand the importance of role clarification?
- How does the quote miss the point of role clarification?
- How does it apply to your team?
- How would you rewrite it to reflect various aspects of roles on your team, such as role conflict, role ambiguity, role efficacy, and role expectations?

**IN THIS AISLE YOU HAVE FOUND MANY VIEWS OF TEAM ROLES** as well as advice on how to clarify roles as a way of getting your team back on track. While role clarification may be your greatest need, you might want to wander over to the aisles that deal with goal clarity, work planning, and accountability as these are often related to role issues.

 **AISLE 4**

# REEXAMINE THE TEAM'S EMPOWERMENT CHARTER

## OVERVIEW

**EMPOWERMENT!** What is it? Everyone wants it or assumes they have it or believes managers won't give it. There's lots of confusion about what it is . . . about who has it . . . about who can give it . . . about when to use it . . . about why it's important for successful teamwork.

Mature teams are assumed to possess it. It's believed that if you've been around for a while, you must be empowered. Not true! Many teams operate for years with no clear authority to do anything except what they've been told to do.

And yet, empowerment is related to other key business strategies. Speed: Time to market for a new product, turnaround time on customer orders, cycle time on getting a product out the door, and response time to customer inquires are all considered to be indicators of competitive advantage. Speed, or at least rapid speed, is not possible without empowerment.

Think about it: If a team is required to or believes it is required to obtain approval for all key decisions, it takes time to formulate the request and time for the manager to reply. If there are many decisions along the way, as in the case of a new product development team, much time will be lost. The time lost due to the lack of empowerment may mean that a competitor will get to the market first and gain a major competitive advantage.

Consider this: If a customer calls with a complaint about poor service, and the customer service team says "We'll have to check with our boss about this," the customer will end up being more dissatisfied. If, on the other hand, the team could respond on the spot with a way to correct the situation, the customer's dissatisfaction will diminish.

Empowerment encourages independent action, risk taking, and creative solutions—all things that most organizations say they want from teams. If a team is empowered, members get a sense that management believes in their ability to be responsible and to make well-reasoned decisions that will further the best interests of the organization. It's a matter of respect.

Conversely, a team, especially one that has been around for some time, can develop a sense of failure if the members perceive a lack of empowerment. The implication is that they can't be trusted to make decisions in the best interests of the customer, the organization, and the team.

Your team may be stuck because either you are unclear as to the degree of authority you may exercise or you have received a clear message that your level of empowerment is limited. The tips and tools in this aisle will help you understand the importance of empowerment, assess your empowerment quotient, and demonstrate ways to refocus the energies of the team on issues and decisions that can help you get back on track.

## 122. EMPOWERMENT: WHAT IS IT?

Vogt and Murrell (1990, p. 8) provide a very helpful way of understanding empowerment: "In simple definitional terms, the verb to empower means to enable, to allow or to permit and can be conceived as both self-initiated and initiated by others. . . . [Empowerment] is an interactive process based on synergistic, not a zero-sum, assumption about power; that is, the process of empowerment enlarges the power in the situation as opposed to merely redistributing it." Successful empowerment means that (a) all parties have more power and (b) the organization accomplishes more as a result. Therefore, empowerment should result in both a better quality of work life for all employees and increased output, profit, customer satisfaction, or whatever the measures of success are for the organization.

**QUESTIONS**

- How is empowerment defined in your organization?
- Is it a zero-sum game?
- Is it a synergistic process?
- What impact does that have on your team?

 **TIP** Take a look at the book *Empowerment in Organizations* by Judith F. Vogt and Kenneth L. Murrell (1990).

## 123. EMPOWERMENT IS . . .

Power means "control, authority, dominion." The prefix em- means "to put on to" or "to cover with." Empowering then is passing on authority and responsibility. As we refer to it here, empowerment occurs when power goes to employees who then experience a sense of ownership and control over their jobs. Empowered individuals know their jobs belong to them. Given a say in how things are done, employees feel more responsible. When they feel more responsible, they show more initiative in their work, do more, and enjoy the work more.

> "An organization empowers its people when it enables employees to take on more responsibility and to make use of what they know and can learn."
> —*Wellens, Byham, and Wilson (1991).*

**QUESTION**  Does your organization have the same understanding of empowerment?

## 124. WHAT DO YOU NEED US FOR?

A pharmaceutical company established a series of cross-functional "cycle time reduction teams" to look at ways to reduce the time it takes to get a product to the customer. At first each team was told both the number of days the cycle time for their product could be reduced and ways to reduce the time. At one of the first team launch meetings, the team leader asked, "If you are telling us what to do and how to do it, what do you need us for?" After some embarrassment, management agreed with the implication of the question and decided to open up the process and simply charge the teams with developing their own reduction target and providing recommendations on ways to achieve the goal. It was later discovered that the teams usually came up with more ambitious reductions in cycle time than those originally proposed by management!

**QUESTION**  What's the point of this story?

## 125. EMPOWERMENT AND RESPECT

You respect people when you empower them. This is the message of a wonderful book simply called *Respect* (1999), written by Harvard sociologist Sara Lawrence Lightfoot. One of the six people the author profiles in the book, Jennifer, a midwife in a South Bronx clinic, teaches women to be "in charge," to "eliminate the passivity," to "participate and make choices" about their health care. Jennifer says to the women, "This is about you, your body, your baby. You are problem solving, learning, asking questions. You can decide."

**T I P** Managers who empower teams in their area by encouraging and supporting their efforts to make decisions about various aspects of the work are demonstrating the highest form of respect. It sends a powerful and positive message that says "I value you."

**QUESTIONS**

- Are some teams in your organization sitting around passively waiting to be told what to do?

- If so, one way to get them back on the track to high performance is by demonstrating respect via empowerment. What are some ways you can effectively empower teams in your area?

## 126. EMPOWERMENT DOES NOT MEAN ABDICATION!

Some managers think that if teams are empowered that's a signal for them to adopt a completely "hands-off" policy. This is abandonment. In a team-based organization, managers are available to do the following:

- Coach not control;

- Champion not command;

- Advocate not abdicate;

- Teach not preach; and

- Facilitate not obfuscate.

**QUESTION** What role do managers play in your organization?

## 127. EMPOWERMENT AND SPEED

All organizations want speed. Speed in responding to customer requests, speed in filling orders, speed in new product development; but without empowerment, speed is rarely possible. A famous business story about AT&T's development of the cordless phone known as the 4200 illustrates the point (Dumaine, 1989, p. 57):

> John Hanley, vice president of product development, formed teams of six to eight including engineers, manufacturers, and marketers, with authority to make every decision on how the product would work, look, be made, and cost. The key was to set rigid speed requirements—six weeks say, for freezing all design specs. Because the team didn't need to send each decision up the line for approval, it could meet these strict deadlines. With this new approach, AT&T cut development time for the 4200 phone from two years to just a year, while lowering costs and increasing quality.

## 128. FEAR OF EMPOWERMENT

At one of my clients, employees who were told their natural work groups were going to migrate to self-directed teams expressed a high level of fear about the consequences of the actions. One outspoken team leader said what other folks were thinking: "We'll be held accountable, so if anything goes wrong, we'll get fired!" He meant it. He believed that's what happened to supervisors when they did something wrong. In fact, no one had ever been fired for making a mistake unless it was a truly reckless act such as being drunk on the job. Despite these facts, many workers continue to oppose the transfer of responsibility and authority to their teams.

**QUESTIONS**

- What's going on here?
- Why the fear of empowerment?
- How can the fear be overcome?

## 129. TO FEEL EMPOWERED

In his book *The Empowered Manager* (1987), Peter Block reminds us that to feel empowered means several things (p. 65):

a. We feel our survival is in our own hands.

b. We have an underlying purpose.

c. We commit ourselves to achieving that purpose.

**QUESTION**   Do you feel empowered?

## 130. IS YOUR EMPOWERMENT CHARTER CLEAR?

One way you can get your team back on track is to work with management to clarify the team's authority. The team should have a "boundaries" discussion with management to determine which decisions are under the team's control, which are reserved for management, and which are decided jointly. Confusion over the empowerment charter can lead to either (a) apathy and inaction or (b) overly aggressive actions and tense relations with management.

## 131. IS YOUR TEAM EMPOWERED?

### Preparation

Prepare and distribute a copy of the form on the next page to each team member. Prepare a copy of the empowerment continuum on a flip chart or projector.

## ARE WE EMPOWERED?*

*Instructions:* Read each of the following statements and respond by selecting the number that most represents the degree to which the statement is characteristic of your team according to the following scale:

1 = Least Like Our Team    2 = Somewhat Unlike Our Team    3 = Sometimes Like Our Team
4 = Somewhat Like Our Team    5 = Most Like Our Team

| | | | | | | |
|---|---|---|---|---|---|---|
| 1. | Our team has significant influence over the development of our goals. | 1 | 2 | 3 | 4 | 5 |
| 2. | Our team has a voice in all decisions that affect our work. | 1 | 2 | 3 | 4 | 5 |
| 3. | Our team openly shares its problems. | 1 | 2 | 3 | 4 | 5 |
| 4. | Our team has all the resources it needs to be effective. | 1 | 2 | 3 | 4 | 5 |
| 5. | Our team interviews and selects new members. | 1 | 2 | 3 | 4 | 5 |
| 6. | People outside our team do not interfere with our decision-making process. | 1 | 2 | 3 | 4 | 5 |
| 7. | People outside our team are unable to influence our work assignments. | 1 | 2 | 3 | 4 | 5 |
| 8. | We set our own goals, standards, and timelines. | 1 | 2 | 3 | 4 | 5 |
| 9. | People outside our team are very committed to our success. | 1 | 2 | 3 | 4 | 5 |
| 10. | People outside our team provide the tools we need to be successful. | 1 | 2 | 3 | 4 | 5 |
| 11. | Our team regulates its own work schedule and work assignments. | 1 | 2 | 3 | 4 | 5 |
| 12. | Our team is kept informed of external actions that might affect our ability to achieve our goals. | 1 | 2 | 3 | 4 | 5 |
| 13. | Our members can select the way they will perform their work. | 1 | 2 | 3 | 4 | 5 |
| 14. | Our members can evaluate what needs to be done and formulate plans to accomplish it. | 1 | 2 | 3 | 4 | 5 |
| 15. | Our team can change plans as long as the new plans do not conflict with those of other groups. | 1 | 2 | 3 | 4 | 5 |

**Total:**

*Reprinted with permission from Parker and Kropp (1994).

## Interpretation

Place your score on the continuum line below.

| Dependent | | Participative | | Autonomous |
|---|---|---|---|---|
| 15 | 30 | 45 | 60 | 75 |

15 to 30   *Dependent.* Teams that score in this range are managed by traditional managers in a traditional structure. Moving to self-direction will take basic work on such issues as decision making, authority, and task management.

31 to 59   *Participative:* Teams that score in this range are moving progressively toward self-direction. Managers make a significant effort to involve all team members in the action.

60 to 75   *Autonomous:* Teams that score in this range are highly self-managed, reflecting an ability to make task-related decisions, manage performance, and determine both membership and leadership.

## Process

- Create a composite team score by computing the average of all the individual scores.

- Plot the individual scores and the team score on the continuum line.

- Facilitate a discussion on the implications of the results.

- Develop an action plan to move toward more self-direction.

# 132. AUTHORITY ASSESSMENT

Here's a quick checkup on the degree of authority your team exercises.

On *key* decisions that affect the work of your team how are these decisions made?

- ☐ 1. Manager decides and informs the team. No input by members.

- ☐ 2. Manager asks for input from team members. Manager decides.

- ☐ 3. Manager and team members jointly make the decision, usually by consensus.

- ☐ 4. Team is empowered to make the decision. Team informs the manager.

 **T I P**  Facilitate a discussion around the results. Look for various definitions of "key" decisions. Ask for examples of past decisions. Discuss how the level of empowerment has impacted the success of the team. Are there key decisions that are not now but should be made by the team? How can you make the business case to support increased empowerment in these key areas?

# 133. RESPONSIBILITY CHARTING—TODAY

A useful tool for establishing a self-directed team is developing a Team Responsibility Chart. The chart is helpful in both defining the boundaries of the team as well as in resolving ambiguities in the decision-making process. It also helps the team and management plan the transfer of responsibility.

## Preparation

Distribute a copy of the Team Responsibility Chart to each team member. Prepare a copy for presentation on an overhead projector or computer screen.

## Process

At a team meeting, facilitate a discussion with the goal of gaining a consensus on completing the Team Responsibility Chart. Specifically, begin by obtaining an agreement on the key tasks or decisions that must be completed. Then focus on the responsibility for the tasks and facilitate an agreement on who is responsible for each task.

# TEAM RESPONSIBILITY CHART—TODAY

*Directions:* List the specific tasks that have to be completed in the left column below. Then identify whether they are management's responsibility, the team's responsibility, or shared responsibility in the right-hand column.

**Task/Decision**                                    **Responsibility**

# 134. RESPONSIBILITY CHARTING—FUTURE

Now, using the same tasks/decisions, prepare a Team Responsibility Chart that presents your vision of the *future* distribution of responsibility among the team, management, and shared. In addition, for those current management tasks/decisions that you plan to transfer to the team or to a shared responsibility, estimate the *date* you expect the change to be implemented.

# TEAM RESPONSIBILITY CHART—FUTURE

*Directions:* List the specific tasks that have to be completed in the left column below. Then identify whether they will be management's responsibility, the team's responsibility, or a shared responsibility in the right-hand column. If you expect to transfer responsibility, include the date by which you will do so.

**Task/Decision**                                **Responsibility**

# 135. SAMPLE TEAM TASKS

We have found that it is sometimes helpful to have a sample list of tasks or decisions to start the process of empowerment. Here's a list you can use as a starting point that was adapted from Wellins, Byham, and Wilson (1991):

- [ ] Sign work orders
- [ ] Schedule vacations
- [ ] Determine and plan for needed overtime
- [ ] Call for help*
- [ ] Complete production/progress reports
- [ ] Troubleshoot equipment problems
- [ ] Schedule and carry out changeover
- [ ] Maintain records and documentation
- [ ] Assign people to jobs/tasks
- [ ] Train employees
- [ ] Plan and lead team meetings
- [ ] Handle disciplinary issues
- [ ] Coordinate work flow
- [ ] Manage interfaces with other departments
- [ ] Attend management meetings
- [ ] Solve problems when they arise
- [ ] Monitor safety
- [ ] Ensure work standards are met
- [ ] Prepare annual budgets
- [ ] Respond to intra-company complaints
- [ ] Conduct performance appraisals

*Write after the item which people or organizations you regularly call for help (for example, maintenance, information technology, human resources).

## 136. FOUR QUESTIONS

Rees (1997) lists four important questions for management to ponder before they empower a team:

1. What decisions will be the *sole responsibility* of the team?

2. What decisions will be made *collaboratively* between the team and management?

3. What decisions will be *reserved for management,* but *with team input?*

4. What decisions will be *reserved for management,* but *without team input?*

 **T I P** You may not be able to answer all these questions in a precise way, but that should not prevent you from trying. And you should revisit the questions periodically to see whether you are ready for some changes.

## 137. "DO WHATEVER IT TAKES"

A publishing company found a successful road to team empowerment that made managers and team members both feel comfortable. Project teams developing new products, enhancing existing products, or preparing new business strategies were required to produce a detailed project plan. The plan included specific objectives, a detailed timetable, and a budget.

The plan was reviewed with the team's sponsor and often revised to conform to overall corporate guidelines. However, once the plan was approved, the team was empowered to "do whatever it takes to accomplish the plan." The sponsor's role was to provide all the necessary support. For this organization, empowerment became the freedom to act within the context of an approved plan.

This scenario, drawn from one of our client companies, was first published in Parker, *Teamwork* (1998).

# 138. "AMBIGUITY IS AN OPPORTUNITY"

Ideally, you would like to have a clear definition of your authority as a team. I recommend that management meet with the team to agree on the "empowerment charter" of the team. Often, however, this process is not followed. As a result, some teams assume that their default empowerment is "little" or "none" and, therefore, they feel the need to go to management for approval of all key decisions. If this is the behavior of your team, you are reducing your ability to be successful.

**T I P** Rather, you should see ambiguity in regard to your level of empowerment as an opportunity for you to assert yourself, to take action, to respond quickly to customer requests, to decide on new business opportunities, and to make a whole host of other key decisions. Assume this posture: As long as you are taking action that is legal, ethical, customer focused, supports business objectives, and does not violate company policy, GO FOR IT! At best, you may be rewarded for it. At worst, well, as we said earlier, "It is easier to get forgiveness. . . ."

# 139. COORDINATING, SEMI-EMPOWERED, AND EMPOWERED: WHICH ONE ARE YOU?

In Parker (1994, pp. 73-74), three types of teams are identified:

1. *Coordinating.* Coordinating teams are task forces, committees, and some quality teams that are set up to develop recommendations, produce a report, or solve a problem. Their product is then presented to management for approval.

2. *Semi-Empowered.* Semi-empowered teams are often aspiring self-directed teams in the early stages or project teams that, while they have considerable influence, still must obtain approval for major decisions.

3. *Empowered.* Fully empowered teams are just that. They control their resources, set their goals, develop their plans, and then make and implement their decisions.

**QUESTION** Where does your team stand on the empowerment continuum?

# 140. THE EMPOWERMENT CONTINUUM OF CROSS-FUNCTIONAL TEAMS

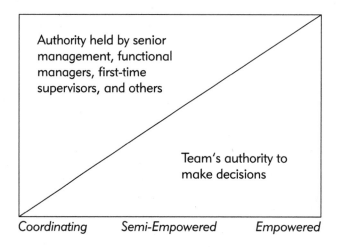

Authority held by senior management, functional managers, first-time supervisors, and others

Team's authority to make decisions

Coordinating      Semi-Empowered      Empowered

# 141. SEMI-EMPOWERED

What does that it really mean to be semi-empowered? Here's a story that helps (Parker, 1994, p. 77):

> At the Texas plant of a major health care company, cross-functional teams are told, "You know what you need to do, so just do it. If you need help from management to make it happen, let us know." However, there are also regular project team review meetings so that management knows what the teams are doing and has an opportunity to comment on their work. While the comments come "after the fact," they obviously have an impact on future team decisions and may even influence the team to be risk-averse.

## 142. "YOU'RE EMPOWERED AS LONG AS I AGREE WITH YOUR DECISIONS!"

While a manager made this statement in jest, it does, of course, reflect an approach to empowerment that is all too often true.

## 143. WHY EMPOWERMENT IS IMPORTANT TO THE SUCCESS OF TEAMS

Here's a simple but powerful exercise for your team to ponder.

### Process

- Ask each team member to think of a time when more empowerment would have improved team performance.

- Ask each person to share his or her story. Probe for the ways that more empowerment would have helped both the team and the organization to be more successful. Look for such outcomes as increased revenues, cost savings, reduced turnaround time, increased customer satisfaction, improved quality, higher employee satisfaction, and other key business indicators relevant to your team.

- Conclude by facilitating a discussion and action plan focusing on presenting a business case to management on increased team empowerment.

## 144. EMPOWERMENT INVENTORY

Developed by Thomas and Tymon (1993), the Empowerment Inventory (available from Consulting Psychologists Press at 800-624-1765) is a brief, self-assessment instrument that measures to what extent team members feel empowered by their jobs and their team. The factors measured are feelings of choice, competence, meaningfulness, and progress.

The booklet includes the questionnaire, scoring instructions, a scoring grid, an interpretative guide, and recommendations for increasing the sense of empowerment based on the results.

## 145. THE ELEMENTS OF TEAM EMPOWERMENT

The article by this name, by Thomas and Tymon (1994), presents three key learnings about empowerment:

1. Empowerment is not something that managers and facilitators *do to* a team. Team empowerment is about a growth process that must occur *within the team itself.* It is a kind of maturation that others can help nurture.

2. Empowerment is not simply a skill-building activity. It involves fundamental changes in the *psychology* of how the team experiences its work. To manage empowerment, you have to know something about the nature of work tasks and the satisfactions that teams can get from them.

3. Work tasks, in turn, are *not just activities* that must be performed. Work tasks are activities directed toward accomplishing *purposes.* Many of the satisfactions of empowerment come from pursuing worthwhile purposes.

## 146. EMPOWERED TEAMS OF OFFICE WORKERS: A VIDEO

This video, "Improving Work Systems," describes the change process to self-directed work teams at IDS Financial Services, the subsidiary of American Express that processes mutual fund transactions. You can buy the video from Blue Sky Productions at 1–800–358–0022. The video does a good job of describing the business case that led to the work redesign and the subsequent formation of customer focused, empowered teams.

## 147. EMPOWERED TEAMS IN A FACTORY: A VIDEO

Another excellent video from Blue Sky Productions is "Redesigning a Workplace for Self-Regulation: The Rohm & Haas Story." It provides some good examples of empowerment in action and the cooperation of labor and management in contributing to the success of the process.

# 148. ECF GRID: BALANCING EMPOWERMENT AND CUSTOMER NEEDS

Here is an exercise to help your team look at the extent of customer and employee focus in your daily work.

*High Empowerment/High Customer Focus.* Teams in this category maintain a healthy balance between the needs of customers and the needs of team members. Team members engage in an ongoing dialogue with customers about their requirements and are empowered to respond quickly to those needs in a manner that both satisfies the customer and maintains the team dynamics.

*High Empowerment/Low Customer Focus.* There is a "We know what's best for you" mentality on the part of the team in its relationship with the customer. The team is empowered to act, but sometimes uses that power in an arrogant, condescending manner toward the customer. The end is likely to be a high level of employee satisfaction, coupled with a low level of customer satisfaction—and often the loss of business. Scientific, engineering, and software development teams are often found in this category.

*Low Empowerment/High Customer Focus.* Teams of this type tend to be so focused on satisfying the customer that they forget about employee needs for empowerment. Team members react quickly to routine customer requests, but have difficulty with requests that do not fit established patterns or past practices. In these latter situations, team members must check with management for decisions, and thus the customer does not receive the desired rapid response. Customer call centers and retail businesses are often found in this category.

*Low Empowerment/Low Customer Focus.* Teams falling in this area tend to be inwardly focused on a series of individual tasks or projects that are determined and directed by management with little concern for the needs of customers. It is not uncommon for basic research teams in the so-called "discovery" or "exploratory" areas to exhibit this type of behavior. The downside of this mentality is a limitation on being able to follow one's instincts and intuition and a lack of concern for the marketability of the potential outcome.

**QUESTION**  Where does your team fit?

**ECF Grid**

**Customer Focus**

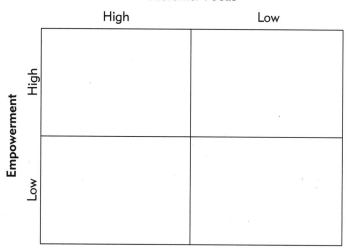

## Preparation

Prepare a copy of the ECF Grid for display on a projector or computer screen.

## Process

- Ask each team member to place the team in one of the four quadrants.

- Record the responses on the ECF Grid.

- Then facilitate a discussion of the responses, probing for the reasons for the placement and examples.

- Conclude by developing a plan of action to move toward the desired location.

# 149. YOU ARE EMPOWERED!

In our experience, most teams have more authority than they realize and utilize. In a rather typical scenario, a manager was asked to approve a team's decision and his response was (somewhat impatiently), "I told them they could decide that. I don't need to approve. . . ."

 **T I P** Take a few minutes to think about some recent team recommendations that you sent up the line for management approval. Is it possible that the team might have been empowered to turn those team recommendations into team decisions?

# 150. I BELIEVE . . .

"When I believe in you, you believe in yourself."
—*Author unknown*

 **QUESTIONS**
- What is the meaning of this quote?
- Have you ever had someone really believe in you?
- What was the impact on you or on someone believing in you?
- What does this have to do with empowerment on our team?
- What can we do about it?

# 151. FORGIVENESS AND PERMISSION

Use this well-known quote to stimulate a discussion of your team's attitude toward empowerment:

"It's easier to get forgiveness than permission."

### QUESTIONS

- Do we believe this is true about our organization?

- Do we act as if this is true?

- What are some examples of actions we have taken without first gaining permission?

- What have been the results of these actions?

- How should we act in the future?

**THIS AISLE PROVIDED INFORMATION, IDEAS, AND TOOLS** for empowerment and ways your team can focus on a better understanding of the dimensions of empowered teams and then facilitate a move to an effective level of empowerment. Since empowerment is a means to effective teamwork and organizational effectiveness, it may be important for your team to seek out other tools in the aisles dealing with goal setting (Aisle 1), role clarification (Aisle 3), and accountability (Aisle 10).

 **AISLE 5**

# REFURBISH THE TEAM'S TALENT BANK

## OVERVIEW

**TEAMS NEED TALENT.** They need skills, knowledge, and what Daniel Goleman (1995) calls "emotional intelligence" to get the job done. You can't have a high-performing team with low-talent team members!

Most teams, like yours, have talent. In fact, usually more talent than they realize. If your team is not living and working up to its potential, the issues for your team are

- Do you have the right people?

- Do all the members want to be on this team at this time?

- Is the talent aligned with the team's current mission?

- What types of development opportunities are needed to refine the team's talent?

- Is it possible to reshuffle the team membership at this time?

- Does the team have a different set of expertise needs at this time?

- If we cannot change the membership, in what ways can we augment the talent bank?

If your team needs to get back on track, you can look at the membership in relationship to the team's mission and its customers. If your customer base has changed, and therefore your mission, it might be time to reexamine the other side of the equation: Do you have the right skill set going forward?

A real issue for some teams is that, despite a need to change the membership composition, such a change is just not possible for a variety of reasons having to do with human resources policy, labor market constraints, organizational politics, and corporate culture. In these situations, it may be necessary to be a little more creative in your approach to refurbishment of the team's talent bank.

In this aisle, you will find a variety of ideas, suggestions, exercises, and scenarios to help you get back on track by focusing on the skills, knowledge, and other expertise of the team's membership. Specifically, a good place to start is an assessment of the talent on your current team—with a view toward future business needs and types of talent that will be required. Sometimes you can change team membership to add what is needed, but often it is just not possible. As a result, this aisle also includes suggestions for getting the talent without changing the composition of the team.

## 152. THE LEADER'S ROLE

Kline (1999) argues that it is the leader's role to develop team members' talents. She believes that the leader should become familiar with each member's knowledge, skills, and abilities (KSAs) and then to match them with the team's needs in the future. Although very time-consuming, this effort can pay big dividends for the team in a number of ways:

1. New members can be added that augment the existing team skill set.
2. Training can be provided that focuses specifically on KSAs needed by the team.
3. Employee satisfaction typically increases when development opportunities are provided.

## 153. MATURITY MAY JUST BE ANOTHER WORD FOR STAGNATION

If you have truly reached the high performing, mature team level, you must be concerned about stagnation. It's a concern of all successful teams—that period just after the launch of a new product, the deployment of a new system, the presentation of a set of recommended organizational changes, the opening of a new customer service center, the successful completion of a leadership development program, or other similar major milestones. Talk to a mountain climber. It's getting to the summit that turns him or her on, not the view from the top. It's the same with team members. When the challenge has been met, most members want to move on to the next challenge, not stick around to evaluate the process or maintain the new system.

If, however, the team does need to keep working on enhancements to the new product, debugging the new systems, helping to implement the organizational changes, managing the new customer service center, or evaluating the leadership development program, it may take a different talent mix.

**T I P** Let the mountain climbers move on to their next Everest and substitute new members with skills, knowledge, and experience in maintenance, evaluation, quality assurance, and management.

## 154. NEW BLOOD = NEW CULTURE

The leader of one of our client teams in telecommunications realized that his management team needed an infusion of new ideas and new talents. He recognized (with some prodding from us) that the team lacked some critical business skills. The solution: Recruit internally (within the corporation) for three people who would bring both technical and marketing talent to the team. What he didn't foresee was the dramatic impact the new talent would have on the overall culture of the organization. The talent infusion led a shift in the culture from a laid-back, family oriented culture to a culture that retained the best of the old while adding a revenue-driven, business culture.

## 155. MISSION IMPOSSIBLE

There is a strong and important relationship between your team's mission and the talent required. It is possible that one reason your team seems to be derailed is that there is a mismatch between your mission and the talent pool of your team.

 **QUESTIONS**

- When is the last time the team reviewed its mission?

- Does your mission reflect your current roles and customers?

- Is the talent mix on your team aligned with your current mission?

- What changes are needed in your mission?

- What changes are needed in your team's talent bank to support the team's current mission?

- How will you go about changing the talent bank?

## 156. A TALE OF TWO TEAMS

As the Chinese market has opened wide to American companies, many organizations have scrambled to position themselves to compete in that marketplace. One telecommunications team prepared itself by stockpiling engineering talent familiar with the language and culture of China. The other team waited and waited . . . and then waited some more . . . until the market really opened and then found it difficult to find the necessary talent to represent them in China.

 **T I P** Successful teams anticipate future talent needs in accordance with their strategic business plans.

## 157. INCLUDE HUMAN RESOURCES IN YOUR STRATEGIC PLAN

When doing a SWOT (strengths, weaknesses, opportunities, and threats) analysis, your team should take a hard look at the current strengths and weaknesses of your human resources against the potential future business opportunities to determine whether the talent bank needs to be refurbished.

**QUESTION** Do you have the required skills and knowledge to meet the challenges of your business in the future?

## 158. DIVERSITY AS A TALENT

When opportunities exist to add new team members or replace members who move on, teams should consider diversifying in terms of gender and ethnicity. A team of white males may work fine in some situations, but in today's global business world, a diverse membership gives your team an edge in communicating with people in many markets throughout the world. While diversity can increase your ability to relate to customers and suppliers, it also adds value to the team's internal planning, communication, and decision-making processes. It is an established fact that diversity in style, perceptions, culture, and experience usually results in more creativity and innovation.

**QUESTION**   Are you satisfied with the diversity on your team?

## 159. DIVERSITY IN PRACTICE

One engineering team saw its diversity as a strategic advantage in obtaining and retaining business throughout the world.

- Several members were born and educated in South America, had worked in various countries, spoke Spanish fluently, and were, therefore, able to effectively manage projects in most areas.

- A number of team members spoke several Chinese languages, some were from Taiwan, some from mainland China, some from Hong Kong, one person from Viet Nam, and together they formed a powerful business team in the Asia/Pacific area.

- The European subgroup included engineers who were from France, Italy, and England and spoke a variety of languages.

In all cases they understood the cultural norms that have an impact on social interactions and business discussions.

## 160. DETERMINING TECHNICAL COMPETENCIES

Our colleague Deborah Harrington-Mackin (1996) has provided us with an effective methodology for determining whether a team has the necessary competencies. First, identify the necessary tasks and then the technical and behavioral competencies to perform each task. Here are a series of questions designed to help identify the necessary technical competencies.

## Technical Competencies

| Competency | What Do They Need to Know How to Do? | What Do They Need to Be Taught? |
|---|---|---|
| *Job Knowledge.* What skills, knowledge, and abilities are needed to complete the task according to accepted procedure? | | |
| *Productivity.* What abilities are needed to meet standard output, efficiency, and follow-through? | | |
| *Quality of Work.* What abilities are needed to meet accuracy, reliability, and appearance standards? | | |
| *Communication Skills.* What abilities are needed to communicate clearly and effectively, both verbally and nonverbally? | | |
| *Equipment.* What abilities are required to use equipment properly and to observe all safety procedures? | | |
| *Environment.* What level of understanding is needed to comply with all relevant customer policies, restrictions, government requirements, and personnel policies? | | |

## Process

- Identify the major team tasks, such as responding to customer inquires.
- Complete a Technical Competencies and a Behavioral Competencies chart for each major task.
- Identify the major skills and knowledge gaps.
- Prepare a training and development plan to fill each gap.

# 161. IDENTIFY BEHAVIORAL COMPETENCIES

Here is the companion chart for behavioral competencies.

## Behavioral Competencies

| Competency | What Do They Need to Know How to Do? | What Do They Need to Be Taught? |
| --- | --- | --- |
| *Interpersonal Skills.* What competencies are required regarding responsiveness to others, including listening and speaking? | | |
| *Dependability.* What abilities are needed to be prompt and reliable and to comply with work procedures? | | |
| *Managing Workload.* What abilities are needed to organize, plan, and prioritize work and to handle pressure? | | |
| *Responsibility.* What competencies are required to take initiative and be open-minded and self-starting? | | |
| *Responsiveness to Authority.* What abilities are needed to follow procedure and instruction and to support the team? | | |
| *Acceptance of Suggestions and Criticism.* What abilities are required to give and receive feedback? | | |
| *Creativity and Risk Taking.* What strategies can be used to encourage and develop creativity? | | |

## 162. TALENT BANK INVENTORY EXERCISE

In most cases, teams do not utilize all of the talent that already exists on their team. The reason? They simply don't know about it! Here's an exercise we use that helps a team create a current inventory of team talents.

### Process

- Ask team members to pair off and interview each other using the following list as a guide to note taking:

  *Past Work Experiences*: types of jobs, projects, and companies you've experienced.

  *Past Team Experiences*: types of teams you've been on, team roles you've played, as well as both successful and unsuccessful experiences you've had.

  *Operational Skills*: things you can do, equipment you can operate, systems you can use.

  *Specialized Knowledge*: information you have, education you've completed.

  *Emotional Intelligence*: interpersonal skills you possess and can use.

- Then ask each person to prepare a summary report, post it on a sheet of flip-chart paper, and present it to the rest of the team.

- Facilitate a discussion designed to clarify anything in the reports.

- After the meeting, ask the team scribe to collect all the reports and publish a complete team inventory.

## 163. CONSIDER NONTECHNICAL TALENT TOO

Over the years, the membership of your team may have evolved in ways that have skewed it away from the team process behaviors that provide the necessary "glue" for team success. To help you assess your talent in this area, we have created a brief survey instrument from a list originally created by Rees (1997).

### Preparation

Prepare a copy of the Assessing Team Behaviors form for distribution to each team member.

## ASSESSING TEAM BEHAVIORS

*Directions:* Look over the list of behaviors in the left column and indicate whether you are satisfied (S) with the team's talent in this area or whether you think the team needs improvement (NI) in this area.

| Typical Team Behaviors | Satisfied | Needs Improvement |
|---|---|---|
| 1. People who see the "big picture." | S | NI |
| 2. People who can do the detail work. | S | NI |
| 3. People who can coordinate and oversee progress. | S | NI |
| 4. People who are creative and who take risks. | S | NI |
| 5. People who can do the research and data collection. | S | NI |
| 6. People who have good collaboration and communication skills. | S | NI |
| 7. People who keep the team linked to the larger organization. | S | NI |
| 8. People who value consensus and work hard to reach consensus. | S | NI |

## Process

- Ask each person to complete the assessment form and return it to you or to an external resource such as human resources or project management.
- Compile the results.
- Report the results to the team.
- Facilitate a discussion about behaviors that need to be strengthened.
- Develop a plan that includes ways to address the areas in the future.
- Alternatively, ask team members to complete the instrument at a meeting and lead a discussion based on their responses.

# 164. CUSTOMER CHANGE = MEMBERSHIP CHANGE

Has your customer base changed? Are you now serving customers in Europe? Asia/Pacific? Latin America? Africa? Have customer needs changed? Are customers now looking for more technical support? More strategic planning? More Internet-based solutions? Less face-to-face consulting? Fewer written documents?

What types of expertise do your customers require? How do your team's talents stack up?

## Process

- Use the following chart to identify your key customer needs and team members' talents that match those needs.

- Write them in the left column.

- Determine whether each of the talents is sufficient (OK) or need improvement (NI).

- Develop a set of action items that address areas that need improvement.

- Alternatively, you may want to involve team members in this exercise. When you identify a talent as NI, write an action plan that specifies how the improvement will be achieved (for example, adding a new member or training an existing member).

---

## ASSESSING TEAM TALENTS AND CUSTOMER NEEDS

| Key Customer Needs/Team Talents | OK/NI |
|---|---|
| _____ | _____ |
| _____ | _____ |
| _____ | _____ |
| _____ | _____ |
| _____ | _____ |

# 165. YOUR STAGE . . . YOUR TALENT

The stage your team is in determines the type of talent needed by your team. What stage are you in? Do you have the right talent?

In his classic article, Tuckman (1965) identified and described four stages of team development.

1. *Forming.* Lack of clarity about the team's task and team member roles and some interpersonal distance.

2. *Storming.* Disagreement and conflict among members about both the task and process of the team.

3. *Norming.* The team agrees on guidelines (norms) about communication, decision making, meetings, and leadership.

4. *Performing.* There is agreement on goals, roles, and relationships, and the team is equally concerned about getting the work done and maintaining the team process.

Here's a brief exercise to show the relationship between talent needs and team development stages. Given the above definitions of the four stages, you will decide what team talents are needed to negotiate each stage successfully.

## Preparation

Prepare a copy of the following chart for projection on an overhead or LCD projector on a personal computer.

# TALENT NEEDS AT EACH STAGE

*Instructions:* Complete this form by identifying the talents, technical and behavioral, that are needed at each stage of team development. Pay special attention to and provide more detail for your team's current stage.

| Stage | Talent Needs |
|---|---|
| Forming | _____ |
| Storming | _____ |
| Norming | _____ |
| Performing | _____ |

## Action Planning

What stage is your team in now? What makes you say this?

What type of talent does your team need now?

## Process

- Display the chart.
- Review the four stages.
- Facilitate a discussion on the talent needs of each stage.
- Write or type the talent needs on the chart.
- Identify your team's current stage.
- Discuss in depth your current and future talent needs.
- Gain agreement among team members on the needs.
- Develop an action plan to ensure the team has these talents.

## 166. USE ADJUNCT MEMBERS

Can't change the membership composition of your team? Consider augmenting your team with adjunct members who can provide the necessary skills and knowledge on an as-needed basis. Adjunct members do not need to attend all meetings, but may be called on to perform certain tasks at certain times.

## 167. ADJUNCT TECHNICAL WRITERS

One software development team needed a technical writer to put together the documentation for a new product release. Since the company only had a few writers, they could not serve as permanent members of any team. However, they joined the team at the time their skill was needed to provide the necessary documentation. It was a win-win for everyone. The team got the skills they needed when they were needed, the writer used her skills in an efficient manner without a lot of wasted time, and the organization made effective use of limited resources.

## 168. EXTERNAL EDUCATION

If your assessment demonstrates a need for new and different skills, a good way to keep your team intact is to send team members to outside courses that provide the skills you need. Let's say your organization is moving from a heavily regulated industry to a more open market environment and now needs to know how to market your services. Instead of recruiting a marketing expert, consider sending one of your current members to a high quality course in marketing.

 **T I P** The American Society for Training and Development (ASTD) is a good source for external education courses. Contact ASTD at www.astd.org.

## 169. REFURBISHING THE PEOPLE MIX
## VS. REFURBISHING THE TEAM'S TALENT BANK

An organizational assessment indicated that the top management team needed an infusion of new people to both provide needed resources to address future business challenges and to "shake things up a bit." However, it was also clear that, since the same team had been together for some time, strong bonds and a positive culture existed. Therefore, rather than "refresh the people mix," the team elected to send individual team members to various external education programs.

## 170. SANITY CHECK

Are you concerned that the culture of your team mitigates against tough assessments of key business decisions? In other words, are members reluctant to speak up and challenge plans, decisions, and other actions made by your team? Some teams, not wanting or able to add new permanent team members, use a "sanity checker." A sanity checker is a person external to the team—a technical or management consultant from inside or outside of the company—who is given carte blanche to provide an honest critique of the team's actions.

## 171. NEW ASSIGNMENTS

One way some teams shake up the talent bank is to give team members new assignments. New roles for team members has a dual effect. The new person brings a new perspective and, one hopes, some new energy to the task that will lead to an increase in team effectiveness. However, a new assignment can also be used as a career development opportunity for the person.

 **T I P** If your team needs an energy boost, move the players around; give people new tasks, new challenges, and new opportunities to stretch themselves and, in the end, bring a new intensity to the team.

## 172. USE MENTORS

Mentoring is another intervention used by teams that cannot or do not want to change the composition of their team. It is possible to assign a mentor to team members who want to develop expertise in a specific area. The mentor can provide advice and counsel as well as directed learning experiences for the team member.

## 173. RESOURCE ON MENTORING

A great new resource is Murray (2001). A "how-to" section of the book includes a readiness assessment, checklists, forms, and solid advice.

## 174. TAKE A SHOT

Consider this quote:

*"You miss 100 percent of the shots you never take."*
    *—Wayne Gretsky*

### QUESTIONS

- What do you think Gretsky meant by this quote?
- What "shots" have you taken lately?
- What "shots" have you not taken? Why?
- Does our team need to "take a shot" now?

## 175. "TALENT WINS GAMES, BUT TEAMWORK WINS CHAMPIONSHIPS"

**QUESTIONS**

- Does your team have the necessary talent?
- Does your team have the necessary teamwork?
- What changes do you need to make in the talent area?
- What changes do you need to make in the teamwork area?

**IN THIS AISLE THERE WERE A VARIETY OF TOOLS** for ensuring that your team's talents match the business environment in which you find yourself. However, you will also find tools that can help in Aisle 2, Refresh the People Mix, Aisle 10, Refocus on Accountability, and Aisle 16, Regain Member Commitment.

 **AISLE 6**

# RECONSIDER STYLE DIFFERENCES

## OVERVIEW

**OVER TIME YOUR TEAM MAY HAVE FALLEN PREY** to a rather typical cause of derailment—style similarity. There is a tendency for mature teams to migrate toward a membership where there is great homogeneity. There is a comfort that comes from everyone thinking and acting within a narrow frame of reference. In fact, the assessment that "We all pretty much think alike" is considered a virtue by many team members.

The tendency toward common styles among mature teams comes from a variety of factors:

- The team leader tends to recruit new members who are similar to the existing members ("I look for people who can fit in"; translation: "think and act like the rest of us").

- Style differences and conflict are not as highly valued.

- Members with different styles that are in the minority tend to move on to other teams.

As a result, a form of complacency sets in. And that can be the death knell for a successful team. When style differences among team members are minimal, it can lead to many unintended results:

- *Boredom.* With everyone going in the same direction, approaching problems in the same way, things can get pretty dull.

- *Lack of Creativity.* Breakthroughs come from a clash of ideas and styles, not from similarities in thinking.

- *Rote Problem Solving.* Instead of brainstorming, in-depth analysis, and examining alternatives, you get quick and clean solutions.

- *Dreary Decision Process.* A so-called consensus comes easily, but the decisions may not be in the best interests of the business because the process was pro-forma.

Therefore, one reason your team may be in need of rejuvenation could be the lack of style differences among the members. In this aisle, we will look at style differences and provide you with tools to get your team back on the winning track. Specifically, you will find a great deal of information about style differences and their impact on team effectiveness, with an emphasis on my Team Player Survey. The nature of the licensing arrangement makes it impossible to reproduce the Survey here, but it can be obtained at minimal cost from Consulting Psychologists Press.

# 176. STYLE?

Your style is a reflection of your behaviors. It describes HOW you go about carrying out your role. In psychological terms, style is often called "type," as in psychological type. Each type or style includes people with similar but necessarily the same characteristics.

## 177. CARL JUNG

We all owe an intellectual debt to the psychologist Carl Jung, who first identified the concept of psychological types (Jung, 1923). His types resulted from two fundamental orientations: (1) introversion and (2) extroversion and then four "functions"—(1) thinking, (2) feeling, (3) sensation, and (4) intuition. Jung combined these factors and created eight types or styles. People familiar with the Myers-Briggs Type Indicator (MBTI) will recognize these types, as the instrument is based on the Jungian types.

## 178. STYLE AND TEAM EFFECTIVENESS

How does the concept of style help us get our team back on track? If your team has lost some of its vigor it may be that:

- The style composition of your team has migrated to a predominance of one style.

- One style is missing and the team is not able to benefit from the strengths of that style.

- Members do not appreciate the style differences that some members bring to the team.

- Members are not willing or able to adjust their styles to current needs of the team.

- Some members are using their strengths to an "excess," resulting in some dysfunctional behaviors.

# 179. PARKER'S FOUR STYLES

In *Team Players and Teamwork* (Parker, 1990, 1996), I identified four types or styles from my research with some fifty companies. "Each style contributes in different ways to the success of the team, and each style has a downside when carried to an extreme . . ." (Parker, p. 63). Briefly, the four styles are

1.  *Contributor.* The task-oriented person who gets the team to focus on the short-term, specific issues facing the team.

2.  *Collaborator.* The goal-directed member who sees the vision, mission, and strategic issues as paramount.

3.  *Communicator.* The process-oriented person who works on the internal dynamics and interpersonal issues of the team.

4.  *Challenger.* This person questions the goals, methods, and process of the team and encourages the team to take well-conceived risks.

# 180. PARKER TEAM PLAYER SURVEY

The *Parker Team Player Survey* (PTPS) is a self-report assessment instrument that helps you identify your style as a team player (Parker, 1991). It yields four scores—one for each of the team player styles: Contributor, Collaborator, Communicator, and Challenger. The purpose of the PTPS is to increase awareness of the behaviors required for effective teamwork. In addition, there is a companion instrument, the *Parker Team Player Survey: Styles of Another Person (SOAP)* (Parker, 1991). Other team members or other similar persons complete this instrument so that the self-report can be compared with the perceptions of others on the team. (Both instruments are available from Consulting Psychologists Press, 3803 East Bayshore Road, Palo Alto, California 94303, 800-624-1765, www.cpp-db.com.)

# 181. OVERLOAD PROBLEM 1: CONTRIBUTOR

If your team is dominated by people whose preferred style is Contributor, be alert to the following behaviors:

- *Data Overload.* Reports that are too long and too detailed.
- *Unrealistic Standards.* Unnecessarily high expectations (higher than the customer's).
- *Perfection Paralysis.* A perception that the work is never quite good enough.
- *Unclear View of the End Goal.* Doing lots of things right, but not necessarily the right things.
- *Lack of Concern for Team Process.* Focused on the details of the task to the exclusion of the interpersonal dynamics of the team.

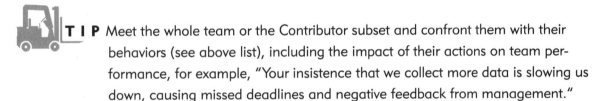 **T I P** Meet the whole team or the Contributor subset and confront them with their behaviors (see above list), including the impact of their actions on team performance, for example, "Your insistence that we collect more data is slowing us down, causing missed deadlines and negative feedback from management."

# 182. OVERLOAD PROBLEM 2: COLLABORATOR

If Collaborators dominate your team, here are some warning signs:

- Lack of attention to basic team tasks and work performance issues.
- Failure to focus on the interpersonal needs of team members.
- Unwillingness to revisit and challenge the team's mission, goals, and plans.
- Complaints about other people who do not think strategically.
- Little interest in managing the effort necessary to implement the team's plans.

**T I P** Negotiate a win-win solution that continues the focus on the strategic plan, but also extract an agreement to develop and implement a new plan that includes a focus on external customers and internal employee development.

## 183. OVERLOAD PROBLEM 3: COMMUNICATOR

When the dominant style of your team is Communicator, you may experience:

- Process being viewed as an end in itself ("Are we having fun yet?")
- Failure to challenge or give constructive feedback to teammates.
- Lack of attention to the completion of team tasks and reaching milestones.
- Overuse and abuse of humor.
- Way too much time spent on planning the next party, dinner, or offsite meeting.

 **T I P** Conduct a project review or other assessment that gets the team to look at progress toward meeting its goals. On the surface the team will think everything is fine because they are having a good time, but they need to see that they can have both positive process and effective task accomplishment at the same time.

# 184. OVERLOAD PROBLEM 4: CHALLENGER

If your team has an overload of Challengers, look for these potential danger signs:

- An excess of disagreements creating a series of stalemates.

- Taking an excessive number of unreasonable risks.

- Excessive rigidity, inflexibility, and self-righteous behavior.

- There appears to be enjoyment in simply challenging and "doing battle."

- Personal attacks on other team members under the guise of discussing the issues.

 **TIP** Revisit and/or establish team norms that deal with such areas as communication, respect, openness, listening, and willingness to back off.

# 185. THE LEADER'S STYLE

It is possible that your team leader has the wrong style. Maybe all team leaders should be Collaborators. Wrong! You can be an effective team leader with any of the four styles. However, it may be that, at this time in the life of your team, the leader needs to be more of one style and less of another. Let's assume that as a result of Step 1 you find that your team needs to develop a new mission, goals, and action plan to address the current realities of the business; then your team leader needs to make greater use of the _____ style.

**Name that style.** *Hint:* It starts with the letter "C." On the other hand, if your team is "doing the same old things in the same old way," then the leader needs to make use of the strengths of the _____ style. The key to being a successful team leader is an ability to "flex" to the style that the team needs at the moment.

# 186. TEAM PLAYER STYLE PROFILE

You can use the primary styles of the individual members of your team to prepare a composite team style profile, like the sample below. Collect the survey results from all of the members and prepare a team grid. In this grid the placement of the "X" indicates the person's primary style.

| Name/Style | Contributor | Collaborator | Communicator | Challenger |
|---|---|---|---|---|
| Sanji | X | | | |
| Rafael | X | | | |
| Joanne | | | X | |
| Saul | X | | | |
| Nathan | | X | | |
| Samantha | X | | | |
| Phil | | X | | |
| Reham | X | | | |
| John | | | | X |

With these data you can begin a discussion of the strengths and potential weaknesses of the team.

## QUESTIONS

- What are the strengths of this team? What things do they do well?

- What are the weaknesses? What are the implications of these weaknesses for such things as team decision making, problem solving, conflict management, and risk taking?

- If the team is unable to change its membership, what can be done to address these weaknesses?

# 187. MISSING PERSPECTIVES

If, as in the previous example, one style does not exist with any degree of strength, there are implications for the overall success of the team. If your team is having problems, it may be due to an imbalance in the style makeup of your team. The absence of the strengths incorporated in the missing style may lead to bad decisions, missed opportunities, poor use of team resources, and overall member dissatisfaction.

 **T I P** Your team may be derailed because one or more perspectives are missing.

# 188. MISSING PERSPECTIVE 1: CONTRIBUTOR

The main problem here is a lack of focus on the task at hand. If your team is missing the strengths of the Contributor, you may experience some or all of the following results:

- Work not completed in an efficient manner;
- Time and resources wasted;
- Meetings poorly planned and executed; and/or
- Performance standards lowered.

 **T I P** Introduce structured planning tools such as PERT charts, tracking systems, meeting agendas, and project reviews.

## 189. MISSING PERSPECTIVE 2: COLLABORATOR

The biggest concern here is unclear direction for the team. If your team is missing the Collaborator's perspective, you may have already experienced these results:

- Out-of-date or nonexistent mission statement;
- Tired, worn-out goals;
- Uninspiring objectives and plans; and/or
- Members "doing their own thing" with no common goal.

 **T I P** Schedule a team retreat where you develop a new vision, mission, and goals and be sure everyone is committed to it before you leave.

## 190. MISSING PERSPECTIVE 3: COMMUNICATOR

Your biggest problem here is the interpersonal climate on the team. If your team lacks the strengths of the Communicator, you may have already seen such things as:

- A formal, even tense atmosphere;
- Most interpersonal interactions being about team tasks;
- Lots of talking but not much listening;
- Little or ineffective use of the consensus method; and/or
- Not much fun.

 **T I P** Establish a set of new or revised norms that focus on the internal climate and interpersonal relationships.

# 191. MISSING PERSPECTIVE 4: CHALLENGER

The key concern here is "groupthink" because of the pressures to "go along" rather than challenge conventional thinking. If your team lacks the perspective of the Challenger, you may experience some of the following norms:

- Lack of candor in team discussions;
- Reservations about team decisions not expressed;
- Decisions made that contradict known data; and/or
- Conservative, risk-adverse decisions.

 **T I P** Appoint a devil's advocate at each team meeting whose role is to raise questions about issues and decisions that are considered by the team.

# 192. STYLE SCENARIO

We worked with one pharmaceutical company team that had only four members. Their PTPS scores indicated that the team was composed of one each Contributor, Collaborator, Communicator, and Challenger. Sounds like a perfect team. And yet, there was great conflict among the members.

 **QUESTIONS**

- Why do you think there was conflict?
- What were the causes?
- What do they need to do to resolve their differences?

 **T I P** The team needed to learn (and they did) the strengths each style brought to the team and how this diversity strengthens the entire team. Conflict was reduced because they accepted and used the differences among their teammates.

## 193. THE STORY OF ANDY

A management team was having some difficulty with one of its members. It seems that Andy was the only team member who would openly disagree with other members of the team. As a result, he was accused by his teammates of not being a team player. However, when the team went through a team-building experience using the PTPS, they realized that the Challenger was an important perspective to have on a team and began to value Andy's contributions. Andy felt legitimized but also learned how to be a more effective Challenger by using questions rather than confrontational accusations.

## 194. TEAM PLAYER VIDEO

A useful support for any session using the *Parker Team Player Survey* is the video, *Team Building II: What Makes a Good Team Player?* The twenty-minute video uses vignettes and humor to depict the four styles and their impact on successful teamwork. It is available from CRM Films, 2215 Faraday Avenue, Carlsbad, CA 92008, 800–421–0833, 760–431–9800 or www.crmlearning.com.

## 195. TEAM PLAYER GAMES

For team-building and training events, a good resource to spice things up and have fun while people learn is *Team Players: Games to Explore Team Player Styles,* available from Workshops by Thiagi, 4423 East Trailridge Road, Bloomington, IN 47408, 812–332–1478. The package includes more than a dozen training activities such as card games, board games, a classification game, and even a card trick!

## 196. STYLE RESOURCE

A comprehensive resource on team styles is the *Team Building Workshop Facilitator's Guide* (Parker, 1997). The guide includes five team training outlines, five team-building designs, six lecturette notes, seventeen team building/training activities, thirteen overhead masters, pre-course assignments, and norms data for the PTPS.

## 197. BELBIN TEAM ROLES

Another well-researched and widely used concept is found in the work of Meredith Belbin (1981). Belbin identified what he called eight team roles (we might call them styles):

1. *Company Worker.* Conservative, dutiful, predictable, with organizing ability and practical common sense who works hard and has self-discipline.

2. *Chairman.* Calm, self-confident, controlled, with a capacity for treating and welcoming all potential contributors on their merits and without prejudice.

3. *Shaper.* Highly strung, outgoing, dynamic, with drive and a readiness to challenge inertia, ineffectiveness, complacency, or self-deception.

4. *Plant.* Individualistic, serious-minded, unorthodox, with genius, imagination, intellect, and knowledge.

5. *Resource Investigator.* Extroverted, enthusiastic, curious, and communicative, with a capacity for contacting people and exploring anything new.

6. *Monitor-Evaluator.* Sober, unemotional, and prudent, with good judgment, discretion, and hard-headedness.

7. *Team Worker.* Socially oriented, rather mild and sensitive, with an ability to respond to people and to situations and to promote team spirit.

8. *Completer-Finisher.* Painstaking, orderly, conscientious, and anxious, with a capacity for follow-through and perfectionism.

## 198. BELBIN'S TEAM ROLES AS A TOOL

The Team Roles can be a tool to get your team back on track because, as Belbin points out, the most consistently positive results come from teams composed of a mixture of all these roles. However, creating such a delicate balance is not easy. Therefore, in practical terms, you are better off with a team whose members are less specialized and are able to cover a number of the roles. Adaptable team members who can shift to a role that the team needs at the moment are the most valued. See www.belbin.com for helpful tools.

 **T I P** Team members who are strong in one area have greater difficulty shifting gears to use the strengths of another style. Therefore, your team may be more vulnerable to derailment if there is a style overload in one or two styles and if the primary style scores for those people are quite high.

## 199. TEAM STYLE ASSESSMENT

Here's a quick way to determine whether style differences are causing team derailment. Respond to the following statements with a yes (Y), sometimes (S), or no (N) in the blank.

_____ 1. Do team members primarily think and act in a manner similar to the leader?

_____ 2. When things go wrong, do some members sit quietly and allow others to dominate the discussions and make all the decisions?

_____ 3. Do members try to avoid or smooth over differences among members?

_____ 4. When things go wrong, do some members "put down" or show a lack of respect for the ideas of other team members?

_____ 5. When the team considers a problem, does everyone seem to agree without considering real alternatives?

_____ 6. If a team member disagrees with a proposed team decision, do other members think of this person as not being a team player?

_____ 7. Is there an unspoken norm on your team that says something like "To get along, you go along"?

_____ 8. Would you characterize team problem solving as lacking in real creativity?

_____ 9. In general, this is a pretty dull team to work with.

_____ 10. Do you get the feeling that most team members really do not want lots of diversity in opinions, ideas, and experiences?

## Scoring

If you responded Y or S to at least five of the questions, read on. Your team needs to reconsider style differences.

 **TIP** If you responded with a Y to at least five questions, present the results to the team members. Facilitate a discussion by asking whether they agree with your assessment.

# 200. TEAM PLAYER STYLE INTERVENTION

A powerful team-building intervention for an intact team is to use both the PTPS and the SOAP (see Tool 180, Parker Team Player Survey). With a typical team of fewer than ten members, each person completes the PTPS and one copy of the SOAP for each of his or her teammates. At the team-building meeting, each team member receives a report that includes their self-assessment from the PTPS and the scores of their teammates from the SOAP. The SOAP also includes written comments on the person's strengths, weaknesses, and ways that he or she can improve. After reviewing the feedback report, people team up with other members to explore the data and receive additional feedback. At the conclusion of the activity, each person prepares and presents a plan for increasing his or her effectiveness as a team player. In addition, team members begin to appreciate the different strengths that each member brings to the table.

# 201. STAGES AND STYLES: A MARRIAGE MADE IN TEAM-BUILDING HEAVEN

Tuckman's four stages (1965) help us understand the development of a team. However, we also know that team members can influence the growth and development of a team. Effective behaviors can move a team forward; ineffective behaviors can result in arrested development. We also know that the strengths of certain styles can be critical to a team's ability to negotiate a stage successfully. Some strengths are needed more than others at each stage.

**QUESTION** From what you know about the four stages and the four styles, can you guess which styles are more needed at each stage?

# 202. FORMING STAGE AND COLLABORATOR STYLE

The most significant aspect of the Forming stage is a lack of clarity about the team's purpose. The members' primary need is to know what they are expected to do and what their roles are on this team. Therefore, the strengths of the Collaborator are most in demand at this stage. Collaborators can help the team by ensuring that they spend a chunk of time on the front-end developing a mission, goals, and objectives. The team also needs to know the big picture—where their mission fits with the overall strategy of the organization.

# 203. STORMING STAGE AND COMMUNICATOR STYLE

Among the four styles, the Communicator feels most comfortable and potentially has the most to contribute during the Storming stage. Communicators understand conflict and can help facilitate the open expression of ideas, active listening, and resolution of differences crucial to the successful negotiation of this stage.

## 204. NORMING STAGE AND CONTRIBUTOR STYLE

All styles have a role to play here, but the Contributor is especially important because once the norms are embedded, task accomplishment is set to go forward. The Contributor can help the team focus on getting the work done, maintaining quality standards, and developing the skills and knowledge of team members.

## 205. PERFORMING STAGE AND CHALLENGER STYLE

Challengers are key players at the Performing stage because they can address the potential complacency that lurks in the background of the successful product launches, parties, and awards. They can help the team confront the internal developments (new leader, members, and tasks) and external challenges (increased competition, new regulations, business changes).

## 206. AND THE WINNER IS . . .

Among the four team player styles, which one do you think is the most common?

- ☐ Contributor—Task Oriented
- ☐ Collaborator—Goal Directed
- ☐ Communicator—Process Focused
- ☐ Challenger—Question Oriented

**QUESTION** Why do you think this?

## 207. AND THE WINNERS ARE COLLABORATOR AND CONTRIBUTOR

In our database of more than two thousand people in business, the most frequently reported styles were Collaborator and Contributor.

### QUESTIONS

- Why do you think this is true?
- Is it true for your team?

## 208. WOMEN ARE CHALLENGERS!

Among people with a single primary style, 25 percent of the women are Challengers, making it the second highest category among women. However, Challengers account for only 19 percent of the men, making it the lowest style among men.

### QUESTIONS

- Why do you think this is true?
- Is it true for your team?

## 209. YOUR STYLE CAN CHANGE!

At least your strengths and weaknesses can be altered to increase your effectiveness as a team player. After interpreting your survey results, obtaining feedback from your teammates, and developing an understanding of the potential areas for change, you can prepare a personal change plan. In the plan, you can decide to add certain behaviors to your existing strengths, expand your repertoire to incorporate the strengths of other styles, and try to minimize your ineffective behaviors. Self-directed change, while not easy, can be effective.

# 210. CHANGE IS ENHANCED WITH SUPPORTS

You are more likely to implement and sustain changes if there are supports in place to encourage and reward you for implementing your plan. Some supports we have used include:

- Sharing your plan with your teammates and asking for help with implementation;

- Regular reviews of your change plan;

- Regular feedback from your teammates on how they perceive you and the new behaviors in your plan; and

- Incorporating the behaviors in your change plan in your corporate performance management plan.

# 211. APPRECIATION OF OTHERS

"Appreciation is a wonderful thing; it makes what is excellent in others belong to us as well."
—*Voltaire*

**QUESTIONS**

- What does this quote mean to you?

- What does it have to do with effective teamwork?

- What does it have to do with style differences?

- What can we do to have more "appreciation" on our team?

**IN THIS AISLE YOU HAVE FOUND IDEAS AND RESOURCES** for increasing the value of style differences on your team. Use of a style intervention may help get your team back on track. However, do not limit yourself to tools in this aisle. Style differences are often related to role clarification (Aisle 3), conflict resolution (Aisle 13), and trust (Aisle 14). Therefore, you may want to wander over to those aisles.

# REESTABLISH TEAM NORMS

## OVERVIEW

**WHILE THERE ARE MANY REASONS FOR A TEAM TO DERAIL,** very often the cause can be found in their norms or the lack thereof. Norms are the behavioral guidelines or expectations that members have of one another. We call them the "rules of the road." In other words, "If you are a member of this team, this is how you are expected to act around here."

As teams evolve, the norms must evolve to deal with the new reality of the team. In many instances when we conduct a team diagnosis, we find norms that can only be described as anachronistic. That is, the existing guidelines are not appropriate, or worse they are counterproductive given the current needs of the team. As teams mature, they need to revisit their norms:

- To determine whether the list of behaviors is still being followed;
- To assess the relevance of the behaviors to the current team environment;

- To codify norms that have evolved naturally and that the team believes are helpful;

- To agree to delete norms that are no longer helpful; and

- To develop new norms that address issues faced by the team.

If your team needs to look at their norms as a basis for getting the team back on track, this aisle includes a variety of tools to help. You will find information that updates your knowledge of the power of norms as a shaper of team culture, tools to assess the usefulness of your current norms, and activities designed to create a new set of norms.

## 212. WHAT ARE NORMS?

The textbook definition is: "Standards of behavior a group expects of its members." The key words are "standards" and "behavior." It's what teammates come to expect from each other in terms of behavior. Some teams have extended the definition to include agreed-on procedures or procedural norms that will guide the team, such as "We will have an agenda for every meeting" or "The agenda will be sent to members at least forty-eight hours prior to the meeting."

## 213. EVERY TEAM HAS NORMS

What we mean is "Every group has norms whether they know it or not." Even if your team does not have a written list of norms, there are still norms guiding the behavior of team members. Think of the first team in your life—your family. There were understood and usually unspoken norms about how family members were to treat each other, such as "Do not argue with dad about your curfew" or "Call if you will be late for dinner." The key for your team is to uncover the current norms, including those that are unwritten, to see if they still make sense.

**QUESTION**  What are the "unwritten" norms on your team?

## 214. ELEVATOR NORMS

I use this example to highlight and explain the concept of norms, especially the idea that there are unwritten norms everywhere. Since just about everyone has been in an elevator at one time or another, they are aware of the guidelines for acceptable behavior in an elevator. Begin by asking the team, "What are the behavioral expectations for a group of people in an elevator?" The typical answers are

- Do not talk.
- Do not make eye contact.
- Look up.
- Face forward.
- Maintain spatial distance.

It is then useful to ask:

- Do any of these "rules" make sense today?
- Which ones should be changed or simply violated?
- Do we need any new elevator norms for today's world?

## 215. ELEVATOR NORMS IN ACTION

This is a true story. While waiting for the elevator on the 52nd floor of a large downtown hotel, it became apparent that the elevator was delayed or not working. Within five minutes, five people were gathered on the 52nd floor in front of the bank of elevators. At first there was no talking among the five people, but then a new norm emerged to address the situation. One person suggested that we use the house phone near the elevator to call the front desk. Once that happened, a new set of norms developed to deal with the problem faced by the *group* that had now become a *team* of people with a common purpose and a willingness to work together to achieve that purpose. Lots of sharing of ideas for problem solving took place, and finally we discovered a freight elevator on the floor that took us to the lobby. By the way, many of the old elevator norms were discarded in that freight elevator as we talked to each other, made eye contact, and did not feel the need to look up for the whole trip.

# 216. TEAM MEMBERS' BEHAVIORS

Rees (1997) suggests that team members' behaviors can be separated into three major categories. You can use these categories as a model for developing or revisiting your team norms to ensure you have sufficient norms in each of these areas:

1. Behaviors that contribute to the *cohesiveness* of the team;

2. Behaviors that contribute to the *productivity* of the team (behaviors that focus on the task at hand); and

3. Behaviors that *undermine* or *block* team progress (behaviors that hurt team relationships or block the effective completion of the team's task).

# 217. COHESIVE BEHAVIOR

Examples of cohesive behaviors include:

- Be open to different ideas.

- Show up on time for all team meetings.

- Actively listen to the contributions of your teammates.

- Be willing to go along with a consensus decision, even if you disagree with it.

- Ask questions to seek clarification.

# 218. PRODUCTIVE BEHAVIORS

Examples of productive behaviors include:

- Freely share your knowledge, skills, and information.

- Deliver your action items in a timely and quality fashion.

- Don't promise things you can't deliver.

- Suggest a process for helping the team make a decision or solve a problem.

- Summarize the key ideas and propose a consensus.

## 219. BLOCKING BEHAVIORS

Included in this category are

- Disagreeing without offering a rationale or alternatives.
- Attacking other members of the team or in other ways being disrespectful.
- Monopolizing a discussion or discouraging others from participating.
- Excessive use of humor that diverts the focus of the team.
- Repetition of one's own ideas or refusing to let go of an issue that's been decided.

## 220. NORMS: THE MOST POWERFUL DRIVER OF TEAM MEMBER BEHAVIOR

Norms tell team members how they are expected to behave. But how does a norm influence a person's behavior? First, the person must be aware of the norm. A proactive team accomplishes this awareness by creating and publishing its list of norms. Then each person becomes aware that other team members are following these norms and therefore knows that he or she is also expected to live by these same rules. At the beginning of the team process, members follow these norms because they are reminded of their existence, receive positive feedback if they follow them, and receive negative feedback if they violate them. In the end, our goal is to have members simply live by the norms without thinking about them, much like we follow certain societal norms. High performing, mature teams rarely discuss norms because they are embedded in the culture and, therefore, the behavior of the members.

**QUESTIONS**

- What norms are embedded in the culture of your team?
- Are they all positive (that is, contribute to the cohesiveness and productivity of the team)?
- Do you have some negative or blocking norms?

## 221. LEARNING ABOUT TEAM NORMS THE HARD WAY

When I was a high school student, I had a part-time job as a delivery person for a fabric company in New York City. My job was to deliver small packages and boxes to companies in the garment center, a twenty-five-square-block area in Manhattan. My first day at work, I was asked to deliver a package to a company in the area. I returned in forty-five minutes and was greeted by the other employees in the shipping department, who "informed" me that the typical time for a delivery of that distance was about an hour and half. They also indicated that if you returned "early" there would probably not be another delivery for a significant period of time and thus you would be assigned to the hated task of dusting the bolts of fabric on the storeroom shelves. So I learned my first norm: Double the actual time required making a delivery and do not return until then. By the way, many years later it occurred to me that the company contributed to the negative norm by requiring the useless dusting task instead of looking for more productive alternative tasks, such as teaching the delivery staff some of the other shipping functions.

 **T I P** Some negative norms evolve in response to organizational policies, management procedures, or corporate norms that team members find illogical. If your team has some negative norms, look for the reasons or supports for the norms. In some cases the supports can be easily changed or no longer exist.

## 222. BEHAVIORAL VERSUS PROCEDURAL NORMS

I often suggest that a team create lists of two types of norms:

1. *Behavioral Norms.* Norms in this category deal with expectations members have about how they will treat each other. Here you will find norms such as the cohesiveness, productivity, and blocking norms described above.

2. *Procedural Norms.* Procedural norms are those guidelines that describe the rules of the road for team meetings and other activities. Included here you will often find such norms as

- "There will be an agenda for each team meeting."
- "The agenda will be sent to all members twenty-four hours prior to the meeting."
- "If you are unable to attend a meeting, inform the leader as soon as you know."
- "If you are unable to attend and you owe the team an action item, give the work to the leader or other member prior to the meeting."
- "The role of scribe will be rotated among all team members."
- "Meeting minutes will be distributed no later than forty-eight hours after the meeting."

# 223. TARGETED NORMS

Mature teams, even those with a well-developed set of norms, may need what we call targeted norms to address specific issues facing the team. Targeted norms cover specific topics or situations that the team is facing. These norms often cover an area in some depth. For example, your team may suddenly have to deal with:

- The addition of a number of members from other countries;
- A number of members attending a meeting via teleconference rather than in person;
- A decision involving poor performance or inappropriate behavior by one team member; or
- Conflicting views among team members over an important decision.

When it appears that targeted norms are needed, the leader or facilitator will lead the team through a process that begins with something like: "What guidelines do we need to ensure that we include the views of new members from outside this country?"

# 224. SAMPLE TARGETED NORMS: OPEN COMMUNICATION

Here are some sample norms designed to ensure that members feel free to speak their minds:

- "Everyone will be given an opportunity (if they want) to speak on the issue before we make a decision."

- "We will allow each person to finish his or her thought without interruption."

- "We will use active listening skills (such as paraphrasing) to ensure we clearly understand the contributions of our teammates."

- "No personal attacks on one of our teammates."

- "It's OK to disagree with a contribution but not OK to 'put the person down' for the idea."

- "We will ask questions to seek clarification of a teammate's contribution."

- "All communication in team meetings is considered confidential. It will not be shared with outsiders unless agreed to by the team."

# 225. SAMPLE TARGETED NORMS: CONFLICTS

Here are some norms developed by a team that knew there would be a great deal of conflict over an upcoming decision:

- "We will look at both the advantages and disadvantages of each alternative."

- "We will allow people to complete the presentation of their position without interruption."

- "We will always keep in mind the needs of the customer when considering alternatives."

- "We will seek a 'win-win' decision that is responsive to the customers' needs."

- "We will not agree to a compromise that only 'splits the differences.'"
- "If you disagree with an alternative, you have to provide the reasons for your position."

# 226. GUIDELINES FOR THE ESTABLISHMENT OF TEAM NORMS

Johnson and Johnson (2000) put together a helpful set of guidelines for embedding norms in a team. Here is our adaptation of their list:

1. If you want members to accept and live by the norms, they must first recognize that the norms exist, that other members accept and follow them, and feel some internal commitment to following them.

2. Norms will be followed if members understand how the norms will help the team accomplish its goals. Therefore, it is important to clarify how following the norms will support the team's efforts to get its work done.

3. Members will accept norms that they "own." Therefore, it is important that team members develop and agree to the norms for their team.

4. The entire team is responsible for enforcing the norms. When a norm is followed or violated, other team members should acknowledge the behavior with either a supportive comment or a caution.

5. Members need examples of the norms in practice so they have models to follow. Therefore, when a norm is established, it is helpful to provide behavioral examples for members to follow and/or adapt.

6. Since norms exist only to help a team be successful, they should be flexible and subject to change over time. Therefore, it is important for a mature team to periodically look at its norms to determine whether the list is still relevant to today's environment and goals.

# 227. THE TEAM OF YOUR LIFE

Here's a quick activity that serves as both an icebreaker and a norms building exercise.

## Process

- Explain that members' experiences on past teams will provide the data they need to understand the dimensions of an effective team and to use as the basis for developing a set of norms for the team.

- Ask each member to (a) describe his or her best experience as a team member—either formal, informal, on the job, or off the job (for example, community group), and (b) explain what made the experience special— what happened, what worked, what specific things the team did or did not do that are worth remembering.

- Suggest that team members take notes on the key elements of the experiences as they are being presented by their teammates.

- After all the stories have been told, facilitate a discussion on the key elements that emerge from the stories and post the responses on a flip chart.

- If necessary, explain the concept of norms. Then ask team members to create a list of norms for their team using the ideas from the stories but incorporating other ideas as well. One way of categorizing the norms is to create two columns on the flip chart, as shown below.

### Our Team Norms

| Wants | Don't Wants |
| --- | --- |
|  |  |

# 228. WHAT ARE YOUR TEAM'S NORMS NOW?

You can do a simple exercise to identify the current norms of your team.

## Process

- Begin by creating a series of categories such as interpersonal communication, problem solving, decision making, meetings, accountabilities, electronic communication, risk taking, conflict resolution, and empowerment.

- Then assign each of the categories to a team member or a subgroup and ask them to draft a list of current norms in that category.

- Facilitate a discussion on each of the lists, with the goal of reaching a consensus of the team's current norms.

- Distribute a copy of the final list to each team member. Review the norms at a subsequent meeting.

# 229. WHAT SHOULD BE THE NORMS OF YOUR TEAM?

After the team has had some time to absorb the list of current norms, facilitate a discussion around such questions as:

- Which current norms are still viable and should be preserved?

- Which current norms should be deleted entirely?

- Which current norms should be edited or revised to address the current reality?

- What new norms do we need to help us move forward as a team?

# 230. NORMS CARD GAME I

Another way of identifying current norms is to use a deck of "norms cards."

## Preparation

Begin by creating a deck of approximately fifty to one hundred cards each, with a different norm statement printed on one side of each card. Create your own list by brainstorming with several employee focus groups, asking a sample of team leaders, or drawing on some of the lists in this section. Here are some typical norm statements from a deck created for a specific client:

- "Work requiring cooperation between units gets accomplished with minimal friction."
- "Goal setting is a 'drill' people go through because it is required by management."
- "People who 'don't rock the boat' are rewarded."
- "Disagreements are dealt with openly and honestly."
- "People with new and different ideas receive a fair hearing."
- "People feel free to make suggestions to management to improve performance."
- "When something new is introduced, people respond, 'Here we go again.'"
- "Few people are surprised when goals are not met."
- "Attempts to review a project critically are seen as negative and harmful."
- "When things go wrong, people are most concerned about 'covering themselves.'"

## Process

There are several ways to use the deck. In each case the goal is to select the cards that represent the current team norms. One approach is to ask each team member to go through the deck individually and select the cards that are pertinent. Another approach is to have the entire team select as a group, trying to reach a consensus on the final selection.

# 231. NORMS CARD GAME II

Once the current norms have been identified, it is helpful to analyze the current norms to determine why the norms persist.

## Process

- Begin by making a list of the current norms down the left column of a flip chart or electronic file.
- Then create another column called "supports" on the right.
- In this column write aspects of the organization's culture, systems, and structure that support the norm, as seen by the team.
- As a practice exercise, suggest some possible supports for the norms shown on the sample flip chart below.

| Norms | Supports |
|---|---|
| People who "don't rock the boat" are rewarded. | |
| People with new and different ideas receive a fair hearing. | |
| Few people are surprised when goals are not met. | |

- After the supports have been identified, engage the team in a discussion of ways to change, eliminate, or continue the supports.
- Develop an action plan or design to implement the changes.

# 232. NORMS CARD GAME III

You can also use the deck to develop a set of norms for the future. Simply ask team members to go through the deck and select the norms they would like to adopt for their team. In each case ask what new systems, cultural changes, or structural changes are needed for the norm to have some chance of becoming embedded.

## 233. QUICK HIT NORMS EXERCISE

### Process

- After you have explained the concept of norms and given a few examples, divide the team into subgroups and ask each group to come up with six "Wants" and Don't Wants" for team member behavior.

- Post the lists on a flip chart, overhead transparency, or in a computer file.

- Facilitate a discussion leading to agreement on a list for your team.

## 234. NORMS ICEBREAKER

Use the idea of your family as your first team experience and your first experience with team norms as the basis for this exercise.

### Process

- Ask each person (or subgroup) to identify a few norms from their early childhood experiences that focused on what was acceptable and unacceptable behavior for family members.

- Provide some examples from your own childhood to get the ball rolling, such as "complete your homework before watching television or playing music" or "make your bed every morning before you go to school." Keep it playful and fun.

- Discuss how people learned about the family norms and then lead into how team members learn about norms.

# 235. GOING BEYOND NORMS

Some high performing teams go beyond simply creating a list of norms. They provide a behavioral description and/or sample actions to help team members act on the norms. Here are some examples:

| Norm | Description |
| --- | --- |
| Summarize the key ideas and proposes a consensus | Pull together ideas that have been discussed in a sentence or two and then present a possible solution, decision, or recommendation |
| Actively listen to the contributions of teammates. | Paraphrase the ideas of others using such phrases as "What I hear you saying is . . ." |
| Ask questions to seek clarification | Ask others for more information or examples of what they mean to eliminate confusion |

# 236. SHORT AND SWEET SAMPLE NORMS

Here's a list provided by Justice and Jamieson (1998):

- "Sessions start on time. There will be no review for those who are late."
- "Phone messages will be delivered at breaks except for personal emergencies."
- "One person talks at a time."
- "What is said here, stays here."
- "If you miss a meeting, support the decision made in your absence."
- "Listen first as an advocate for the other person's idea."

## 237. LONG AND SWEET NORMS

Another but much longer list of norms is found in Parker (1997). We use the list, which includes thirty norms, as the basis for a team exercise called "Developing Team Norms." We ask team members to go through the list and check the ones they think should be adopted by their team. A list of thirty norms is simply too long to be effective. However, the list is helpful for those teams that need help in generating potential norms for their team. Go to the Team Tool Shed to pick up a copy of the thirty norms.

## 238. TEAM CULTURE SURVEY

An "off-the shelf" survey that your team can use to understand your team's culture and norms is the "Team Culture Survey" found in Parker (1998). You can find a copy of the survey in the Team Tool Shed.

## 239. NORMS ARE RESISTANT TO CHANGE

Since norms, once established, generally have the strong support of team members, they are tough to change. Therefore, for a mature team that finds itself with a number of archaic norms, the challenge to eliminate these norms and install others is great. I point out this phenomenon to alert you to the need for (a) patience and (b) a detailed change plan.

 **T I P** The tools in this aisle, such as Force-Field Analysis and involving key players, can facilitate the change process.

## 240. CHANGING TEAM NORMS USING FORCE-FIELD ANALYSIS

When you find a norm that is particularly resistant to change, consider using that old facilitator's standby, Force-Field Analysis.

### Process

Let's say a norm that is difficult to change is "Members do not speak their minds when the department manager attends the team meeting." Begin by making two lists:

1. *Driving Forces:* The factors that are pushing or driving the team to change, that is, speak up during the meetings when the manager is present.

2. *Restraining Forces:* The factors that are supporting the current situation or resisting the change, that is, remain silent or rarely speak when the manager is present.

It has been established that it is more effective to reduce the restraining forces than it is to add driving forces. Therefore, begin by prioritizing the restraining forces, eliminating forces that cannot be changed by the team, and developing action plans for addressing the key forces that remain.

## 241. CHANGING NORMS VIA GROUP FACILITATION

There is also evidence that changing norms can be made easier by (a) discussing the value of existing norms and (b) gaining a consensus on the need to discard some old norms and adopt some new ones. Involvement in the decision-making process breaks down the resistance to changing the existing norms and agreeing to new norms.

 **T I P** Set aside time for an open but purposeful discussion of your existing team norms and their relevance to the current goals of the team.

## 242. CHANGING NORMS USING KEY TEAM PLAYERS

Experience and some research indicates that norms can be changed by involving high status or informal leaders of the team in leading the effort. It seems that members who are perceived as hard workers, big producers, technical leaders, or others are able to influence the other members. These key players must be seen as having the best interests of the team in mind in order for their norms advocacy to have impact.

 **T I P** Identify the "movers and shakers" on your team and enlist them in your change effort.

## 243. GOLDEN GROUND RULES

Another good resource is Hanson (1998).

## 244. "IF YOU FOLLOW ALL THE RULES, YOU MISS ALL THE FUN"

*—Katherine Hepburn*

 **QUESTIONS**

- This quote seems to fly in the face of the need for norms. Does it?
- What "rules" do you think she was talking about?
- In what ways do our team rules (norms) inhibit our ability to have fun?
- Katherine Hepburn consistently violated many societal norms because she thought they were archaic. Do we have any archaic team norms that need to be (or already are) violated?

## 245. "AS A RULE OF THUMB, INVOLVE EVERYONE IN EVERYTHING"

*—Tom Peters*

### QUESTIONS

- Do you agree with this statement? Why? Why not?
- Is the culture of our team, reflected in our norms, participative?
- Are there some team areas where we could involve people more?

**IN THIS AISLE YOU HAVE FOUND** tools for identifying your current norms, along with tools for changing your norms to help refocus your team. You will find related tools in the next aisle dealing with climate, as well as in the aisles containing tools for dealing with team meetings (Aisle 11), communications (Aisle 15), and conflicts (Aisle 13).

 **AISLE 8**

# RE-CREATE A RELAXED CLIMATE

## OVERVIEW

**THE EVIDENCE IS PRETTY CLEAR**. Team members, and by extension teams, do their best work with an informal and relaxed climate. So if your team has come unglued, you can probably look around and find a formal, stiff, and very tense atmosphere.

When the climate is tense, some or all of the following will result:

- Problem solving will be rigid;

- Decisions will be conservative;

- Creativity will be "inside the box";

- Product and service development will be extensions of last year's model;

- Risk taking will be nonexistent;

- Conflicts will be resolved by "sweeping them under the rug";

- Meetings will be boring;
- Leadership will be "by the book";
- Work area discussions will be pretty dreary and negative; and/or
- The whole team atmosphere will be spiritless and not much fun.

If more that a few of these items describe your team, it is time to look at ways to get back to the informal, relaxed climate that probably marked your team in the beginning. Use the ideas in this aisle to help your team loosen up and get the joy of collaboration back.

In this aisle you will find information on the importance of climate to successful teamwork, many instruments to assess your team's current climate, and ideas for changing the climate to a more positive upbeat environment.

# 246. CLIMATE VERSUS CULTURE

People often confuse these two "C" words, but they are quite different. *Climate* measures and describes how satisfied team members are with various aspects of their team. Thus, a climate survey uses questions that ask people how satisfied they are. *Culture* describes how things really get done in the organization. As Deal and Kennedy (1982) put it, "A strong culture is a system of informal rules that spells out how people are expected to behave most of the time."

In the context of the *Team Depot,* we define climate as "the feeling tone or emotional atmosphere of the team."

# 247. CLIMATE AND RISK TAKING

What is the tolerance for failure on your team? If the climate does not permit "good trys," you are not going to get much innovation or change. A high performing team allows and even encourages risk taking. A climate that supports reasonable risk taking is more likely to get innovation in new product development and service delivery, rethinking and revitalization of key processes, and creativity in the organization and management of the enterprise.

**QUESTION**  How would you describe the climate for risk taking on your team?

## 248. CLIMATE AND PRODUCTIVITY

People simply get more and better work done when the climate is informal and relaxed. Team members are motivated to work hard and do their best when the atmosphere is supportive and positive.

### QUESTIONS

- How would you describe your team's productivity?
- In what ways does the team's climate have an impact on the team's productivity?

## 249. CLIMATE AND DECISION MAKING

In a positive and upbeat climate, decisions are more likely to be forward-looking and creative. On the other hand, when the climate is conservative and risk-averse, team members are likely to be so concerned about making a mistake that they take the path of least resistance rather than the high road. Business breakthroughs occur most often when the team is open to new ideas, willing to experiment, and not afraid to fail.

### QUESTIONS

- How would you describe the decision-making process on your team?
- In what ways does the team's climate have an impact on the quality of your decisions?

## 250. CLIMATE AND LEADER BEHAVIOR

The style and behavior of the team leader is a key factor in determining the overall climate of the team. You might say, "As the leader goes, so goes the team." If the leader is relaxed, open, and informal, the members are likely to model his or her behavior. On the other hand, if the leader wears a conservative business suit, rarely smiles, conducts team meetings in a formal manner, and is generally rigid, the atmosphere of the team will be humorless and efficient—but not necessarily effective.

 **TIP** Loosen up!

## 251. CLIMATE AND PERSONALITY

Research indicates that the personality of some people is affected by the weather. When the atmosphere is dark and dreary for extended periods of time, some people report becoming depressed. However, when the weather is sunny and bright, their personality is similarly positive and upbeat. We think it is quite possible to extend that argument to the social climate of a team. That is, when the team climate is positive and fun, team members are more likely to enjoy the experience and be positive contributors to the team.

 **QUESTION** Do you agree?

## 252. THE CLIMATE WAS "TOO POLITE"

Some teams carry the idea of a relaxed, friendly climate to the extreme. A company president complained that his board meetings were useless because everyone was "just too darn polite." As a result, none of the vice presidents was willing to disagree with anything said by the president or any of the team colleagues. The board had been through team building where there was an emphasis on collegiality and consensus. However, the team took collegiality to the extreme such that it prevented any form of civilized disagreement. The vice presidents felt they had been given the message that any disagreement would destroy the delicate balance of harmony on the team.

**QUESTION**   Is your team too polite and too civilized?

## 253. "I WAS AFRAID TO DISAGREE"

During the course of a data-collection interview in the same organization, one vice president reported the following incident:

> "At a board meeting, the president asked, 'How's morale in the organization?' The first vice president to respond said, 'On a scale of one to ten, I'd say it was an eight.' After that everyone said either seven or eight. When my turn came, I really wanted to tell the truth and say, 'Around three or four,' but I was afraid to disagree."

**QUESTIONS**

- Can you imagine this scenario happening on your team?
- What can your team do to avoid the consequences of this type of climate?

## 254. RISKY BUSINESS

Your team's climate may be at risk if:

- Subgroups of members meet or trade e-mails discussing what's wrong with the team, the leader, or management;
- Members are absent from meetings when key decisions are on the agenda;
- Members sit quietly and show their displeasure with a variety of nonverbal gestures (rolling eyes, folding arms, leaning back from the table);
- You hear that members have complained to colleagues or their boss about the team; and/or
- Members "straddle the fence" when asked for their opinions or expert advice.

**QUESTION**   Is your team's climate "at risk"?

# 255. CLIMATE DESCRIPTORS

- How would you describe the climate of your team at this point in time? Check as many as apply.

  ☐ Relaxed

  ☐ Collaborative

  ☐ Stressful

  ☐ Frantic

  ☐ Open

  ☐ Fun

  ☐ Boring

  ☐ Rigid

  ☐ Conservative

  ☐ Progressive

 **T I P** Use this list as a starting point for an assessment of the team's climate. Ask each member to complete the checklist individually and then facilitate a discussion based on the responses. Conclude with a list of action items designed to improve the climate.

# 256. TEAM CLIMATE ASSESSMENT

Here's another quick and easy climate assessment tool. It's also fun. Feel free to add other cars to the list.

## Preparation

Prepare a copy of the The Auto Climate for each team member.

## Process

- Ask each person to complete the survey.
- Create subgroups of three to four people.
- Ask the groups to discuss their responses and the reasons for their responses.
- Ask the groups to arrive at a consensus on the one car that best describes the team.
- Ask one person from each group to present the consensus.
- Conclude the meeting with a summary of the responses.
- If time permits, discuss ways to change to a more positive climate.
- As an alternative, you can ask people to select the car that represents the climate that they would like to have in the future.

# THE AUTO CLIMATE

*Instructions:* Review the list of automobiles below. Then select one car that best describes the culture of your team today. Be prepared to explain your answer and, if possible, to provide examples.

_____ *Mercedes Benz*—a well-engineered (and well-oiled) machine

_____ *Cadillac*—a conservative, safe machine

_____ *Mustang*—a lively, fun machine

_____ *Chevy Blazer*—a tough, resilient all-road machine

_____ *Porche 911*—a fast-paced, exciting machine

# 257. HOW DO YOU CREATE A "SUNNY CLIMATE"?

If your team climate has become dark and dreary, formal and formidable, cold and cheerless, spend a few minutes at the end of your next meeting engaging the team in a brainstorming exercise designed to come up with ideas to change the climate.

## Process

- At the top of a sheet of flip chart paper or a computer projection screen, place the words, "Ways to Create a Sunny Team Climate."
- Then ask for ideas which, in turn, you record.
- Discuss the list, eliminate items, and then rank order them.
- Select one or two of the best ideas for implementation.
- Then ask subgroups of team members to take responsibility for their implementation.

# 258. QUICK CLIMATE QUIZ

Here's a brief data-collection tool to get a quick reading on your team's climate.

## Process

- Ask each team member to complete the instrument and then return it to you for summarization.
- Prepare a summary of the responses, including the number of responses for each answer (for example, how many people circled "almost never" for question 1).
- Present the summary at the next team meeting.
- Facilitate a discussion of the results.
- Conclude with a list of action items to improve the climate.

# QUICK CLIMATE QUIZ*

*Directions:* Please review each question and then circle one answer.

1. To what extent do I feel safe, relaxed, and myself as a member of this team?

   Almost Never      Rarely      Sometimes      Occasionally    Almost Always

2. To what extent do I have private thoughts or unspoken opinions that I do not feel comfortable expressing?

   Almost Never      Rarely      Sometimes      Occasionally    Almost Always

3. To what extent do we work to get out the opinions and ideas of all team members prior to making a decision?

   Almost Never      Rarely      Sometimes      Occasionally    Almost Always

4. To what extent are differences openly shared and discussed on this team?

   Almost Never      Rarely      Sometimes      Occasionally    Almost Always

5. To what extent would you describe the climate on this team as "open, informal and relaxed"?

   Almost Never      Rarely      Sometimes      Occasionally    Almost Always

Comments:

*Adapted from Dyer (1975).

# 259. WHEN ARE YOU MOST RELAXED?

A great way to help the team create or re-create a relaxed climate is to ask team members to share their answers to these questions:

- When are you most relaxed?
- Why are you relaxed in this situation?
- What aspects of that situation can we bring into our team environment?
- What aspects of our team environment can we change to make it more like the situation in which you are most relaxed?

## Process

Facilitate a discussion based on these questions, with the goal of identifying ways to adjust the climate of the team to get it back on a "relaxed track."

# 260. EVERYONE LIKES FOOD!

Food at a meeting tends to spark conversation, and the more unusual the food, the more animated the conversation. So surprise the team with something different and fun. One of the most popular we've seen was an all-chocolate break. The table included a myriad of chocolate snacks such as brownies, Kisses®, M&Ms®, cookies, chocolate milk, and . . . well, you get the idea. We have also seen people go in the other direction with a table of healthy snacks such as fruit, cold vegetables, granola bars, and fruit juices. There is also a message inherent in the choice of snack that says we care about you and, consequently, we even gave some thought to the food.

## 261. GROUPTHINK AND OPENNESS

A great way to start a discussion and come up with some ideas for improving the team climate is to show the video, "Groupthink." The video uses the Space Shuttle Challenger disaster as a dramatic example of the natural tendency of teams to achieve unity in spite of contrary facts or potential consequences. Included in the video are ways for groups to overcome groupthink. A leader's guide provides ideas for using the video as a kick-off for an action-planning exercise designed to reduce the groupthink tendency on your team. The video and guide are available from CRM Learning at 1–800–421–0833 or online at www.crmlearning.com.

## 262. DECORATE THE MEETING ROOM

You can change the climate by changing the look and feel of the team's meeting room. Change the setup of the tables and chairs to make it less formal and more conducive to open communication. Try to add some posters to the wall with humorous and motivational quotes. Two fun little books by Doug McCallum, *The Speed of the Leader . . .Determines the Rate of the Pack* (1996) and *Don't Send Your Turkeys to Eagle School* (1994) can provide you with a rich inventory of quotes. Another good source is *Winning with Teamwork* (Karvelas, 1998).

## 263. CHANGE OF VENUE

Sometimes just changing to another location for your meeting can change the emotional atmosphere of the team. Try moving to another meeting room, use a quiet table in the cafeteria during off hours or an off-site facility, or, when weather is nice, meet outside under a tree.

## 264. PLAY SOME GAMES

Take five minutes at the beginning or end of your meeting to play a game. Try to make it a game that connects with some work of the team or makes a point about team climate. Instructional puzzles or perception exercises are quick jolts that can be fun, educational, and positive. A good source is www.thiagi.com

# 265. USE RELAXATION TECHNIQUES

You can introduce the team to simple relaxation techniques as a prelude to making a key decision. Instead of plunging headlong into the discussion and debate, the team spends five minutes relaxing and clearing their minds. The result: A climate change at that meeting that may extend into the future of the team. A good source for simple relaxation techniques is *The Relaxation and Stress Reduction Workbook* (Davis, McKay, & Robbin-Eschelm, 2000).

# 266. MASSAGE TRAIN

A good little break exercise we use is called the Massage Train. Team members line up facing the backs of the people in front of them. Each person is instructed to massage the shoulders of the person directly in front of him or her. After a minute, instruct the team members to turn and face in the opposite direction and repeat the massage with the people who are now in front of them.

**THIS AISLE INCLUDED INFORMATION ON THE IMPORTANCE OF CLIMATE,** ways to assess your team's climate, and ideas for returning to a more positive climate. Don't limit yourself to this aisle. Take a look at the aisles that focus on team celebrations (Aisle 20), rewards and recognition (Aisle 19), team meetings (Aisle 11), and norms (Aisle 7).

 **AISLE 9**

# RECONSTITUTE
# THE WORK PLAN

## OVERVIEW

**IN TODAY'S FAST-PACED BUSINESS WORLD,** planning is often short-lived or nonexistent. The frequency of change is usually cited as the reason for the failure to plan. The typical response is "Why prepare a plan when you know it will just have to be changed?"

Our response is "If you don't have a plan, you have nothing to change." Teams, especially project teams, without a plan tend to spend lots of time in a reactive mode . . . responding both to immediate problems and to every opportunity. They lack a context in which to prioritize problems and opportunities, so they feel compelled to respond to everything that comes their way. A reactive team can get bogged down and stressed out. Members are very busy doing lots of work but have the feeling they may be doing the wrong work.

A plan can help get a team back on track. Perhaps more important than the plan itself is the process a team goes through to develop the plan. The project planning process provides members with a sense of purpose and direction, and, most importantly, it brings the team together again. A good project planning process should result in the conclusion that "We're all in this together."

The tools in this section will help your team assess its attitude toward planning, decide whether you need a plan or if yours needs modernizing, and get it done.

## 267. PROJECT PLANNING PHASES

The typical phases of a project plan include:

1. *Project Scope.* During the first phase, the team prepares the scope of the project, the objectives, and deliverables and selects the project team. If the team already exists, certain adjunct members such as subject-matter experts, are identified.

2. *Task Breakdown.* Here the team comes up with a list and description of the required tasks.

3. *Responsibility Charting.* The team matches the tasks with the team members responsible for each, along with the level of effort involved.

4. *Sequencing.* In this phase the team prepares the sequencing of the tasks.

5. *Resource Availability and Scheduling.* Here the team determines the scheduling of their resources to ensure that the project is appropriately resourced.

6. *Budgeting.* The team prepares an estimate of the various costs needed to complete the project.

7. *Risk Analysis.* The team plays various "what if?" scenarios and prepares contingency plans for the project.

# 268. DEFINE YOUR PROJECT

The most important phase of a project plan is the definition and scope of the project. Often when a team's planning process breaks down it is because the team did not take the time at the outset to define the project scope. Here's a simple but powerful protocol for this activity.

- *Who?* Who are the project end users or customers? For whom are we doing this work?

- *Why?* Why is the project needed? What problems or opportunities does the project address?

- *What?* What are the main deliverables? What are the critical success factors?

- *When?* When will the project begin and end? When are the critical milestones?

- *How?* How will the project meet its objectives?

# 269. OBJECTIONS TO PROJECT PLANNING

Many team members object to preparing a project plan because they are unable to fully understand the dimensions of a project at the outset. As a result, they say "Why plan?" If such an attitude is blocking your efforts to institute a planning process for your team, we suggest you spend some time exploring the dimensions of this objection. Begin with a simple analogy that just about everyone can relate to: Planning a family vacation. Let's make it something exotic like a trip to Paris.

Begin by putting together a plan of action with a list of the tasks, responsibilities, and costs. But, you say, I've never been to Paris so how can I know all of the things I'd like to do? True enough, but prepare your plan based on the data available from existing resources, such as guide books, travel agents, or friends. At this point, your plan is sufficient for starting the project (vacation).

However, you should consider your plan a work in progress. Therefore, once you reach Paris and acquire more tangible and current information, you can adjust your plan. For example, your hotel concierge may suggest some historical sites and restaurants that were not in any of your initial planning resources. As a result, you alter your action plan and budget accordingly.

 **T I P**  Facilitate this vacation planning exercise with your team. Ask them to identify the knowns and unknowns at the outset. Then ask team members to identify things that might alter their plans later in the process.

## 270. PROJECT PLANNING PRACTICE

Let's go back to our vacation project. Now, using our planning protocol, answer the following questions for the vacation in Paris.

Who? _____

_____

Why? _____

_____

What?_____

_____

When?_____

_____

How?_____

_____

# 271. DO YOU NEED A WORK PLAN?

This checklist will help team members determine whether they need a work plan.

## Preparation

Prepare a copy of the checklist on the next page for each member of the team. You may also want to give it to your key stakeholders.

## Process

- Provide each person with a copy of the checklist. Ask that they complete it.

- Facilitate a discussion based on the results. Discuss each question separately and try to reach a consensus on a team response.

- Conclude with a summary of the need for a work plan. If a plan is needed, use other resources in this aisle.

- Alternatively, distribute the survey and ask members to return it to you or to an external resource for summarization. Present the summary at the next meeting and facilitate a discussion as indicated above.

## DO WE NEED A WORK PLAN?

*Directions:* Please answer yes (Y) or no (N) to the indicators below by circling your responses.

| | | | |
|---|---|---|---|
| 1. | Are you wasting resources (technical and human) now? | Y | N |
| 2. | Have you missed any important deadlines in the past three months? | Y | N |
| 3. | Are there many last minute rush jobs? | Y | N |
| 4. | Are team members very busy at times and underutilized at other times? | Y | N |
| 5. | Are you viewed as a team with solid planning skills? | Y | N |
| 6. | Do team members know how to use planning tools such as Gantt charts? | Y | N |
| 7. | Do you track progress of your work? | Y | N |
| 8. | Do you have methods of assessing the performance of your work? | Y | N |
| 9. | Do you document the results of your work? | Y | N |
| 10. | Are stakeholders aware of the progress of your work? | Y | N |

A "yes" to any items 1 through 4 and "no" to any items 5 through 10 are all indicators of a need to take a look at a team's ability to plan.

# 272. PROJECT REVIEW MEETING

One way to get your team and its project back on track is to hold a project review meeting. The key to a successful review is, you guessed it, planning! Let's be clear . . . a project review meeting is not a team meeting. In fact, the team should meet prior to the review meeting to plan for the project review. The project review meeting is for stakeholders such as subject-matter experts, customers, senior management, and support personnel. A good project review meeting is based on several assumptions: (a) you are confident of your accomplishments to date and (b) you have been communicating progress with your stakeholders all along.

The purpose of a review meeting is to present your interim results, get feedback and recommendations from the participants, and agree on project changes. The meeting format should include a set of norms targeted for a review meeting. The agenda of the meeting should include:

1. A brief summary of the project plan and progress to date.

2. A list of potential project problems, ideas for saving time and resources, and suggestions for process improvements.

3. Discussion of each item on the list and disposition of the item.

4. Summary of agreed on changes in the project plan.

Following the meeting prepare a summary of the items discussed and decisions made and distribute it to all the stakeholders, along with a note of thanks to the meeting participants.

# 273. QUOTABLE QUOTES

How would you describe your team's current approach to project planning? Are you satisfied with the current approach? Is the current approach appropriate to the current environment? Try this exercise as a way to help your team back on track (Parker & Kropp, 1992).

## Preparation

Prepare a copy of the Quotes for each person. Prepare a copy for projection on an overhead or LCD projector or computer screen.

## Process

- Ask the subgroups to share their answers.
- Facilitate a discussion on the responses.
- Find out whether there is a consensus on one or two quotes.
- Then ask the subgroups, "In the future, which of the quotes would you like to be known by?"
- Once again, facilitate a discussion on the responses and determine whether there is a consensus on one or two quotes.
- Take it one step farther by working with the team to develop an action plan to get from the current to the future quote.

# QUOTES

*Instructions:* Pair up with another team member. Together review the list of Quotes. Then decide which quote best describes the team's current approach to planning.

Nothing Ventured, Nothing Gained

Go for the Gusto

A Place for Everything and Everything in Its Place

Ready, Fire, Aim

Time Waits for No One

Slow But Sure

Look Before You Leap

Opportunity Knocks But Once

When in Rome, Do as the Romans Do

Seize the Day

In Touch with Tomorrow

Think Different

People Finding a Better Way

Where Do You Want to Go Today?

Go Your Own Way

Don't Stop Thinking About Tomorrow

## 274. GET THE WORK DONE

Enough talking, enough planning. It's time to get to work. Perhaps your team has a plan but still doesn't get much done. Maybe your team needs some "targeted norms" that focus on taking responsibility for accomplishing the objectives and delivering on the actions in the work plan. Here is a list of "get the work done" norms to start off your discussion.

▶ Deliver on your commitments.

▶ Ask for help when you need it.

▶ Offer to help your teammates when they need it.

▶ Be responsive to your teammates by returning phone calls and e-mails, providing requested information, offering suggestions, and sharing your expertise.

▶ Communicate regularly with your teammates about the status of tasks and other project-related issues.

▶ Bring concerns and problems about the work to the team as soon as possible.

▶ Be responsive to customer requests and complaints.

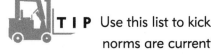 **T I P** Use this list to kick off a session on work norms. Begin by asking which of these norms are currently in place on your team and which ones need to be incorporated. Then ask what other norms need to be added to the team's list.

## 275. RESOURCE ON PROJECT MANAGEMENT

One of the best training resources on project management is Project Mentors. You can reach them via the web at www.projectmentor.com.

## 276. NEWSLETTER ON PROJECT MANAGEMENT

A good electronic newsletter is available at www.projectworld.com/newsletter/home/htm. It includes lots of good, practical articles on project management. Go to the site and sign up.

## 277. ALICE IN PLANNING LAND

In Lewis Carroll's *Alice in Wonderland,* Alice arrives at the intersection of main roads; looking up, she sees the Cheshire Cat smiling from the tree above. She asks the cat, "Which road should I take?" and he responds, "Where is it you'd like to go?" Alice replies, "I really don't know." The cat responds:

_____

_____

**QUESTION**   What do you think the cat said to Alice?

## 278. "SMALL PROBLEMS . . ."

Use this quote to start a discussion about your team's approach to work.

**"Small problems are difficult to see but easy to fix. However, when you let these problems develop, they are easy to see but difficult to fix."**
—*Niccolo Machiavelli*

**QUESTIONS**

- What types of small problems do we have that often grow into larger ones?

- To what extent do we allow small problems to go unsolved until they are big?

- Are these small problems truly hard to see until they become larger and more difficult?

- What are some examples of problems that were allowed to grow before we addressed them?

- What can we do to address problems when they are small and easier to fix?

## 279. "READY, FIRE, AIM"

This is a well-known and oft-repeated quote from the early, fast-paced days of the computer business. Use it to begin a discussion of your team's approach to planning.

### QUESTIONS

- What does this quote mean to you?

- To what extent does it describe your team?

- If it does describe your team, what causes it to be true?

- Should we try to change our approach?

- Why would it be helpful to have a plan?

- What next steps should we take to incorporate planning?

**AMONG THE TOOLS IN THIS AISLE** were tools to develop a work plan, understand the planning process, and deal with the traditional objections to planning. Other aisles that include complementary tools are the ones that focus on goals (Aisle 1), accountability (Aisle 10), and performance management (Aisle 18).

 **AISLE 10**

# REFOCUS ON ACCOUNTABILITY

## OVERVIEW

**ENOUGH TALKING AND PLANNING.** Let's get back to work! Let's get some real work done and stop talking about getting the work done. We've revisited our goals, reviewed our plan, and reworked our norms. Now it's time to get back to producing goods or providing service to our customers. Now is the time to come up with an innovative new product, reducing the defects in our existing products, speeding up the turnaround time on customer requests, or whatever else is central to our mission.

If your team is experiencing a retreat from its original task focus and, as a result, your metrics are down, use this time to refocus the energy of the team on plain, old-fashioned production. In addition, refocus on establishing both a culture and a process of accountability.

Another issue is the question of whether you are doing the right tasks. Mature teams should be taking on more supervisory and administrative tasks that were previously the responsibility of management or the team leader. Therefore, a part of your team's ability to get back on track is to take on different work tasks.

Use the ideas is this aisle to get your team back on the task track and the fast track to accountability. The aisle includes tools to understand the concept of accountability, ways to assess your team's culture of accountability, and ideas for increasing the level of accountability among members on your team.

# 280. BEING ACCOUNTABLE

A key aspect of being a team player is to be accountable for tasks and projects. We define "being accountable" as accepting personal responsibility for the satisfactory completion of a task, activity, or project in a timely manner. Accountability is at the heart of teamwork and collaboration and serves as the foundation of trust. As members make commitments to one another, they establish a contract and set up a series of expectations. The degree to which team members honor those commitments impacts the overall culture and effectiveness of the team. When team members do not honor their commitments, trust decreases, conflicts increase, and the performance of the team is diminished.

**QUESTION**  Does your team have a culture of accountability?

# 281. CULTURE OF ACCOUNTABILITY

Take a look at some of these norm statements. To what extent are they true about your team?

- On this team, members are willing to be personally measured against the outcomes of a project.

- Around here, you can trust your teammates to deliver on their commitments.

- Members of this team provide honest assessments of a project.

- On this team, you can expect members to report early warning signs that a project is in trouble.

- Around here, members do not sugarcoat results or minimize problems.

- Members of this team are willing to face the consequences of their decisions.

- On this team, members will say (in so many words) "The buck stops here."

- Around here, members do not cover up or run from mistakes, errors, or problems.

- On this team, when things go wrong members look to solve the problem, rather than avoid or hide it.

- Members of this team give an honest estimate of the time and resources required to carry out a project.

 **T I P** You can turn these ten statements into an assessment instrument by adding a rating scale and directions such as the following:

Please read each statement and indicate the extent to which the statement is true about your team according to the following scale:

1 = Not at All
2 = To Some Extent
3 = To a Moderate Extent
4 = To a Great Extent
5 = To a Very Great Extent

# 282. PRODUCTION BEHAVIORS

Take a look at the following behaviors and see to what extent they exist on your team. Better yet, turn this list into a self-assessment survey.

To what extent do team members (you) exhibit the following behaviors on the job:

\_\_\_\_ Deliver on commitments

\_\_\_\_ Produce quality error- and/or defect-free work

\_\_\_\_ Get work done on time

\_\_\_\_ Ask for help when needed

\_\_\_\_ Offer to help and/or train teammates when needed

\_\_\_\_ Follow up with teammates by returning calls, providing requested information, offering suggestions, and responding in other ways

\_\_\_\_ Accept responsibility for assignments

\_\_\_\_ Communicate regularly about the status of tasks and/or projects

\_\_\_\_ Make effective and efficient use of team resources

\_\_\_\_ Always deal with agenda items at team meetings

 **TIP** You can turn these ten statements into an assessment instrument by adding a rating scale and directions such as the following:

Please read each statement and indicate the extent to which the statement is true about your team:

1 = Not at All

2 = To Some Extent

3 = To a Moderate Extent

4 = To a Great Extent

5 = To a Very Great Extent

# 283. POSITIVE PROCESS SKILLS THAT SUPPORT TASK COMPLETION

Positive process skills (Parker, 1994) include:

- Asking questions that bring out ideas and stimulate discussion;
- Using paraphrasing and other active listening skills to ensure effective communication;
- Managing groups discussions to encourage quiet members to participate and talkative members to adhere to limits;
- Establishing an informal, relaxed climate where members feel free to candidly express their points of view;
- Using the consensus method to reach decisions on key team issues;
- Involving members in the setting of goals and objectives;
- Implementing good team meeting guidelines, including agenda planning and time management;
- Insisting that team members respect each other and that each person's contribution is valued;
- Identifying and dealing with team members' dysfunctional behaviors;
- Celebrating the achievement of milestones and other team accomplishments; and
- Using recognition methods, task assignments, and other techniques to motivate team members.

 **T I P** Use this checklist of behaviors to create an assessment tool for team leaders by adding a rating scale and directions such as the following:

To what extent does he or she [your team leader] demonstrate the behaviors according to the following scale:

1 = Not at All
2 = To Some Extent
3 = To a Moderate Extent
4 = To a Great Extent
5 = To a Very Great Extent

## 284. TASK-ORIENTED LEADERS

Another perspective to consider is excessive task focus. Many team leaders focus so much on getting the work done that they inhibit the success of their teams. In many cases they get a lot of work done but (a) it may not be the right work and (b) it may not be the best work possible. In these cases, and I have seen many such situations, the emphasis on task completion while minimizing group process has resulted in member dissatisfaction, unresolved conflict, miscommunication, and curbed creativity. The best way to get back on an effective task track is to utilize positive process skills.

## 285. LEADER BEHAVIORS FOR A MATURE TEAM

Here's a checklist that is based on the work of Wilson, George, and Wellins (1994). Take a look at these mature team leader behaviors and see how you stack up as a team leader.

- ☐ Clarifies the organizational mission and how the team supports the mission
- ☐ Encourages the team to develop specific plans that support the mission
- ☐ Helps the team eliminate unnecessary tasks
- ☐ Is proactive in seeking out opportunities, potential problems, industry trends, and improvement initiatives that support the team's goals
- ☐ Takes responsibility for cross-organizational integration opportunities that support both the team and the organization
- ☐ Sees both the big picture and long-term picture for the team

## 286. LEADERSHIP RESOURCE

A great resource is J.M. Wilson, J. George, and R.S. Wellins with W.C. Byham (1994), *Leadership Trapeze: Strategies for Leadership in Team-Based Organizations*. Chapter 12, "Mature Team Leadership: Encouraging Focus, Direction, and Initiative," is especially helpful.

## 287. ARE WE DOING THE RIGHT THINGS?

To what extent do you agree with this scenario?

Our team seems to lack focus. There are people on this team (including myself at times) who spend a lot of time and energy on things that do not seem to be central to our stated mission. Yes, we work hard, but I question whether it is the *right* work. We seem to downplay the important aspects of our overall purpose and give higher priority to tangential tasks.

1 = Strongly Disagree

2 = Disagree

3 = Neutral/Neither Disagree or Agree

4 = Agree

5 = Strongly Agree

*Note:* This scenario and the ones that follow are based on materials in Rubin, Plovich, and Fry (1978).

# 288. OPEN SEASON

In this book I provide many ideas that include team reviews or assessments. While I value diagnosis as the starting point for redirecting a team, we recognize the potential dangers in such reviews. Team members and outside stakeholders can use these review meetings to "take shots" at people and their work. Consider this scenario, which is a composite of many meetings I have observed:

> The small conference room is crowded. People are standing in the back along the wall. It seems that there is a great deal of interest in this Wireless Window Design Review. Soon after the project team leader opens the meeting, while he is reviewing the agenda, the questions start flying. It is clear that people are here to criticize and find fault with the design. Team members try to respond to questions, but often they are not allowed to complete their answers before being interrupted by negative comments and more questions. The tone is definitely unfriendly, and the intention is not to help but simply to find fault.

 **T I P** There are a number of ways to deal with this type of situation:
- Limit the number of people on the list of invitees;
- Set meeting behavior norms;
- Send the norms out to invitees with the agenda;
- Use an outside facilitator to manage the meeting process;
- Ask invitees to submit questions in advance and then respond to those questions; and/or
- Do not hold the meeting until you are ready to respond to questions.

# 289. AM I DOING THE RIGHT THINGS?

To what extent do you (and your teammates) agree with the following?

> I find it hard to get my work done. Many people both inside and outside of the team ask me to do different things. Often there is not enough time to do all of these tasks . . . and do all of them well. I find it difficult and frustrating to not be able to meet everyone's requests. I feel like a juggler

most of the time . . . a bad juggler. I want to get the work done, but it is just not happening.

1 = Strongly Disagree

2 = Disagree

3 = Neutral/Neither Disagree nor Agree

4 = Agree

5 = Strongly Agree

## 290. WE REDO THINGS

To what extent do you (and your teammates) agree with the following?

When we sit down to discuss something, I never walk away clear about what we decided and what I am supposed to do. We never seem to get anything done. If I am given an action item from one of these get-togethers, I am rarely clear about what I am supposed to do and often I do not agree with it. As a result, the task does not get done or has to be redone because it was not what was wanted by others. We seem to be spinning our wheels.

1 = Strongly Disagree

2 = Disagree

3 = Neutral/Neither Disagree nor Agree

4 = Agree

5 = Strongly Agree

## 291. THE LEADER MAY BE THE PROBLEM

If you (the leader) are still doing lots of traditional supervisory tasks for the team, then you may be the problem.

> *Rule of Thumb:* If you are spending more than 20 percent of your time on reactive, administrative, and supervisory tasks, then your team is not mature. And you may be preventing them from moving on and up to the mature team level.

## 292. "NO ONE FEELS ACCOUNTABLE"

In one organization, the division manager is a consensus builder to excess. He goes to an extreme to create a positive, supportive environment. For example, at team meetings people accept task assignments with vague or nonexistent due dates and quality standards. He will say something like, "Sara, I'd like you to take responsibility for the next division meeting." That's it. There is no further clarification of the assignment. And there is little or no follow-up to ensure successful completion of the work. As a result, dates slip; and when the work is submitted, it may not resemble what the division manager had in mind. For example, he asked a manager to plan an offsite division meeting. The manager formed a planning team that, in turn, researched and recommended a site for the meeting. The team presented a rationale and a budget for the meeting. His response was "Oh, that's too much, we can't spend that much on the meeting." The planning team was deflated and angry because they felt he should have told them about the budget limits when he created the assignment. Valuable time was lost, and the original dates for the meeting had to be pushed back to allow additional time to locate another site. There is a similar attitude toward customer requirements. The net effect is a culture where "no one feels accountable" if assignments are late or incomplete. And yet, the division manager is one of the most likeable and revered leaders in the whole company.

**QUESTION**   How does a process-oriented, consensus building leader such as this change to become more task oriented without losing the positive aspects of his style?

## 293. "I CAN'T GET MY WORK DONE BECAUSE I HAVE TO ATTEND TOO MANY MEETINGS!"

If this is a typical response to a meeting notice, you may have a problem. It's important to understand that meetings do take people away from their basic work tasks. Many organizations, in their zeal to become team-based and inclusive, schedule entirely too many meetings. One reason your team may be off track is that too much time is spent in meetings, especially bad meetings.

**QUESTION** Does your team spend too much time in meetings and not enough time on getting the work done?

 **T I P** Go to Aisle 11 for tips for reducing the number of face-to-face meetings, teleconferences, and other similar tasks.

## 294. MATURE TEAMS NEED FEWER MEETINGS

High performing teams need fewer and shorter meetings to make decisions, solve problems, and communicate information. Mature teams include empowered members, embedded norms, and shared goals. As a result, they have more time to focus on production and service because issues do not require lots of discussion and a lengthy decision-making process.

 **T I P** One way to refocus your team on getting the work done is to ensure that the basic process issues, such as roles, goals, and norms, are in place.

## 295. REDUCING PROJECT REVIEWS

Many teams have reduced the number of project reviews because the preparation for a review is so time-consuming. These teams have balanced the need to keep working on the tasks necessary to complete the project against the need for feedback and find they can do with less feedback or can obtain it by other means. When teams take a hard look at project reviews, they find that the reviews are often done simply to impress senior management.

- Are all your project reviews necessary?

- Can your reduce the number and/or scope of your reviews?

# 296. MCTASK REVIEW

A McTask review is a "fast food" version of the full project review described in the previous aisle. A McTask review is an internal team session attended only by team members and perhaps the team coach and facilitator. The purpose and agenda of the meeting are focused on four outcomes:

1. Compare actual current tasks with the project specifications.

2. If variances exist between plan and actual, determine the causes and analyze the impact.

3. Decide on a course of action to address variances.

4. Make changes, if necessary, to the project specifications.

# 297. REVISIT TASK NORMS

One way to refocus on getting the work done is to revisit your team norms. Consider an open discussion of your existing norms that looks specifically at the norms that address task focus, accountability, quality standards, and completion dates. Ask:

- How can we change our norms to increase our focus on task completion?

- What do we need to do to be more accountable?

- What norms should we add to emphasize the importance of due dates?

- How do we address the issue of "consequences"?

## 298. REWARDING TASK ACCOMPLISHMENT

One way to reestablish a culture of task accomplishment is to provide a system of rewards. There are various methods, such as the following:

- *Spot Bonus.* When a manager sees a team or an individual complete an important job while meeting all quality and cost requirements, the manager provides the person or team with a reward, such as cash or a gift certificate. The reward is discretionary and provided after the fact.

- *Project Team Reward.* Project teams that come together for a limited period of time to complete a specific task are given specific goals and rewards tied to those goals. If the team accomplishes the goals, the rewards are automatic.

For more background see McAdams (1996). For examples of team rewards from twenty-seven organizations, see Parker, McAdams, and Zielinski (2000).

## 299. "SOMETIMES YOU JUST HAVE TO ASK"

A project team leader at a major telecommunications company was frustrated because a team member from a key functional area was not delivering his task assignments. The team was falling behind on its schedule and was in danger of not meeting the due dates for major deliverables. The project manager went to the functional manager for the area and put it on the line. In so many words, he said, "This project requires a major contribution from your people, and we're not getting it. As a result, we're behind schedule. Therefore, I need either of two things: (1) your current representative to do the necessary work or (2) a new person who is both able and available to complete the tasks." A new person was assigned to the team with clear instructions to give the project up to 50 percent of her time—and more if necessary. As the project team leader said to me later, "Sometimes you just have to ask."

 **T I P** Be direct. Explain the problem and the impact. Then ask for what you need.

# 300. USE A COORDINATOR

Does your team have many tasks that need to be done? Are some of these tasks not being done? Are tasks being done late? Perhaps your team needs a coordinator to get things back on track and to keep them on track. Sure, the team leader can be the coordinator, too, but another team member may have both the time and the talent to do it better.

The coordinator's role is

- To maintain the list of action items and other task assignments;

- To check with team members to see whether they need help on their assignments;

- To remind people of their due dates;

- To prepare reports of outstanding tasks;

- To arrange team meetings to discuss task assignments; and

- To distribute communication to team members and stakeholders about tasks.

 **T I P** Nothing breeds team enthusiasm and a positive climate like task accomplishment and meeting deadlines. When work involves many tasks, it takes coordination to make it happen.

# 301. MOTIVATING TASK ASSIGNMENTS

Maybe the problem is the work assignments of team members. Is it possible to change or enhance work assignments? Some teams rotate members to new projects as a way of instilling motivation. Some team leaders provide members with opportunities to learn a new skill, operate a new type of equipment, or teach someone else their specialty. A new assignment as a motivator builds on the work of Frederick Herzberg (1968) whose Motivation/Hygiene Model says that certain conditions lead employees to apply greater effort to their work. These motivators include such non-monetary factors as positive feedback, increased responsibility, greater opportunity to learn, more challenging work, recognition, and increased stature. By the way, more challenging work does not just mean "more work." Piling it on does not usually motivate anyone.

**QUESTION**  Have you considered giving team members new assignments, new tasks, or opportunities to learn a new function?

# 302. BEING ACCOUNTABLE: A SELF-ASSESSMENT

An instrument that helps individuals assess their current level of accountability is found in Parker (1998). Go to the Team Tool Shed for a copy of this instrument.

# 303. SOFTWARE SOLUTION

You may want to look at a piece of software that can help. It's called *Managerpro* and information about it can be found at www.performancesolutionstech.com.

## 304. EFFICIENCY OR EFFECTIVENESS?

Use this quote from Peter Drucker to kick off a discussion with team members:

**"It is important to distinguish between efficiency—doing things right—and effectiveness—doing the right things."**
*—Peter Drucker*

### QUESTIONS

- Are we doing the right things?
- Are we doing things the right way?
- What more could we be doing?
- What should we be doing less of?
- How should we change the way we are doing things?

**IN THIS AISLE YOU HAVE BEEN ABLE TO LOCATE A VARIETY OF TOOLS** designed to raise the level of accountability on your team. However, there are many tools to upgrade your team's approach to accountability in other aisles including Aisle 1, Revisit Your Team Goals; Aisle 9, Reconstitute the Work Plan; Aisle 16, Regain Member Commitment; and Aisle 18, Reassess Team Performance.

# AISLE 11

# REJUVENATE TEAM MEETINGS

## OVERVIEW

**"UGH, ANOTHER MEETING."** If that is the typical response to a meeting notice, then it is time for your team to look for some ways to get your meetings back on track. This section includes a number of tips, tools, and samples to help you start.

Although a good deal of teamwork takes place in the daily interactions among members, meetings are the most visible expression of teamwork. Therefore, if a meeting is poorly run, it is there for all to see. As a result, people will think the team is ineffective. The formula is simple: bad meeting = bad team. Some teams, even teams that in other ways see themselves as "mature," accept the inevitability of bad meetings. But it doesn't have to be that way. You don't have to accept the idea that your team meetings are as good as they are going to get or—a more typical reaction—"They're not THAT bad."

Your meetings can be better . . . they can even be very good, productive exercises. As the old saying goes, "It ain't rocket science." Effective meetings are more about discipline than they are about creativity. The key to a successful meeting is planning and then executing that plan.

In this aisle you will find a variety of tools to help you understand the components of successful ways to assess your current meeting, plan your next meeting, format an effective meeting notice and agenda, facilitate a meeting, develop meeting norms, and hold virtual meetings.

## 305. THE COST OF A MEETING

Did you ever think about the real cost of your team meeting? Do some simple math and you may be in for a shock. Simply multiply the average hourly wage of the members of your team by the length of the meeting to obtain the dollar cost. If the average wage is $30 per hour, then the cost of a two-hour meeting for ten people is $600. Beyond the direct costs of a meeting are the ancillary costs of a bad meeting is terms of such things as:

- Negative impact on the performance of members in the next meeting they attend;

- Discussion (complaining) that takes place among members after the meeting;

- Miscommunications during the meeting that result in such things as tasks not completed, incorrect and duplicate work being done, and wrong information given to stakeholders; and/or

- A bad attitude at the next team meeting.

 **T I P** Estimate the cost of your last meeting. Then ask: Did the value of the meeting exceed the cost?

## 306: THE KEY IS THE PLAN: MEETING MECHANICS

The key to a successful meeting is not what happens *during* the meeting but what happens *before* the meeting. Pre-meeting planning involves:

- Contacting members to gather items for the agenda;
- Arranging for a meeting room with sufficient space;
- Ensuring that the appropriate equipment will be in the room;
- Obtaining a "bridge number" for members who will attend via teleconference;
- Preparing the meeting agenda;
- Preparing and/or gathering the necessary materials;
- Arranging for refreshments as appropriate; and
- Sending the agenda and materials to members prior to the meeting.

## 307. THE KEY IS THE PLAN: MEETING DYNAMICS

In addition to having all the mechanics of the meeting in place prior to the meeting, it is also important to anticipate the interpersonal dynamics of the meeting. Consider the following checklist of team dynamics items as you plan your team meeting:

- ☐ Determine who should be invited to the meeting;
- ☐ Brainstorm possible issues and problems that will be raised;
- ☐ Prepare responses to and/or strategies to deal with the issues and problems;
- ☐ Anticipate potential conflicts and consider ways to resolve them;
- ☐ Develop tools for involving people in the discussions;
- ☐ Anticipate potential problem behaviors and ways of dealing with them;
- ☐ Identify decisions or other actions that must come out of the meeting;
- ☐ Prepare the opening statement of purpose for the meeting; and
- ☐ Develop tentative closing for the meeting.

# 308. GUIDELINES FOR AN EFFECTIVE AGENDA

A good agenda should:

- Begin with the most important or most complex topic;

- Include an approximation of the time needed to complete each topic;

- Indicate what action the team will be expected to take on the item;

- Use clear descriptions of each agenda item, not just one- or two-word titles;

- Specify the person(s) responsible for each agenda item;

- Indicate both the starting and the ending time for the meeting; and

- List the materials to be read prior to the meeting.

# 309. SAMPLE MEETING NOTICE AND AGENDA

On the next page is a format I use.

# MEETING NOTICE

| | |
|---|---|
| *Meeting Title:* | Work and Family Action Team |
| *Meeting Date:* | January 12 |
| *Starting Time:* | 2:00 p.m., ET |
| *Ending Time:* | 3:15 p.m., ET |
| *Location:* | North Conference Room B |
| *Pre-Work:* | Review the Work and Family Institute Website; read the Action Team Recommendations |

# AGENDA

| Topic | Action | Responsibility | Time |
|---|---|---|---|
| Action Team Recommendations | Decision | P. Chin | 30 min. |
| Feedback from Employee Survey | Consensus on key conclusions | K. Dunn | 20 min. |
| Additional Data Collection | Decision on what and who | M. Perillo | 15 min. |
| Presentation to Department | Who will present? | J. Vargas | 10 min. |

# 310. MEETING BEHAVIORS

One way to get your meetings back on track is to establish or revisit team meeting norms. Many organizations post standard meeting behaviors in all conference rooms. Here are some typical meeting norms I like:

- Arrive (or call in) just prior to the scheduled starting time of the meeting.
- Stay for the duration of the meeting.
- Do your "homework" by reviewing the agenda, considering the issues, and reading the materials prior to the meeting.
- If you are unable to attend, inform the meeting planner as soon as you know.
- If you are unable to attend, provide your action items to another member prior to the meeting.
- If you are unable to attend and decide to send a substitute in your place, provide that person with an orientation to the work of the team and the authority to act in your place.
- Ask questions when you don't understand an issue or decision.
- No "multi-tasking" during the meeting (that is, doing other work).
- Turn off all cell phones and beepers.
- Do not leave during the meeting.
- What is said here, stays here.
- Support the facilitator's efforts to involve people and complete the agenda.
- No "put-downs," sarcasm, or other demeaning actions toward teammates.
- Be willing to listen to and consider all ideas.
- Help the group work toward common ground and a consensus.
- State your disagreements in the meeting.
- Do not monopolize or give long lectures.
- Volunteer for meeting roles such as scribe and timekeeper.
- Help clean up the room after the meeting.
- If you miss a meeting, support decisions made in your absence.

# 311. GUIDELINES FOR TELECONFERENCE MEETINGS

Since many team meetings are now done completely or partially by phone, we believe it is necessary to develop new rules for these meetings. One of the problems is that teams are trying to use the old norms for this new meeting format. A full teleconference meeting involves all members participating via the telephone. A partial teleconference meeting involves some members sitting in a conference room while a few participate by phone. Here are guidelines we recommend:

- Prior to the meeting, send each person a copy of the agenda and the reading material.

- Ask for volunteers for the roles of scribe and timekeeper.

- Begin by asking people to identify themselves.

- If time permits, ask people to indicate where they are calling from, the weather there, and other icebreakers. By asking that people say a few words, it makes it easier later to identify them when they speak.

- Refer to the agenda, review the items, and state the overall purpose of the meeting.

- Review the norms, especially the ones about "no multi-tasking."

- At the beginning ask people to identify themselves before they speak and, if necessary, to specify to whom their remarks are directed.

- If some people do not speak on an issue, call their names and ask if they have opinions.

- Summarize all decisions and other agreed-on actions as they are completed during the meeting.

- When conflicts arise, carefully state, or get members to state, both sides of the issue. Recognize that it is more difficult to resolve conflicts during a teleconference meeting. Resolution may require some off-line discussions.

- Because all members cannot see a flip chart or projector, be careful to summarize key items at the end of the meeting. However, be aware that there are computer programs that allow all participants to see the same information during the meeting, provided they have access to a personal computer.

## 312. HOW LONG SHOULD A MEETING BE?

The guidelines are pretty clear, although most of us violate the rules all the time. Psychologists tell us that after about ninety minutes of meeting time the effectiveness of a team diminishes. After two hours it drops off dramatically. Therefore, the ideal meeting runs one hour!

**QUESTION** How often do your team meetings go beyond ninety minutes without a break?

## 313. MEETING BREAKS

Let's set this rule: No team meeting should go beyond ninety minutes without a break. However, if your meeting is scheduled to run for two hours, take a ten- to fifteen-minute break after one hour. Breaks should neither be too long (more than fifteen minutes) to ensure members do not lose focus nor too short (five minutes) to give people ample opportunity to refresh. One exception that I employ: A stretch break of one minute sometimes incorporating a Massage Train (see Aisle 8). For example, you can have a ten-minute break at 10 a.m. and then stretch at 11:15 a.m.

## 314. STAY ON THE TIME TRACK

Ever have a problem getting people to return on time from a break? We've lessened the problem with a great little piece of software called *Time's Up*®. It allows you to flash the break time on the screen from your LCD projector and then count down the time remaining. You can buy *Time's Up*® from Trainer's Warehouse at 800–299–3770 (508–653–3770) or www.trainerswarehouse.com.

## 315. WHEN TO MEET?

Sometimes there is no choice, but more often you have options. So follow these guidelines:

- Meet when your members are best able to deal with issues in a group setting.

- Ask your members when they prefer to meet.

- Avoid Monday mornings when people may have weekend issues to address or they like to use that time to plan their week.

- Avoid Friday afternoons when the energy level is low and people have assignments that need to be completed by the end of the week.

- Avoid the time period right after lunch when the body systems let down and people tire.

- Avoid very early morning meetings because parents may take their children to day care and may not be able to come to work early.

- A good time is just before lunch because it allows members to have lunch together after the meeting.

- Other good times are mid-morning (10 a.m.) or mid-afternoon (2:00 p.m.).

- Consider the time in other time zones when your team consists of geographically dispersed members.

## 316. HOW MANY?

Maybe your team meetings are just too large. If your group is large, the best agenda, the greatest facilitator, the most complete set of norms, and clear goals—all will have minimal impact. Team meetings designed for problem solving and decision making get best results with four to seven members. Anything over ten participants and effectiveness drops dramatically.

### QUESTIONS
- How often do your meetings include more than ten people?
- Do you believe that the effectiveness of your meeting would increase if fewer people attended?

# 317. REDUCING THE NEGATIVE IMPACT OF LARGE GROUP MEETINGS

There are a number of actions you can try to get the group down to a manageable size:

- Eliminate guests who are pure observers and not contributing to the team process.

- Ask members who are subject-matter experts whose expertise is only needed on certain occasions to only attend at those times.

- Consider reorganizing the team into two groups: (1) a small core group of key people who are charged with setting the direction and making the major decisions (this group meets frequently) and (2) the full team, who meet less frequently to hear status reports and serve in an advisory capacity.

- Divide the team into several small task groups charged with various aspects of the work or the project (hardware, software, marketing, service). The subgroups do the basic work and report back to the total team periodically.

- Use subgroups on an ad hoc basis during team meetings. When an important issue arises, divide the team into several small subgroups that are given a limited amount of time to consider and report their recommendations.

# 318. FORMAL ROLES

Every team member assumes a role at your team meetings. While most of these roles are informal (for example, devil's advocate, gatekeeper), there are some formal roles that all teams should consider. If your team meetings are less than effective, consider designating certain roles at all your team meetings. The designations can be permanent or can be rotated among all members. There are advantages and disadvantages to both approaches.

- *Permanent Roles.* The advantage of permanent assignments is that the members get a chance to develop some real expertise in carrying out the role. The disadvantage is that only a few members have an opportunity and other members may become resentful.

- *Rotating Roles.* The advantage is that everyone has an opportunity to develop new skills and it spreads the burden around. The disadvantage is that the quality of team meetings may suffer because some members are just not good at carrying out a particular role.

## 319. MEETING ROLE: TEAM LEADER

The leader ensures that the team stays on track by such things as maintaining a focus on the goals of the meeting, completing the agenda, reminding the team of the overall goals of the organization, reinforcing the role of the team in meeting those goals, providing technical and policy information, and highlighting the importance of nurturing effective external relationships.

## 320. TEAM ROLE: TEAM FACILITATOR

This person manages the process aspects of the meeting with tools such as active listening, open-ended questions, and nonverbal communication to get everyone involved, resolve differences, summarize ideas, achieve a consensus, and have fun. The leader may also serve as facilitator, although at times an outside expert or another team member may play this role.

## 321. MEETING ROLE: TEAM RECORDER

Sometimes called the scribe, this team member is responsible for capturing the team's decisions, action items, and task assignments. The recorder sends out these meeting "notes" after the meeting to all members.

## 322: MEETING ROLE: PARKING LOT ATTENDANT

This team member collects all those ideas that are brought out at the meeting but not discussed at the time. He or she collects these ideas in the "parking lot" for inclusion in the agenda of future team meetings.

## 323. HOW TO BE A MEETING PARTICIPANT

We spend so much time on the leadership roles we forget about the role of meeting participant. Team members can increase the effectiveness of their team meetings by:

- *Doing Homework.* Review the agenda, be clear about the items to be discussed, prepare opinions on the agenda items, read the required materials, and complete action items.

- *Being on Time!* Enough said except perhaps: Arrive early to talk with your teammates and get focused on this meeting.

- *Participating.* Ask questions, seek clarification, offer opinions, share knowledge of the subject, challenge assumptions, actively listen to other points of view, and help resolve conflicts.

- *Taking Notes.* Don't wait for and depend on the formal meeting minutes. Use the agenda as an outline for taking notes. Take down all decisions and action items, especially your own action items.

- *Helping the Leader or Facilitator.* Think of the meeting as your meeting, a meeting that you want to be successful. Let's face it. You don't want to waste your time. So, help the team stay on the agenda, get others involved by asking questions, look for common ground when differences arise, and summarize key ideas and decisions.

- *Not Being a Problem.* Don't monopolize the discussions, engage in side conversations, be unnecessarily argumentative, attack other members, or do other work during the meeting.

- *Being There.* Stay focused on this meeting and the topic under discussion. Try not to let your mind stray.

## 324. BEING A TEAM PLAYER

A web-based course on meeting behavior and a whole lot more is *Being a Team Player,* available through www.iti4training.com. A description of the course and a link to a demo is found on my website at www.glennparker.com/Products/web-being-a-team-player.html

## 325. DON'T REVIEW DISCUSSION FOR LATE ARRIVALS

Many teams adopt this norm because they believe it encourages members to arrive on time and, conversely, it insults members who are present at the beginning of the meeting and are forced to sit through the review.

**QUESTIONS**
- What do you think? If a member or several members come late, should you review what happened earlier in the meeting?
- What if the late arrival is your vice president?
- What if the late arrival asks for a review?
- What's the norm on your team?

## 326. IS A MEETING NECESSARY?

We know of too many teams that meet because there is a meeting scheduled . . . and not because a meeting is necessary. Unnecessary meetings are, of course, a waste of time and money but, perhaps more important, an unnecessary meeting is a drain on team morale. Members feel they have wasted their time and come to resent their membership on the team. Use our checklist to see if your next meeting is necessary.

## Is This Meeting Necessary?

1. *Is There a Clear Purpose for the Meeting?* A clear purpose looks something like this "to develop a procedure for handling customer complaints." The regular Monday morning staff meeting may not be necessary if there is no reason to meet this week.

2. *Should We Meet Now?* While you may have a clear purpose, the time may not be right because:

   - All the required information or equipment is not available.
   - All the key players are not available.
   - An appropriate meeting facility is not available.
   - An important organizational change that has impact on the purpose of the meeting is about to be announced.

3. *Is There a Better Alternative?* The purpose will help you determine whether another meeting method will accomplish your goal more effectively. If the purpose is to review and edit a document, then some electronic means might be better, while a project status update can be accomplished via a teleconference, and orienting members to an impending change might be better handled with one-on-one sessions.

4. *What If the Meeting Is Not Held?* If your answer is "nothing" or "members will cheer loudly" you have your answer.

# 327. MEETING MISTAKES

One way to rejuvenate your meeting is to eliminate the typical meeting mishaps, mistakes, and monsters. Have you taken for granted that certain things are inevitable or impossible to change? Do you feel you just have to put up with long, boring meetings? Are "do nothing" meetings taken for granted? You can do better. Here's our Elite Eight of Meeting Mistakes.

**T I P** As you review the list, be honest with yourself. Do these things happen on your team? If so, commit to implement the changes suggested.

*1. Too Many Meetings.* Simply reduce the number by (a) asking "Is this meeting necessary? (see above); (b) point out the cost of a meeting and ask: "Is it worth it?"; (c) use electronic methods to facilitate team communication.

*2. Meetings Are Too Long.* Add time allocations to your agenda (see sample agenda above), reduce the number of action items, handle typical agenda items electronically or off-line, and use your facilitation skills to stick to the agenda.

*3. Agenda Has Too Many Items.* Clarify the purpose of the meeting and then only include those items relevant to the purpose. Once again, use electronic communication to handle noncontroversial issues.

*4. Too Many People at the Meeting.* Limit invitees to those people who can realistically contribute to the purpose of the meeting. If people still insist on attending, arrange the seating so that the required people sit around the conference table while the others are asked to sit around the perimeter of the room. Keep in mind that it's difficult to engage in problem solving and decision making with a large group.

*5. Meetings Are Dull and Boring.* Use icebreakers, small group activities, and props to liven up the meeting. A good source for ideas is Silberman (1999).

*6. Not Enough Is Accomplished.* Start the meeting on time, remind members of the team meeting norms, follow the agenda, manage the discussion, record action items and people responsible for each item, identify follow-up work, and deal with problem behaviors.

*7. Participants Do Not Cooperate.* Listen to their concerns. Maybe, just maybe, their concerns are legitimate and you might learn something that can improve team meetings. Otherwise reestablish positive meeting norms and use them, speak privately with the "problem people," confront the behavior when it happens in a meeting, or, when appropriate, speak with the person's supervisor.

*8. Nothing Happens as a Result of the Meeting.*    Summarize key decisions as they happen and then again at the end of the meeting, agree on action items and the persons responsible for them, ensure that minutes reflect decisions and action items, and then follow up individually with members to see whether they understand their assignments and/or need help.

## 328. USE GROUPWARE

A number of websites and software packages offer computer-based support for so-called "virtual meetings." One site we like is www.sametime.com. This site provides support for online meetings, presentations, editing documents, and chats.

## 329. VIRTUAL TEAM MEETINGS

Lots of great tips for selecting meeting technology, planning the agenda, and facilitating a virtual team meeting are found in Chapter 8 of Duarte and Snyder (1999).

## 330. 3M MEETING NETWORK

This is a frequently updated website that provides lots of tips for improving the quality of meetings and for facilitating meetings. You will find information about meeting practices, tools, and services. You can sign up for the monthly 3M Meeting News. Check it out at www.3M.com/meetingnetwork/

## 331. TEAM MEETING ASSESSMENT

 A good place to start getting your team back on track is with an assessment tool. This assessment provides data on the four key determinants of an effective meeting: (1) planning, (2) procedures and mechanics, (3) group dynamics, and (4) closing and follow-up. Go to the Tool Shed to find the Team Meeting Assessment (Parker, 1998).

## 332. VIDEO: BE PREPARED FOR MEETINGS

Most people know about the wonderful John Cleese video, *Meetings, Bloody Meetings* (Video Arts), but I like a great little video called *Be Prepared for Meetings,* part of the Toastmasters International Communications Series. The video is distributed by Kantola Productions, 56 Sunnyside Avenue, Mill Valley, CA 94941, 415–381–9363. It's not very funny, but it teaches and demonstrates the basics of a well-run meeting that is both practical and believable.

## 333. VIDEO: MEETING ROBBERS

As the name implies, this great video covers all the various things that team members do to "rob" the team of valuable time and effectiveness. *Meeting Robbers* include the Show-Off, the Critic, the Rambler, the Whisperer, the Assignment Misser, and the Super Seller. The video explores strategies for stopping them. It is available from CRM at www.crmlearning.com

## 334. THE COMPLETE GUIDE TO FACILITATION

The authors, Tom Justice and David Jamieson (1998), are serious when they call it "complete." A big book of more than six hundred pages (also available on CD-ROM), it stands as the most comprehensive source of practical information on meetings and group dynamics.

# 335. "A MEETING IS NO SUBSTITUTE FOR PROGRESS"

This rather interesting quote by an anonymous author can form the basis for good discussion on the meaning of meetings.

### QUESTIONS

- What does this quote mean?
- What is the author trying to say?
- In what ways is a meeting a sign that a team is making progress?
- In what ways is a meeting a signal that a team is not making progress?
- In what ways IS a meeting a substitute for progress?
- How can we avoid a team meeting serving as a substitute for progress?

**THIS AISLE WAS LOADED WITH TOOLS FOR PLANNING AND FACILITATING** a successful meeting. However, many related tools are also found in the aisles dealing with team norms (Aisle 7), climate (Aisle 8), conflict (Aisle 13), and celebrations (Aisle 20).

# AISLE 12

# REHABILITATE EXTERNAL NETWORKS

## OVERVIEW

**WE ARE STILL VICTIMS** of outdated thinking about teams. Most of the underpinnings of what we know about teams comes from group dynamics. Group dynamics focuses on the internal aspects of a team, specifically, such issues as:

- How members interact with one another;
- The importance of shared leadership;
- Fostering harmony among members;
- Group decision-making processes;
- Communication among members;
- The influence of groups norms; and
- The interpersonal competence of members.

As a result, most team-building interventions and team training programs deal with improving interpersonal relationships and internal team dynamics. In addition, most books on team effectiveness and facilitator guides provide tools and techniques that have as their goal bettering interior teamwork. And yet, "managing the outside" is thought by some to be the critical differentiating factor in team success. In the age of partnering, relationship management, network organizations, and cross-functional teams, your team's ability to build and sustain external relationships is critical.

The concept is "no team is an island." No team can exist in isolation and have any hope of success. Teams exist in a constellation replete with other teams, numerous support groups, and a bevy of key stakeholders. As people begin to shed old paradigms, successful teams are collaborating with suppliers, customers, vendors, and even competitors!

It is possible to have a team with solid goals, clear roles, excellent interpersonal relationships, and a positive, relaxed climate that still is frustrated by a lack of success. And if your diagnosis focuses exclusively on the internal dynamics of the team, you may miss the real cause of your derailment.

Therefore, in this aisle, you will find tools to help you to think about your external relationships.

- Who are the key stakeholders who can either support your efforts or create barriers to your success?

- How would you characterize your relationship with these stakeholders?

- What efforts have you undertaken to develop and nurture these relationships?

- What more can you do to improve the quality of your team's external interactions?

## 336. WHAT IS A STAKEHOLDER?

Since we're using the term, let's define it. A stakeholder is a person, team, or organization that has a "stake" in the success of a team. In other words, they have an interest in seeing the team succeed, hold resources that can help the team, can provide assistance the team needs, or can clear away barriers that may block the team's path toward its goal. Members also have a "stake" in the team, but in this context we are referring to people who are not members.

## 337. EXTERNAL VERSUS INTERNAL RELATIONS?

We use the word "external"; that does not necessarily mean outside the organization, although it may. Confused? An external relationship refers to any stakeholder who is not a direct member of your team. Therefore, an external stakeholder may be another employee of the organization, but an external stakeholder may also be a customer or supplier who is not an employee. In both cases a positive relationship may be essential to your success.

 **T I P** Get used to using the word "stakeholder" to designate everyone is this category and eliminate use of "external."

## 338. THE INVISIBLE TEAM

 Colin Hastings and his associates (1987) were some of the first team experts to think about the importance of "the invisible team." Invisible team members include customers, clients, users, vendors, support groups, and sponsors.

**QUESTION** Who are the members of your Invisible Team?

Use the following form as the basis for a discussion with your team.

## TEAM STAKEHOLDERS

| Category | Examples |
| --- | --- |
| 1. Customers and Clients | |
| 2. Users | |
| 3. Suppliers and Vendors | |
| 4. Sponsors | |
| 5. Support Groups | |

# 339. EXTERNAL TEAM NEEDS

What types of help does your team need? Typically, teams need the following:

- *Information.* Teams need accurate and current information, such as customer and market data, production and safety records, research results, and quality and customer reports. Information usually comes from support groups, customers, and even suppliers.

- *Resources.* Teams need all kinds of resources, such as people to provide expert opinions and assistance, statistical and laboratory research, production of prototypes, and the preparation of test samples. Support groups, vendors, sponsors, and customers are usually in a position to provide resources.

- *Support.* Teams need intangibles such as easy, no-hassle, timely approvals, opportunities to take risks and try out new ideas, and occasional expressions of interest in the work of the team. Sponsors and support groups are the major support providers.

- *Budget.* Teams need money and the freedom to spend it when needed for equipment, software, travel, and other items that support the team's goals. Sponsors are typically the stakeholders who furnish the funds.

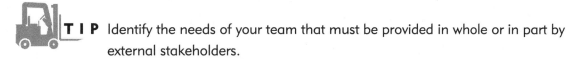 **T I P** Identify the needs of your team that must be provided in whole or in part by external stakeholders.

## 340. GAME PLAN FOR REHABILITATING YOUR EXTERNAL RELATIONSHIPS

Here is a template adapted from Parker (1994) that can form the basis for getting your external networks back on track. Edit the approach to fit your current situation.

- *Identify Key Stakeholders.* Prepare a list of the people you need to ensure your team will succeed. Focus especially on people and organizations with which your relationship needs to improve. Don't forget to include people who have something to gain from your work and people who may have something to lose.

- *Look for Commonalities.* Expand your thinking. Don't be selfish. Go beyond what you need from these stakeholders to identify ways you can help them succeed. The outcome of this activity should be a set of common objectives, the umbrella you can both get under.

- *Communicate Information.* Find ways to tell your story. Don't forget the obvious: reports, meeting minutes, presentations, and company publications. However, since verbal communication still works best, look for opportunities for informal communication with stakeholders in the hallway, at the coffee machine, in the cafeteria, and just prior to or after meetings. Another approach is to invite a key stakeholder to one of your meetings.

- *Select Boundary Managers.* A boundary manager is a team member who manages the "boundary" or interface with a key stakeholder. Many teams assume the team leader is the only person who should be responsible for relationship management. Not true. In some cases the leader may be the wrong person to handle a relationship. The best boundary manager for a particular stakeholder may be the team member with the relevant technical expertise, good past relationship, or good style fit.

- *Identify Potential Barriers.* Before jumping into rebuilding a particular relationship, ask yourself if there are any outstanding issues that need to be addressed or fixed before proceeding. For example:

  - Are there any technical or interpersonal problems hanging around?

  - Does this group see us as a competitor?

  - Will this person or organization potentially stand to lose something as a result of our work?

  - Does this group or person respect and value the work of our team?

  - Do we respect this person or group?

- *Be Credible.* None of this works unless your team is credible in the eyes of this stakeholder.

**QUESTIONS**

- Are you dependable?

- Are you honest?

- Do you deliver on your promises?

- Anything in your past relationship with this stakeholder that has strained credibility?

 **T I P** Before you quickly answer "yes" to any of these questions, ask yourself: How would a key stakeholder answer these questions?

# 341. BARRIERS TO BRIDGE BUILDING

Despite all the good reasons why cross-group collaboration is necessary for success, breakdowns do occur, poor relationships evolve, and conflicts happen. Why? Let's look at some of the major causes and, as we do, see if any of these factors exist on your team.

- *Stereotyping.* Team members have preconceived, negative ideas about stakeholders.
- *Competition.* Teams compete with stakeholders they should be cooperating with.
- *Differentiation.* Organizations create barriers by erecting functional silos.

**QUESTION**  Do any of these factors exist on your team?

# 342. STEREOTYPING

Plain old-fashioned prejudice. We "pre-judge" people in other teams and organizations, and these perceptions color our interactions with them. Negative stereotypes such as the following are typical (Parker, 1994):

- *Senior Management.* "All they care about is the bottom line." "They don't know what it is like out there in the real world."
- *Functional Department Managers.* "All they care about is meeting their personal objectives." "They love our help but don't like to give anything back."
- *Customers and Clients.* "All they want is more for less." "They can't tell us their needs up-front, but they sure have a lot of complaints on the finished product."
- *Support Groups.* "Ask those market research folks for some help and they dump a stack of useless data on you." "Ever try getting a fast answer out of an engineer?"

**QUESTION**  Do any of these stereotypes exist among members of your team?

# 343. COMPETITION

There is nothing wrong with healthy competition between units in an organization. However, when one team tries to achieve its goals at another's expense by, for example, withholding resources, that is negative competition. Teams compete with each other for all sorts of things: recognition, budget, projects, and resources. In some organizations, the culture encourages competition among teams. The net result: Reduced cross-group collaboration.

**QUESTION** Does your team compete with other groups with whom you should be collaborating?

# 344. DIFFERENTIATION

In a breakthrough study, Lawrence and Lorsch (1969) said that groups in organizations need to be differentiated (that is, all the accountants work together in the accounting department). Although this differentiation is helpful in getting the work done efficiently, it also can be a barrier when cross-organizational teaming is required. Each group in the organization develops its own culture and work practices that can make it difficult for the group to "network" with other groups.

**QUESTION** Do you see barriers created as a result of so-called functional silos?

# 345. TYPES OF EXTERNAL ACTIVITIES

Ancona and Caldwell's (1992) study of forty-five product development teams found that team members engaged in three different types of interactions with external stakeholders:

- *Ambassador.* Activities that involved representing the team to outsiders and protecting the team from interference.

- *Task Coordination.* Activities designed to coordinate the team's work with others.

- *Scouting.* Activities that involved seeking out information about markets, technology, and competition.

## 346. AMBASSADOR EXTERNAL ACTIVITIES

Ancona and Caldwell found that external ambassador activities included: (1) building support for the team and its work; (2) reporting the team's progress to sponsors and other senior managers; (3) understanding the company's strategy and its impact on the team; and (4) protecting the team from outside influences that might have a negative impact on the work of the team.

**QUESTION** To what extent does your team engage in successful Ambassador activities?

## 347. TASK COORDINATION

Task coordination activities involved coordination with colleagues and support groups to discuss issues and to obtain feedback and other information in an effort to ensure smooth transitions and handoffs.

**QUESTION** To what extent does your team engage in effective coordination with other groups?

## 348. SCOUTING

Ancona and Caldwell characterize these activities as "scanning" for information about new developments in markets, the competition, and technology.

**QUESTION** To what extent does your team "scan" the organization for information relevant to the team's work?

## 349. SUCCESSFUL EXTERNAL RELATIONS

Ancona and Caldwell's work suggests that the key to success is (1) to develop solid relationships with senior management; (2) to work with other support groups to negotiate schedules and resolve design questions; and (3) to minimize efforts to obtain technical information from others, such as changes in technology, markets, and the competition. In other words, you should spend more time on Ambassador and Task Coordination activities and less time on Scouting.

# 350. BUILDING BRIDGES EXERCISE

We use this activity to create a plan to develop a positive relationship with a team's key stakeholders. For a complete description of this exercise, see Thiagarajan and Parker (1999).

## Preparation

- Use The Invisible Team (number 338 in this aisle) to identify your key stakeholders.

- Prepare a copy of the Building Bridges handout below for each team member.

## Process

- Distribute copies of the Building Bridges handout to all members of the team.

- Form subgroups and ask each subgroup to address one stakeholder from the list.

- Ask each team to present a report on its stakeholder.

- Facilitate a discussion on the reports.

- Conclude with a summary of next steps for each stakeholder.

# BUILDING BRIDGES

1. Identify a person, department, or other stakeholder that your team needs to develop a successful relationship with.


2. What specific types of help do you need from this stakeholder?


3. What kinds of assistance does this stakeholder need from your team?


4. Identify common objectives you share with this stakeholder.


5. What potential barriers may prevent this stakeholder and your team from working together effectively?


6. What member of your team would be the best person to be the main contact with this stakeholder?


7. What specific steps can you take to develop a positive relationship and obtain the necessary assistance from this stakeholder?

# 351. "IT'S ALL JUST PR"

When many team leaders hear that cross-group collaboration involves developing relationships with key stakeholders, they don't value the work. As one leader said, "It's all just PR," while another person jumped up and said "Yeah, you've got to 'smooze' with your bosses." For many team leaders, calling these activities "relationship management," "networking," or "boundary management" does not make them any more important and any more valued. It is their view that their teams should be known and respected solely on the basis of the quality of their work.

 **T I P** Use the research by Ancona and Caldwell (1992) to show team leaders the importance of "ambassador" and "coordination" activities. You can also make the point that it does no good to do good work if no one knows about it. You should be proud of your efforts and want other people to know about them. In addition, not all networking is about gaining support from senior management. Some networking is designed to get help from support groups whom the team needs to provide information, samples, prototypes, and ideas.

# 352. YOUR NETWORKING STYLE

How would you characterize your team's approach to building external networks? Please select one primary (P) and one secondary (S) style and write your letters in the blanks below.

_____ *Businesslike.* Provides regular progress reports, circulates minutes, and makes periodic presentations.

_____ *Smoozers.* Uses many informal opportunities to "sell" the team at other meetings, in the cafeteria, in the hallways, and in other venues.

_____ *Efficient*. Develops a plan that identifies key stakeholders, what they can provide, what they like and what they dislike and assigns specific team members to network with each stakeholder.

_____ *Serendipitous*. A happy-go-lucky, somewhat haphazard approach that takes advantage of networking opportunities as they naturally occur.

_____ *Ostrich*. Takes no direct measures to network, believing instead that the quality of the team's work will create all the support necessary to succeed.

_____ *Integrative*. Believes in the power of networking and therefore combines some aspects of the businesslike, efficient, and "smoozer" styles.

 **TIP** This is a good icebreaker to get the team started on a discussion of rehabilitating your external relationships.

# 353. ZERO SUM? A CROSS-TEAM COLLABORATION GAME

 This activity addresses destructive competition between teams in a fun and engaging way (Thiagarajan & Parker, 1999). You can find the game in the Team Tool Shed.

# 354. WISDOM: AN INTER-GROUP TEAM GAME

 Another similar activity that demonstrates the value of cross-group collaboration is Wisdom (Parker & Kropp, 2000). You can also find this game in the Team Tool Shed.

## 355. THREE-WAY TEAMWORK

This is a more involved and time-consuming simulation that focuses on the barriers to cross-functional teaming (Parker, 1997). It is found in the Team Tool Shed.

## 356. TRICKY TALES

This is another game that demonstrates both the difficulty and the need for cross-group collaboration (Parker & Kropp, 2000). Go to the Team Tool Shed for a copy of this activity.

## 357. "NO TEAM IS AN ISLAND"

Use this quote to kick off a discussion of the need to rehabilitate your external networks.

**QUESTIONS**

- What does this quote mean?
- In what ways is our team operating as an "island" now?
- In what ways are we functioning interdependently with other people and groups?
- What alliances with other people and groups do we need to establish and/or rehabilitate?

## 358. BEING RESPONSIBLE

Use this quote to stimulate a discussion about your relationships with stakeholders.

**"A decision is responsible when the group that makes it has to answer for it to those who are directly or indirectly affected by it."**
*—Charles Frankel*

### QUESTIONS

- Which groups are affected by our decisions?

- How would you characterize our relationship with these groups? Very positive? Friendly? Open? Hostile? Neutral? Suspicious?

- In what ways do we consider our key stakeholders when we make a decision? Senior management? Support groups? Functional departments? Suppliers?

- How do you think these stakeholders would respond to the previous two questions? Why?

- What can we do to take into account key stakeholders when we make a decision?

# 359. "AGAINST THEIR WILL"

Here's another great little quote for your team to consider.

**"Those convinced against their will are of the same opinion still."**
—*Dale Carnegie*

### QUESTIONS

- What application does this quote have to our team?

- How do we typically try to convince our stakeholders that we're right?

- Are there any stakeholders who have been "convinced against their will" to do something for our team? What's been the impact?

- When we are aware that a stakeholder does not support us, how do we typically approach the person? How successful have we been?

- What things could we do more of or less of to win people over to our point of view?


**IN THIS AISLE YOU HAVE FOUND TOOLS TO IDENTIFY** your key stakeholders and a variety of ideas for increasing the quality of your relationships with those stakeholders. However, there are tools in other aisles that can help your team build more effective external relationships. For example, you will find helpful tools in the aisles dealing with accountability (Aisle 10), commitment (Aisle 16), conflict (Aisle 13), and role clarification (Aisle 3).

# AISLE 13

# REDUCE CONFLICT SUCCESSFULLY

## OVERVIEW

**CONFLICT!** It's a dirty word! We don't like the sound of it. It sounds negative or, at best, unpleasant. Clearly, it is something to be avoided at all costs. Is that true? Is that how your team sees it? Do you try to avoid conflict at all costs? Or is your team one that seems to enjoy conflicts among team members?

In our experience, teams derail when they have either (a) too little or (b) too much. Conflicts are a natural part of the team experience. Disagreements, in fact, are to be encouraged and accepted as an inevitable part of the dynamic of a healthy team. With norms encouraging open communication, expression of opinions, looking at both sides of an issue, and candor, we should expect disagreements. Therefore, when a team experiences little or no conflict, there is something radically wrong with the team process. The results of too little conflict are

- Good ideas are not expressed and considered;

- Creativity and innovation suffer;

- Opportunities are missed because they are not surfaced;

- Decisions are made but the alternatives may not be considered;

- Problem solving is routine and unimaginative;

- Meetings are boring; and/or

- Members lose interest in the work of the team.

On the other hand, when a team experiences too much conflict, it may get off track and lose focus on its primary mission. The differences among members absorb the team, and progress is stalled because there is no consensus on the issues. Members lack basic conflict-resolution skills and the team lacks norms that encourage harmonizing and consensus building. In some cases, members actually enjoy the battles and discourage efforts to minimize or resolve the conflict. Consequences for a team that has too much conflict are

- Decisions are not made or, at best, are delayed;

- Opportunities are missed because too much time is taken deciding what to do;

- A negative climate emerges on the team;

- Focus drifts away from the basic mission;

- Customers do not like working with the team;

- Members face personal attacks;

- Meetings are characterized by lots of heat and not much light; and/or

- Ideas are surfaced but few are put into practice.

If your team is bogged down or derailed because of too much conflict, too little conflict, or a lack of conflict-resolution skills, the tools in this aisle can help. You will find information to help you understand conflict in teams and how ineffective resolution techniques can immobilize your team. There are also many tools designed to assess your current approach to conflict and tips for increasing the effectiveness of conflict resolution on your team.

## 360. RESOLVING CONFLICTS ON TEAMS

Teams react to and resolve conflicts in a variety of ways. The way your team resolves its conflicts is a reflection of the degree of maturity on your team. Mature teams see conflict as something to be encouraged because they believe the best ideas emerge in this environment and they are confident in their ability to resolve their differences. One signal that your team is off track is to look at how you resolve differences. There are typically five ways of addressing conflict in teams (Parker, 1996): denial, smoothing over, power, compromise, or problem solving.

 **TIP** As you read over the following descriptions, think about how your team typically approaches a conflict. Ask yourself: What is our primary style?

## 361. DENIAL

Denial is simply denial. Team members do not acknowledge the existence of any disagreements. They continue to go about the business of the team, having meetings, implementing plans, and so forth, without any reference to the discord. The only reaction is a non-reaction. If someone asks about the "problem" or "issue" or even "the conflict," the reaction will be something like "I don't understand what you're talking about."

 **QUESTION** Is this how your team handles conflict?

## 362. SMOOTHING OVER

This method is closely related to denial. The conflict is acknowledged to exist but is characterized as "unimportant" and "not worthy of consideration." The differences are seen as "trivial," "no big deal," "a healthy discussion," "a good exchange of ideas," or "that's just normal around here."

The reaction is a little like hiding under the covers and hoping it will all go away soon. One pervasive thought is that talking about conflicts only makes them worse. So the team members minimize them and don't give them a lot of "air time." Another way that teams using this mode smooth over a conflict is to use humor to relieve the tension, get everyone laughing and, as a result, off the subject.

**QUESTION**  Does this method of dealing with conflict sound like your team?

## 363. POWER

It's simple, easy, and, above all, fast. When a conflict arises, one or two people make the decision because of their position (team leader, manager) or influence (expertise, experience). In a subtle version of this approach, the team is asked to discuss an issue, solve a problem, or make a decision, but when a conflict arises, the power person steps in and decides "in the interests of time" or to "move things along."

**QUESTION**  Does this happen on your team?

## 364. COMPROMISE

It looks good on the outside, but the results are not very satisfying or productive for the team if all conflicts are resolved by compromise. In its crudest form, compromise is "splitting the difference." For example, say you want a performance objective of "a patient will be seen by a doctor within ten minutes of arriving at the ER," while I propose twenty minutes as more realistic. We settle on fifteen minutes as a compromise. Sound good? In fact, we have simply minimized our dissatisfaction and have not worked through the issue to find a solution that is best for the patient and the organization. Compromise produces an answer with a minimum of stress, but it does not fundamentally reduce the roots of the conflict.

**QUESTION**  What are some recent "compromises" that your team or some team members participated in?

## 365. PROBLEM SOLVING

In this approach to conflict resolution, the team does not deny or smooth over the conflict, allow one person to decide, or accept an easy compromise. On the contrary, the team first acknowledges the conflict, looks at all sides of the issue, identifies the root problem ("patients need immediate treatment"), collects data, develops possible solution scenarios, debates the pros and cons of each solution, and comes to a consensus on a decision. Problem solving is more difficult, more time-consuming but, in the end, more likely to be permanent and satisfying for team members.

## 366. YOUR TEAM'S CONFLICT RESOLUTION STYLE

How would you characterize your team's approach to conflict? Use this survey to answer the question. You can check the predominate style of your team and then discuss everyone's answers in the group or rank them in the order in which they reflect your style, with "5" being most reflective and "1" being least reflective.

_____ 1. **Denial.** "Problem? There's no problem."

_____ 2. **Smoothing Over.** "There're some differences of opinion, but it's no big deal."

_____ 3. **Power.** "It's my way or the highway."

_____ 4. **Compromise.** "Let's split the difference."

_____ 5. **Problem Solving.** "Let's look at the problem and then figure out what's best for the organization."

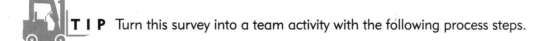

**T I P**  Turn this survey into a team activity with the following process steps.

## Process

- Distribute a copy of the survey to each person.

- Provide a brief explanation of the five approaches.

- Ask each person to rank the styles in the order in which they think they reflect the team's current approach to conflict.

- Facilitate a discussion based on the responses.

- Conclude with a summary and a list of actions to be taken by the team that are intended to embed the problem-solving approach.

# 367. CAUSES OF TEAM CONFLICT

Lois Hart (1981) has identified eight causes of conflict. As you review the list, try to identify the primary causes of conflict on your team. Different causes will require different interventions. In addition, some causes are more reflective of an immature team.

- Unmet needs and wants;

- Values;

- Perceptions;

- Knowledge;

- Assumptions;

- Expectations;

- Different backgrounds; and

- Willingness and ability to deal with conflict.

## 368. UNMET NEEDS

Conflicts occur when people's basic needs are not met to their satisfaction. These needs may be such things as security (income, job), comfort (work/meeting space), affiliation (feeling a part of the team), affection (closeness to other team members), and recognition (positive feedback). Mature teams should have already addressed these needs.

 **T I P** If conflicts seem to be caused by unmet needs, you may need to do some re-forming activities.

## 369. VALUES

Conflicts among team members are generated by differences in beliefs about central issues such as leadership (roles), time (management), goals (accountability), compensation (fairness), collaboration (providing help), and trust (delivering on promises). A mature team should have worked through and resolved value differences.

 **T I P** Value differences should be reflected in team norms.

## 370. PERCEPTIONS

One of the major and ongoing sources of team conflict is our natural tendency to filter the data we absorb. Since we all have different filtering systems, the possibilities of seeing things in different ways or believing things are more or less important can create an endless stream of conflicts. Sharing values, experiences, and styles are ways of minimizing differences, but they will never go away.

 **T I P** Different perceptions are helpful to the team because we want to be able to look at an issue from a variety of perspectives.

# 371. KNOWLEDGE

When one member has different knowledge or expertise, this can create conflict when that knowledge is not shared. However, this obstacle can be reduced, even eliminated, by a conscious effort to share knowledge that is relevant to the issue at hand.

 **T I P** Mature teams should not experience this problem.

# 372. ASSUMPTIONS

Another ongoing source of conflict is assumptions members make about other people and issues. Conflicts escalate when the assumptions focus on the motives of the other person, as in "You continually come late to our meetings because you don't value what we do."

 **T I P** While this problem may never go away, developing norms against making assumptions about people's motivation can minimize it, and training in asking open-ended questions in place of accusations can also help.

# 373. EXPECTATIONS

This issue was discussed in Aisle 3. Mature teams need to have a session in which expectations about other team members' roles are shared and clarified. Differing expectations about roles often leads to conflicts among members, as in "I thought you were responsible for that function."

 **T I P** If there are still lingering issues around expectations, go back to square one and facilitate a role-clarification process.

## 374. DIFFERENT BACKGROUNDS

Since there are so many global teams with members who come from different cultures, this can be a source of conflict. It can also be a source of strength. Members need to share and discuss their different orientations to such team issues as resolving conflict, open communication, leadership styles, listening, and candor, among others.

 **T I P** A sure sign of maturity on a cross-cultural team is the open discussion of different backgrounds.

## 375. WILLINGNESS AND ABILITY TO DEAL WITH CONFLICT

Skill-building training in conflict management can provide team members with the *ability,* and team-building sessions can help a team develop the *will* to address conflicts in a professional manner.

 **T I P** A sure sign of a mature team is the ability and willingness to resolve its conflicts in an open and effective manner.

## 376. CAUSES OF CONFLICT ON YOUR TEAM

Use this instrument to identify the key sources of conflict on your team.

### Preparation

Prepare a copy of the survey for each member of the team.

### Process

- Distribute a copy of the survey to each team member.
- Provide a brief explanation of each of the causes for conflict.
- Ask each person to check the three most important causes on the team.
- Facilitate a discussion based on the results leading to (1) identification of the major causes and (2) action plans to address the causes.

# CAUSES OF CONFLICT ON YOUR TEAM

*Directions:* Check the three most important sources of conflict on your team.

☐ Unmet needs and wants

☐ Values

☐ Perceptions

☐ Knowledge

☐ Assumptions

☐ Expectations

☐ Different backgrounds

☐ Willingness and ability to deal with conflict

## 377. LEARNING FROM CONFLICT

The *Learning from Conflict* handbook for trainers and group leaders by Hart (1981) is a great resource with workshop designs, lots of activities, and theory inputs. The sections include topics such as reacting to conflict, searching for the causes of conflict, preventing conflict, and resolving conflicts.

## 378. THOMAS-KILMANN CONFLICT MODE INSTRUMENT

The classic instrument, the *Thomas-Kilmann Conflict Mode Instrument,* helps each team member identify his or her predominant mode of dealing with conflict (Thomas & Kilmann, 1974). The five conflict positions taken by people are avoiding, accommodating, competing, compromising, and collaborating.

The instrument can be used to help team members understand the various ways people respond to conflict, learn how to resolve conflict with another person, try some methods for getting to win-win solutions, and increase their personal effectiveness in dealing with conflict.

The instrument is available from Consulting Psychologists Press at www.cpp-db.com or 800-624-1765

## 379. AVOIDING

Avoiding is closely related to denial. Here the person is very unassertive and very uncooperative. There is no attempt to either satisfy your needs or the needs of the other party. This method is useful only in situations in which the issues are of little importance or it is clear there is no chance of addressing team concerns.

**QUESTION** Think back to those on your team with this style of dealing with conflict. How effective was it in the long run?

# 380. ACCOMMODATING

Similar to smoothing over, the accommodating mode focuses on being very cooperative in an attempt to satisfy the needs of the other person. There is no effort to satisfy one's own needs. While this position can be frustrating to the person using it, it may be necessary when the goal is to maintain harmony with another person or organization.

**QUESTION** Can you describe some situations when you felt forced to accommodate another person or team?

# 381. COMPETING

Not unlike the power style, competing focuses on satisfying your needs while demonstrating little effort to address the needs of the other person. High assertiveness and low cooperation characterize competing. Competing is sometimes called for in cases of extreme emergency or when rules must be strictly enforced.

**QUESTION** When were some times when the competing style was called for on your team?

# 382. COMPROMISING

Serving as a midpoint between competing and accommodating, this mode seeks to "split the difference" by being moderately assertive and moderately cooperative. Compromise does not produce the best solution, but it may result in the only solution possible in certain situations wherein goals are incompatible or the problems are too complex to be addressed in the time available.

**QUESTION** Are there times when your team could benefit from compromise in a conflict situation?

## 383. COLLABORATING

This most desirable mode of dealing with conflict demonstrates both high assertiveness and high cooperation in an effort to satisfy the needs of everyone. This approach is very useful when a team wants to build positive relationships, deal with important issues, and achieve a true consensus.

**QUESTION** Which method of conflict resolution is most prevalent on your team?

## 384. IS CONFLICT HEALTHY?

Is conflict really healthy for a team? Most people would rather avoid conflict, and yet we keep saying conflict is a *good* thing. What's the problem here? Team-building consultants say conflict is desirable for a team, but most team members would just as soon avoid it.

**QUESTIONS**

- Can you point to a time on your team when conflict was helpful?
- What types of conflict are healthy? What types are unhealthy?
- If conflict is so useful, why do we tend to avoid it or try to get over it quickly?
- Should we try to encourage more conflict on our team?
- If we do have more conflict, are we ready to deal with it?
- What are the key skills needed to effectively resolve conflict?

# 385. IS CONFLICT A SIGN OF MATURITY?

In our experience, there is a tendency on the part of so-called mature teams to avoid or smooth over conflict. Why?

Teams that have been in existence for a long period of time tend to resist surfacing conflicts among team members for the following reasons:

- Overt conflict is viewed as a sign of an ineffective team;

- Disagreements among members are associated with the "storming" stage;

- They do not want to shake the delicate balance and outward harmony that characterizes the team;

- Disagreements are perceived as a sign of immaturity; and/or

- There is a belief that there should no longer be any conflicts at this stage in the team's development.

### QUESTIONS

- Do you agree with any of these statements?

- Are any of them true for your team?

**T I P** Facilitate a discussion with your team beginning with the question: "Is conflict a sign of maturity?" and then bringing in some of the above bullet points.

# 386. COMMUNICATING ABOUT CONFLICT

If you decide you need to go back to square one to develop a common understanding and some agreements about conflict, consider this exercise (Parker & Kropp, 2000). The handout lists a series of incomplete sentences, which members take turns completing. With good facilitation, this exercise can produce an action plan designed to establish effective conflict resolution norms.

Go to the Team Tool Shed to take a look at this exercise.

# 387. CROSS-FUNCTIONAL TEAM CONFLICT SURVEY

This survey focuses on your ability to work cooperatively on a cross-functional team with members from many other departments in the organization. It can also be adapted to be a peer feedback tool, with teammates providing their perceptions of you. Among the thirty items are such statements as:

- Work toward the "best" solution for the team rather than one that just meets the needs of my department.

- Treat team members from other departments as collaborators rather than as competitors.

- Keep team members from other departments informed of issues that affect them.

- Do not spend excessive amounts of time defending my own or my department's point of view.

A copy of the survey is found in the Team Tool Shed.

# 388. VIDEO: DEALING WITH CONFLICT

This twenty-minute video uses realistic vignettes to demonstrate the five modes of dealing with conflict and their impact on conflict resolution. The video works extremely well in conjunction with the Thomas-Kilmann Instrument. You can order the video from CRM Learning at www.crmlearning.com

# 389. RESOLVE CONFLICTS WITH THE CRITERIA GRID

This simple but effective tool is used to help a team decide among several possible choices. The process begins with the team brainstorming possible criteria for deciding between two or more alternatives. They can select up to seven criteria by using consensus, multi-voting, or some other technique. They then create a grid with the criteria listed across the top and the alternatives listed down the left side, compare each option against each criterion and, if it meets the criterion, please an X in the box at the intersection. Alternatively, the team can use a five-point scale to rate each option.

You will find the Criteria Grid in the Team Tool Shed.

# 390. RESOLVE CONFLICTS WITH MULTI-VOTING

This tool helps a group quickly prioritize a list of items. It identifies which are considered most urgent or promising by the team.

## Process

1. Brainstorm a list.

2. Count the number of items on the list (for example, thirty-six items).

3. Divide the list by three (36 ÷ 3 = 12).

4. Each team member selects the twelve items he or she likes best (only one vote per item).

4. By a show of hands, tally the number of votes per item. Write the number of votes received next to the item.

5. Circle the top vote-getters or create a new list of the winners.

6. Alternatively, use stick-on red dots. Give each person as many dots as the number identified in Step 2.

7. Each person votes by placing a dot next to the item. Tally the dots to create the rank-ordered list.

## 391. WORKPLACE CONFLICT RESOURCE CENTER

A good source for information on resolving conflict is found at www.mb.imag.net/~rbacal/conflict/index.htm The site includes lots of good advice and articles dealing with conflict on teams, between team members, and with supervisors and customers.

## 392. CONFLICT WITHIN PROJECT TEAMS

A good source for information on conflict within project teams is found at www.projectconnections.com/knowhow/fasttrack/conflict.html. The site contains articles, tips, book lists, and focused discussions by project managers.

## 393. GETTING PAST NO

This excellent book, *Getting Past No: Negotiating Your Way from Confrontation to Cooperation,* is by William Ury (1993), co-author of *Getting to Yes.*

**AS YOU LEAVE THIS AISLE,** keep in mind that there are tools in many other aisles that also may help address team conflict issues. Take a look at the aisles that address team meetings (Aisle 11), goals (Aisle 1), roles (Aisle 3), style differences (Aisle 2), climate (Aisle 8), communication (Aisle 15), and trust (Aisle 14).

# AISLE 14

# REBUILD A CLIMATE OF TRUST

## OVERVIEW

**YOUR TEAM CANNOT GO ANYWHERE WITHOUT TRUST.** If team members do not trust one another, then:

- The climate is tense;
- Members do not honor their commitments;
- Communication is guarded;
- Risk taking is minimal;
- Meetings are formal;
- Creativity is stifled; and
- No one feels empowered.

A lack of trust among members usually translates into a low level of trust with other teams and key stakeholders. External relations that are marked by a lack of trust means that other teams:

- Do not believe your estimates;

- Question the quality of your work;

- Are skeptical of your promises;

- Wonder whether you will support their goals;

- Think you may take sole credit for joint efforts;

- Closely examine the veracity of your requests; and

- Wonder about the truthfulness of your reports.

If you believe that diminished trust is a factor in the current culture of your team, then you must immediately begin the journey of rebuilding trust and trustworthiness among members and with your external partners. This will not be a quick fix because, as Elledge and Phillips point out:

> "There is no structured process to guide a trustless team, nor will there be a specific outcome to measure. There is no magic cure. It is not as simple as developing a mission statement or establishing problem-solving guidelines. Two days of team building do not undo three years of shared experience. Trust is established only over the long haul. It accumulates from observations and judgments of everyday, routine interactions."
> (1994, p. 51)

Begin your journey down this aisle by first understanding a little more about trust in teams. Then try to uncover the breakdowns in trust on your team. Is the trust issue more significant among team members or in your interactions with outsiders? Next, move to specific actions that you can take to rebuild the climate of trust.

# 394. TRUST IS . . .

A working definition of trust has been provided by Shaw (1997, pp. 21–22). Trust is the "belief that those on whom we depend will meet our expectations of them." In other words, "We trust those who meet our positive expectations." Since trust hinges on expectations, it is important for team members to discuss their expectations of one another. Therefore, many of the tools we suggested in Step 3, Redefine Everyone's Role, and Step 7, Reestablish Ground Rules, are especially relevant to trust and should be reviewed in conjunction with your interest in rebuilding a climate of trust.

 **T I P** Check out the role clarification (Aisle 3) exercises for help in setting expectations among team members.

 **T I P** Revisit your norms to determine whether all members have the same perceptions of what is expected from members of your team.

# 395. TRUST AND TEAMWORK

My colleague and co-author Dick Kropp has some useful thoughts on the impact of trust on teamwork (Parker & Kropp, 2000, p. 7). He takes the idea of expectations a step farther when he says, "The extent to which we believe that our expectations are accurate determines the amount of time and attention we devote to oversight, follow-up, and contingency plans." In other words, when we believe that our teammates will meet our positive expectations of them, we trust that the job will be done efficiently and effectively. By the way, the same view impacts our inter-team interactions.

## 396. TRUST AND PREDICTABILITY

Kropp believes that predictability impacts team effectiveness because it determines the extent to which our teammates are likely to carry out a task in an anticipated manner. We refer to the person's behavior as "reliable." When there is a high level of predictability among teammates, there is little misunderstanding and second-guessing. We are all "on the same page."

**QUESTION**   Is "predictability" always a good thing?

## 397. TRUST AND SAFETY

Kropp's third aspect of trust is safety. When the environment is safe, team members trust that it is acceptable (even encouraged) to take reasonable risks, to explore new ground, to consider a variety of innovative alternatives. Members feel free to advance different ideas, alternative opinions, and "out of the box" solutions. Safety is a cornerstone of trust that in turn expands the possibilities of teamwork.

**QUESTION**   How would you characterize the degree of "safety" on your team?

## 398. TORI

Jack and Lorraine Gibb (1972) developed the TORI model to express a group's movement toward (T) trusting relationships, (O) open communication, (R) self-realization, and (I) interdependence. As teams grow and mature they move from:

- Defensiveness and formality to freer, trusting relationships;
- Distorted and closed communication to openness and candor;
- Competitive problem solving and goal formation to a realization that all members can contribute to team goals and problem solving; and
- Dependence on the formal leader to a fluid form of shared leadership.

Using this model you can identify trust as the central factor in assessing the level of growth or maturity on your team. In a sense, the four bullet points above represent a continuum (or four continuums) of team growth from immaturity (forming) to maturity (performing).

 **T I P** Post four continuums on the wall representing (1) Defensiveness—Trust, (2) Closed Communication—Open Communication, (3) Competitive Problem Solving—Participative Problem Solving, and (4) Leader Dependent—Shared Leadership. Then ask team members to place an X to indicate the current state of the team on each continuum. You can then develop action plans designed to move the team toward maturity.

# 399. TRUST BUSTERS

While we tend to focus on behaviors that build trust, it is instructive to look at the actions that diminish trust. In a study of trust in team leaders, the following were the five top behaviors associated with reducing trust in a leader:

1. Sends mixed messages so that I never know where he/she stands (inconsistent).

2. Acts more concerned about his/her own welfare than anything else.

3. Avoids taking responsibility for actions ("passes the buck" or "drops the ball").

4. Jumps to conclusions without checking the facts first.

5. Hides information or lies to me about things that might affect me.

 This study by DDI/Center for Applied Behavioral Research is summarized and analyzed in Parker (1997, pp. 123–127).

**QUESTION** Do you see any of these behaviors on your team?

# 400. FEAR AND TRUST

In their seminal work, *Driving Fear Out of the Workplace,* Ryan and Oestreich (1991), give us some guidance as to what team leaders, coaches, and managers can do to foster a climate of trust. Here's our edited version of their suggestions:

1. Listen, really listen, demonstrating your active listening skills, to the concerns, questions, and feelings of team members.

2. Be a role model by being open and trusting in your interactions with team members.

3. Be open to feedback about your behavior and demonstrate a willingness to change.

4. Be vigilant to the actions of others that foster mistrust and be ready to address them.

5. Deal with your own fear of speaking up and help others deal with their fears.

6. Be a facilitator rather than a director in meetings and other communications forums.

7. Ask for help in dealing with mistrust and fears among team members.


# 401. TRUSTING AND TRUSTWORTHY

We talk a good deal about trust, trusting, and trustworthy. Are they the same?

- *Trusting behavior* is defined simply as being open with your teammates and freely sharing your ideas, feelings, and information with them.

- *Trustworthy behavior* is the expression of acceptance, support, and a willingness to cooperate with your teammates.

 **T I P** Remember that expressing acceptance and support of your teammates does not mean that you have to agree with everything they say or do.

**QUESTION** A teammate decides to give a customer something beyond what was called for in the contract and you disagree with her decision. How would you express both acceptance and support at the same time as you disagree with her decision?

## 402. WHEN IS IT OK NOT TO TRUST A TEAMMATE?

We say trust is so important to the rebuilding of open communication and trust. But when is it appropriate not to trust another person or another team?

*Instructions:* List some situations in which trust is inappropriate.

1. _____

2. _____

3. _____

4. _____

5. _____

**T I P** Trust is usually not called for when the other person sees him- or herself in competition with you and acts accordingly. However, you may be able to turn a competitive situation into a collaborative one by pointing out the value (if it exists) of working together. For example, your sales team may collaborate with a team from another region to achieve a major sale with the same customer instead of two small sales.

# 403. TRUST AND EXTERNAL STAKEHOLDERS

In a fascinating article, my colleague Ira Asherman (2000) makes a strong case for pharmaceutical companies building a trusting relationship with the Food and Drug Administration (FDA). In the end, Asherman believes that trust between the FDA and a drug company will benefit both organizations greatly. He believes that drug development teams that focus on relationship management, stop "demonizing" the agency, understand the agency's needs, communicate openly about safety issues, and, when appropriate, admit their mistakes will be successful. And success translates into more rapid approval of new drug applications.

# 404. TEAM TRUST TEST

Here's a quick tool to assess the level of trust on your team.

## Preparation

Prepare a copy of the survey for each team member. If you think you will receive honest responses, do it in an open discussion or ask members to sign their names to the form. If you have concerns about the degree of trust, you can administer the test anonymously.

## Process

- After each person has completed the survey, compile the results.
- Then facilitate a discussion on the data, probing for reasons and examples, concluding with ideas for increasing the level of trust on the team.

# TEAM TRUST TEST

*Directions:* Indicate the degree to which the following statements are true for our team, according to the following scale:

1 = Almost Never   2 = Rarely   3 = Sometimes   4 = Most of the Time   5 = Almost Always

1. Members feel free to express their opinions whatever they may be.      1   2   3   4   5

2. Members honor their commitments.      1   2   3   4   5

3. Members' actions are consistent with their words.      1   2   3   4   5

4. Members are empowered to get the job done.      1   2   3   4   5

5. Members feel they can rely on their teammates.      1   2   3   4   5

**Total:**

# 405. TRUST WORDS

Here's another exercise designed to begin the dialogue about the level of trust in your team.

## Preparation

Prepare a copy of the handout for each person. Prepare a master copy as an overhead transparency or as a computer file.

## Process

- Ask each person to select one word and circle it.
- Tally the number of votes received by each word.
- At a team meeting post the results.
- Lead a discussion on the words receiving the most votes and those receiving few or no votes.
- If a consensus emerges on a negative word, probe for the positive word that members want to aspire to.
- Discuss changes needed to achieve the desired state.

# WORDS OF TRUST

*Directions:* Review the following list of descriptors. Select the one word that best describes this team and circle it.

| | | |
|---|---|---|
| OPEN | RIGID | INCONSISTENT |
| EMPOWERED | RESTRICTIVE | DEPENDABLE |
| PRINCIPLED | TRUSTWORTHY | CARING |
| COMPETITIVE | CONSERVATIVE | CAUTIOUS |
| ETHICAL | INTOLERANT | CANDID |

# 406. IS YOUR TEAM TRUSTED BY OTHER TEAMS?

Use the following tool to look at the factors that impact the degree to which you are likely to be trusted by other teams.

## Preparation

Provide each person with a copy of the survey.

## Process

- Distribute the survey to the team.
- Ask the members to complete the survey.
- Facilitate a discussion based on the responses.
- Alternatively, collect the completed surveys, compile the results, and present a summary at a team meeting.
- Summarize the key conclusions of the session.
- Develop a list of actions necessary to develop a higher level of trust with other teams.

# EXTERNAL TRUST

*Directions:* Review the questions and then indicate your response using the following scale. Place your number in the space to the left of the question.

1 = Almost Never    2 = Rarely    3 = Sometimes    4 = Most of the time    5 = Almost always

In your dealings with other teams and key stakeholders:

_____ 1. Do you provide them with delivery dates that you honestly expect to meet?

_____ 2. Do you typically deliver on your commitments?

_____ 3. Do you only ask for what you really need?

_____ 4. Do you provide them with an honest assessment of actual and potential problems?

_____ 5. Do you provide them with a realistic appraisal of potential opportunities?

_____ 6. Do you accept responsibility for problems that arise from work you performed for them?

_____ 7. Do you offer to correct or redo work that you performed for them?

_____ 8. Do you offer to help them when they experience problems?

_____ 9. Do you complain to others about the other team or its members or your relationship with them?

_____ 10. Do you share the limelight with them?

**Total:** _____

# 407. WHOM DO YOU TRUST?

Here's a good activity for exploring the issues of interpersonal trust.

## Process

- Ask each person to think about and then identify a person in his or her work or personal life that he or she trusts.

- Have everyone write the person's name at the top of a sheet of paper and then list all the things the person does that inspire trust.

- Ask team members to pair off and share their lists and develop a composite or consensus list of trustworthy behaviors.

- Ask team members to team up with two other team members to form a group of four and again reach consensus on a list of trustworthy behaviors.

- Have all subgroups share their lists and post the trustworthy behaviors on a flip chart or screen.

- Refine and edit the list to make them specific and behavioral.

- Facilitate a discussion with the goal of gaining agreement on a list of trust norms for the team.

# 408. INTERPERSONAL TRUST ASSESSMENT

Here is a brief assessment exercise for team members.

## Preparation

Prepare a copy of the assessment for each team member.

## Process

- Give copies of the form to all members of the team.

- Facilitate a discussion based on the responses. Probe for examples from members.

- Draw out from members a list of norms that help build interpersonal trust on a team.

- Try to achieve a consensus on the list.

- Conclude with a discussion of next steps.

# TRUST ASSESSMENT

*Directions:* Please read the following statements about your trust-building behaviors and indicate the extent to which you feel they are true about you according to the following scale:

**1 = Strongly Disagree    2 = Disagree    3 = Neither Disagree nor Agree    4 = Agree    5 = Strongly Agree**

_____ 1. I communicate with my teammates openly and honestly, without distorting any information.

_____ 2. I show confidence in my teammates' abilities by treating them as skilled, competent associates.

_____ 3. I listen to and value what they say, even though I may not always agree.

_____ 4. I keep my promises and commitments to my teammates.

_____ 5. I make sure my actions are consistent with my words. In other words, I practice what I preach.

**Total:**

 **T I P** Convert this tool into a feedback activity by changing "I" to "He or She." Then ask each team member to complete a feedback survey for each of his or her teammates. Send all the completed surveys to an impartial person or service and have a report prepared for each team member that includes self-assessment scores and the scores of teammates.

## 409. TRUST TEST FOR LEADERS

The behaviors of team leaders is a major contributing factor to the level of trust on your team. In this case, we are referring to both your team leader and to managers and coaches. Here is a brief assessment tool for team leaders. The behaviors are based on a list created by Zenger et al. (1994) cited earlier.

# LEADERSHIP TRUST

*Directions:* Review the list of leader behaviors below and then indicate the extent to which your team leader demonstrates each behavior according to the following scale:

1 = Never     2 = Seldom     3 = Sometimes     4 = Usually     5 = Always

**Please Circle One Number**

| | | | | | |
|---|---|---|---|---|---|
| 1. Keeps his or her promises. | 1 | 2 | 3 | 4 | 5 |
| 2. Maintains confidences. | 1 | 2 | 3 | 4 | 5 |
| 3. Respects the opinions and feelings of others. | 1 | 2 | 3 | 4 | 5 |
| 4. Willingly admits his or her mistakes. | 1 | 2 | 3 | 4 | 5 |
| 5. Respects the ability of others to do the job. | 1 | 2 | 3 | 4 | 5 |
| 6. Provides others with appropriate credit and recognition for their accomplishments. | 1 | 2 | 3 | 4 | 5 |
| 7. Does not speak in negative terms about 5 people who are not present. | 1 | 2 | 3 | 4 | |
| 8. Delegates important tasks to the team. | 1 | 2 | 3 | 4 | 5 |
| 9. Empowers the team to make key decisions. | 1 | 2 | 3 | 4 | 5 |
| 10. Does not closely monitor the activities of team members. | 1 | 2 | 3 | 4 | 5 |

**Total:**

**TIP** With minimal editing (for example, change "the team leader" to "you"), you can convert this tool to a self-assessment instrument for a team leader. In addition, you can create a feedback activity by combining the data from the leader's self-assessment with a summary of the members' responses.

# 410. MOMENTS OF TRUST

Have you ever experienced a situation where you really trusted another person? What did he or she do (or not do)? What did you do (or not do)? What was that experience like? Let's turn that question into a team exercise.

## Process

- Introduce the activity by asking: "Have you ever experienced a situation where you really trusted another person?"

- Then give each person a few minutes to think about the question and a possible answer. Encourage reflection and note taking.

- If your team is small, facilitate a discussion with the whole group based on the responses. If the group is large, create subgroups for sharing the responses.

- After everyone has had an opportunity to share his or her "moment" ask the team to reflect on the factors that are common to all or most of the stories. Post the responses on a flip chart or projector screen.

- Conclude the activity by facilitating a discussion on norms that support a trusting climate.

# 411. TRUST BAROMETER

Here is a great icebreaker to kick off a discussion of trust on your team.

## Preparation

Prior to the session, post the following signs on the wall about six to seven feet off the ground. On the left side of the wall, post a sign that says "Open and Candid," and on the right side post another sign that says "Closed and Cautious." Post the two signs fifteen to twenty feet apart. Between them, post ten signs, each with one of the following numbers, in order: 1, 2, 3, 4, 5, 6, 7, 8, 9, and 10. Start with the 10 on the *left* side of the wall near the Open and Candid sign, moving to the right, and ending with the 1 next to the Closed and Cautious sign.

## Process

- Ask members of your team to stand under the number that represents their perception of the level of trust and openness of the team. Several members may stand under the same number.

- While the members are still standing, facilitate a discussion using some of the following questions:

  - Why did you select this number?

  - What is it about the climate on our team that led you to take this position?

  - What does it say about the level of trust?

  - How do you react to the numbers selected by other team members?

  - Are you surprised by any of the positions taken by other team members?

  - If we had done this same exercise one year ago, where would you have stood? How about five years ago?

  - What are the implications of the responses?

  - How does this impact our performance?

  - How confident are you we can change the climate of trust to make it more "Open and Candid"? (You can ask team members to move to a number on the scale that represents their level of confidence, with 10 being Very Confident and 1 being Little or No Confidence.)

- Conclude the session by creating a list of actions designed to increase trust on the team.

# 412. TRUST AND MOTIVES

Share this quote with your team and explore its application to the current state of your team:

> "Trust makes it unnecessary to examine motives, to look for hidden meanings, to have it in writing. As trust ebbs, we are less open with each other; we look for strategies in dealing with each other; we seek help from others; or we look for protection in rules, norms, contracts, and law." (Gibb, 1978)

### QUESTIONS

- Has trust ebbed on our team?

- To what extent do we examine the motives of others, look for hidden meanings in what others say, or insist on having things in writing?

- How open are we with each other? With stakeholders outside of the team?

- Gibb seems to be saying that having rules, norms, and written agreements is a bad sign. How do you feel?

# 413. TEAM CLIMATE AND TRUST

Here's a quote from Douglas McGregor (1960, p. 192). Use it as a one-item team assessment instrument.

## Process

- Prepare a handout of the quote and the directions and distribute to everyone.

- Ask each team member to answer the questions.

- Facilitate a discussion based on the responses.

- Conclude with a discussion on ways the team can develop a "climate of mutual trust and support."

# TRUST ASSESSMENT

*Directions:* Please read the following quote by management expert Douglas McGregor and then reflect on the extent to which the statement is true about our team. Using the following scale, select one number that represents your perception of the climate of trust on the team.

"In a climate of mutual trust and support . . . members can be themselves without fearing the consequences."

\_\_\_\_ 1. Not at all

\_\_\_\_ 2. To some extent

\_\_\_\_ 3. To a moderate extent

\_\_\_\_ 4. To a great extent

\_\_\_\_ 5. To a very great extent

## 414. TRUSTLESS TEAMS

A great resource is Module A, "Trustless Teams," in Elledge and Phillips (1994). Here you will find excellent insights and several trust-building exercises.

## 415. FREE CASH: A CASH GAME TO EXPLORE TRUST

This is a wonderful game that demonstrates the effects of lack of trust on teammates (Thiagarajan & Parker, 2000). Go to the Team Tool Shed for a look at this exercise.

## 416. TRUST: THE GREAT TEAMWORK ENABLER

This article by Larry Meeker (1996) discusses trust and empowerment and how trust develops over time. It also includes a new experiential exercise called the "Trust Gauntlet." Read the article in the Team Tool Shed.

## 417. RESOURCE ON TRUST

A good resource for articles and other information is found at www.humanresources.about.com.

## 418. TRUST IS FUNDAMENTAL TO SUCCESSFUL TEAMWORK

Consider this advice to team leaders and managers and how it applies to your team.

"In the team-oriented workplace, trust is fundamental. A team won't fulfill its promise unless you can trust the team to follow through on commitments. And you won't fulfill your promise unless the team can trust you to respect them and their ideas. Ron Deane describes how trust grows at Spectra Physics: 'We set boundaries for the teams and let them know that they can make decisions within those boundaries. Then, as they grow and mature, we increase the boundaries so they can make larger decisions in a greater span of influence.'" (Zenger et al., 1994, p. 37)

**QUESTIONS**

- Does your leader, coach, or manager trust your team?

- Does your team have boundaries?

- How would boundaries help your team?

- Some people argue that boundaries are an indicator of lack of trust. What do you think?

- How does trust help you follow through on your commitments?

## 419. TRUTH AND TRUST

Here's a great quote to stimulate discussion on trust in your team:

**"Tell the truth and keep your promises."**
*—Frank Navran*

**QUESTIONS**

- What has this got to do with trust?

- Why is it important to "tell the truth and keep your promises"?

- Do we always "tell the truth"?

- Do we always "keep our promises"?

- What can we do to improve trust among team members?

- What can we do to improve trust with our external stakeholders?

# 420. ARE YOU TRUSTWORTHY?

Use the following quote to stimulate a discussion of building a climate of trust in your relations with other teams and key stakeholders:

**"You gain trust by being trustworthy."**
    —*Author unknown*

### QUESTIONS

- What does this quote mean?
- How do you become trustworthy?
- To what extent do other teams consider us trustworthy?
- What are the components of trustworthiness?
- What can we do to be more trustworthy?

# 421. TRUST IS THE CORNERSTONE

Use this quote to get the dialogue going:

**"Trust is the cornerstone in a successful team."**

    —*Fran Rees*

### QUESTIONS

- Why is trust the cornerstone?
- Do you think that trust is more important than specific performance objectives? Clear roles? Effective meetings?
- Is trust the cornerstone in our team?
- How would your describe the level of trust in our team?

**THIS AISLE INCLUDES LOTS OF INFORMATION ABOUT CONCEPTS OF TRUST,** ways to assess the level of trust on your team, and exercises designed to increase trust levels. You will also find trust-building tools in other aisles, specifically Aisle 3, Redefine Everyone's Role; Aisle 7, Reestablish Ground Rules; and Aisle 15, Resuscitate Failing Communications.

# AISLE 15

# RESUSCITATE FAILING COMMUNICATIONS

## OVERVIEW

**"WHAT WE HAVE IS A FAILURE TO COMMUNICATE"** is the famous line from the old movie *Cool Hand Luke* starring Steve McQueen. In the case of mature teams that have lost their way, poor communications is very often a significant marker. In other words, one of the first things to go is communication. Members fail to communicate with each other, and the team fails to communicate with external stakeholders.

Poor communication is usually directly related to these other key factors in team breakdowns:

- When we fail to communicate, team trust suffers.

- When we fail to communicate, team climate becomes negative.

- When we fail to communicate, team decision making is less effective.

- When we fail to communicate, team member commitment diminishes.

- When we fail to communicate, our external networks break down.

Mature teams tend to make certain assumptions about communication:

- Members assume that everyone knows what is going on;

- Members assume that others understand their intentions;

- Members assume that external stakeholders do not want to know everything;

- Members assume that others know how they feel; and

- Members assume that other people will ask if they need something or don't understand something.

Assumptions based on poor data can lead to significant team problems—both internal and external. As members perpetuate these "myths," the team starts a downward spiral toward serious dysfunction. On the surface the team seems to be doing well. However, cracks in the foundation start to emerge as a member complains he did not know about a decision, a key stakeholder finds that a report was not sent to her, and a vice president is not made aware of problems with a major customer.

If communication is a problem on your team, there is hope. Poor communication is one of the easier team problems to repair. The biggest barrier is the willingness to admit to a problem and to accept the fact that there is a problem. Once you "own" the problem, tools in this aisle can help you both understand and solve the problem. You will find tools to assess existing communications skills on your team and many excellent exercises designed to increase communication among members of your team.

# 422. YOU CANNOT NOT COMMUNICATE

Think about it. Even when you say nothing, you are saying something. When you do not respond to a team member's request or question, you are sending a message. When you fail to send a report to a colleague, you are sending that person a message. Breakdowns occur because other people attach their own meanings to your failure to communicate.

**QUESTION** Think about some recent situations in which someone did not communicate with you. What assumptions did you make about that person and the message?

# 423. TWO LEVELS OF TEAM COMMUNICATION

It is hard for a team to communicate too much. In fact, most teams do not communicate enough. Team communication operates on two levels:

1. *Interpersonal.* This involves all the verbal and nonverbal interactions among members.

2. *Informational.* This involves all the knowledge, facts, data, and advice that is communicated among members and with external stakeholders.

# 424. INTERPERSONAL COMMUNICATION

**QUESTIONS**

- How effective is the communication among members on your team?

- How open and trusting is the communication?

- Do members freely share ideas, information, disagreements, and problems with one another?

- Are members sensitive to the nonverbal cues that pass between people on the team?

- How would you characterize the interpersonal relationships with key stakeholders?

 **T I P** Use these questions to facilitate a discussion of communication issues.

# 425. INFORMATIONAL COMMUNICATION

### QUESTIONS

- Is there a free flow of information to and from the team?

- Do members receive the information they need to do their jobs and do they keep others informed about their work?

- How do external stakeholders feel about the quality, quantity, and timeliness of information flow from your team to them?

 **T I P** Use these questions to facilitate a discussion of communication issues.

# 426. COMMUNICATION AND TRUST SCENARIO

The management team of a business unit developed a strategic plan for the organization. They "assumed" that each manager would communicate the plan to his or her organization. As a result, information distribution was haphazard—some people in the business unit were aware of the plan while others knew little or nothing about it. The net result was that people wondered why some people received the information and others did not. Communication broke down and, more importantly, resulted in a breakdown in trust.

 **T I P** Spend almost as much time on a communications plan as you do on developing the information in the first place.

# 427. EFFECTIVE COMMUNICATION TIPS: SENDING MESSAGES

Perhaps members of your team are not sending messages to each other in a way that they can be understood. Here are some tips for sending messages effectively:

- ☑ *Own Your Message.* Take responsibility for your communication by using "I" messages. Say something like "I do not believe this project will work," rather than "Some people feel this project will not work."

- ☑ *Be Specific.* Provide the receiver with as much background information and data as possible to ensure that he or she understands the basis for your message. For example, it facilitates effective communication to say, "Data from the Michigan site report for January indicates that the dosage is too low."

- ☑ *Align Your Verbal and Nonverbal Messages.* Make sure your nonverbal cues, such as tone of voice and gestures, support your verbal message. Eliminate sarcasm, especially in cross-cultural teams. Do not roll your eyes and say, "Sure, I really think this product will sell," when you mean it will not sell.

- ☑ *Use Multimedia.* You have a better chance of your message being understood if you send it via several communications methods. For example, use audio (your voice) and visual (slide) to send the same message. One caution: Do not insult the receiver by simply reading the slide to the person.

- ☑ *Tailor Your Message.* Put your message in a format that can be understood by the receiver. If you're an engineer communicating with a group of non-engineers, use analogies and metaphors such as "Think of this as your television set . . ."

 **T I P** Use this list as the basis for a training exercise. Take a message that is important for you to communicate to another person and apply these tips to the message, that is, make it specific, tailor it to your audience, and so forth.

This list is based on a similar list found in Johnson and Johnson (2000).

# 428. ONE-WAY VERSUS TWO-WAY COMMUNICATION MODEL

Here is a quick way to understand the communication process and the causes of breakdowns in the process. Present this model to facilitate a discussion of the causes of communications breakdowns on your team. Explain that in this model, the sender (S), the originator of the message, attempts to send a message to another person, the receiver (R). However, the message the receiver ($R_2$) actually receives is different from the message that the sender intended the receiver ($R_1$) to receive.

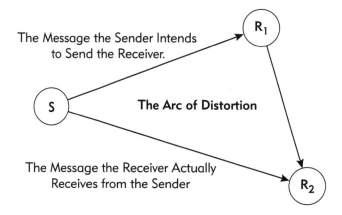

The Message the Sender Intends to Send the Receiver.

$R_1$

**The Arc of Distortion**

S

The Message the Receiver Actually Receives from the Sender

$R_2$

## QUESTIONS

- What causes "distortions" among members on your team?
- What are the factors that cause the actual message received to be different from the intended message?
- How do you reduce the "arc of distortion" on your team?

## 429. EFFECTIVE COMMUNICATION

Effective communication is simply a situation in which the message the sender sends is received by the receiver in the same way it was intended by the sender. In other words, you have a message you want the other person to receive, and he or she receives it. It looks like this:

## 430. LISTENING IS THE KEY

It is pretty well-established that listening is the most critical communication skill for team members. When team members use high level active listening skills, effective communication takes place and overall team effectiveness in problem solving and decision making increases. If your team provides customer service, creates new products or services, or delivers products or services to customers, effective listening is a critical skill. And yet, little effort is put into improving listening as compared with, for example, presentation and speaking skills.

**QUESTION** When was the last time your team participated in listening skills training?

# 431. LISTENING AND CONSENSUS

Work done by Human Synergistics indicates that active listening and clarifying are critical to the successful completion of consensus-building activities such as their *Desert Survival Situation* (Human Synergistics, 1987). Further, teams that are composed primarily of women do better than men in these exercises because, it is believed, women are more skilled in active listening. For more information on their simulations, go to www.humansynergistics.com.

# 432. INFORMATIONAL COMMUNICATION ASSESSMENT

It is important to take a look at your current situation regarding communication links to and from your team. In this way, you can identify the source of the breakdown. The results will point the way to actions required to get your team back on track. Here is good way to start.

## Process

- Distribute a copy of the assessment form to each person.

- Ask each person to complete the form.

- Create subgroups of three or four people and ask them to share their answers and come to a consensus.

- Bring the subgroups together for a sharing of their responses.

- Facilitate a discussion on the answers.

- Conclude with the development of an action plan that addresses ways to obtain the information needed by the team.

# INFORMATIONAL COMMUNICATION ASSESSMENT

*Directions:* Please answer the following questions individually. Then get together with your teammates to summarize and compare your responses.

## Top Down

• What information do we need from upper management?

• Where and when should we get this information?

• How satisfied are you with the information flow from top management to your team? Circle the answer that best describes your level of satisfaction.

| Very Dissatisfied | Dissatisfied | Neither Satisfied nor Dissatisfied | Satisfied | Very Satisfied |

Comments:

## Bottom Up

• What information should we send up to management?

• How and how often should it be sent?

• How satisfied are you with the information flow from our team to senior management? Circle your answer.

| Very Dissatisfied | Dissatisfied | Neither Satisfied nor Dissatisfied | Satisfied | Very Satisfied |

Comments:

## Lateral

• What other groups depend on us/do we depend on for information?

• How and when should be provide this information?

• How satisfied are you with the information flow to/from other groups? Circle your answer.

| Very Dissatisfied | Dissatisfied | Neither Satisfied nor Dissatisfied | Satisfied | Very Satisfied |

Comments:

# 433. IMPROVING COMMUNICATION: AN ACTION PLAN

Use the data from the communication assessment to prepare a plan to get your team back on track.

## Process

Complete the chart on this page as a team activity.

---

## COMMUNICATION ACTION PLAN

### Directions

1. First, post all information that needs to be transmitted or received by your team.
2. Then indicate who should receive the information or from whom your team is supposed to receive the information.
3. Finally, indicate actions you will take to improve the situation.

| 1. What | 2. To/From Whom | 3. Improvement Actions |
|---------|-----------------|------------------------|
|         |                 |                        |

# 434. EXPLORING INTRA-GROUP COMMUNICATION

Here is another tool for assessing the communications climate on your team.

## Process

- Ask each person on the team to complete the form and then send it to a neutral third party for scoring.

- The summary should include the frequencies of the responses for each statement and the mean (average) response for each statement.

- Present the composite results at a team meeting.

- Facilitate a discussion and develop plans for improving team communication.

- Alternatively, simply have team members complete the form and then hold an open discussion on their answers.

# INTRA-TEAM COMMUNICATION

*Directions:* Please read each statement and indicate the extent to which it is true for you according to the following scale:

1 = Not at All     2 = Rarely     3 =Somewhat     4 = Most of the Time     5 =All of the Time

1. I am willing to share information with other members of this team.                1  2  3  4  5

2. I am willing to share my personal feelings with other members of this team.       1  2  3  4  5

3. Members of this team freely share information with me.                            1  2  3  4  5

4. Members of this team freely share their personal feelings with me.                1  2  3  4  5

5. There are no hidden agendas or "secret plan Bs" on this team.                     1  2  3  4  5

6. Members of this team communicate directly with each other rather than complain to a third party.   1  2  3  4  5

7. Members of this team use active listening skills to facilitate effective communication.            1  2  3  4  5

8. Members of this team can be depended on to say what they mean.                    1  2  3  4  5

9. I feel I can be honest in my communication with my teammates.                     1  2  3  4  5

10. I can depend on my teammates to respond to my queries in a timely manner.        1  2  3  4  5

# 435. TEAM MEMBER LISTENING PROFILE

This assessment instrument measures a team member's listening skills in four areas (Parker, 1998):

- *Being a Relaxed Listener.* Good listeners do not interrupt, they concentrate on the other person, and they do not finish a teammate's sentences.

- *Being a Focused Listener.* Good listeners stay with the person and the subject, do not formulate their answers while the other person is speaking, and usually take notes on what is being said.

- *Being a Feeling Listener.* Good listeners pay attention to the nonverbal cues to help them understand the feelings as well as the facts.

- *Being an Active Listener.* Good listeners are proactive partners in the communication by paraphrasing, reflecting, questioning, and summarizing.

You will find this assessment in the Team Tool Shed.

# 436. ONE-WAY VERSUS TWO-WAY COMMUNICATION

This is a classic, but we still use it because it makes a powerful point about the value of two-way communication. We first saw it in Pfeiffer and Jones (1969). Here is a brief summary of the process.

## Process

- Select one person to be the official communicator.

- Give each person on the team two blank sheets of paper and a pencil.

- Give the communicator a sheet of paper containing five squares connected in various ways to each other.

- Explain that the communicator will describe what is on his or her sheet of paper and that each person is to draw the squares exactly as instructed.

- Ask the communicator to sit with his or her back to the group, covering the sheet with the five squares so it is not visible to the group. Explain further that the group may not ask any questions during the demonstration or in any other way communicate with each other or with the communicator.

- At the end of the demonstration, record the amount of time elapsed.

- Ask each person how many squares he or she *thinks* he or she drew correctly and record that number.

- Give the communicator a sheet of paper with a second set of five squares.

- Explain that the communicator will again describe the squares, but that this time he or she will face the group and answer any questions from members of the group.

- At the end of the second demonstration, record the amount of time elapsed.

- Again ask each person to estimate how many squares he or she drew correctly and record that number.

- Determine the median or mean for the guessed accuracy for both demonstrations and record that number.

- Show the sheet containing the five squares for both demonstrations.

- Ask each person to indicate his or her actual accuracy for both demonstrations and record those numbers.

- Calculate the mean or median for actual accuracy.

- Facilitate a discussion on the results, looking at time, actual accuracy, and confidence (guessed accuracy) and the differences between the two demonstrations.

Typically, people will have more confidence and achieve greater accuracy during two-way communication. However, two-way communication takes longer. Is it worth it?

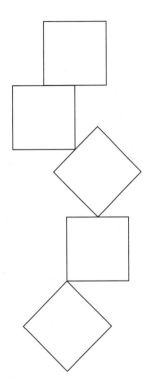

**Chart 1**

*Instructions:* Study the figure shown above. With your back to the group, instruct the other team members to draw what you see. Begin with the top square and describe each in succession, taking particular note of the relationship of each to the preceding one. Do not answer any questions from the group.

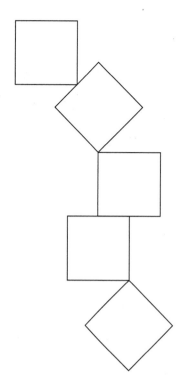

**Chart 2**

*Instructions:* Study the squares in the figure above. Face the group and instruct the team members how to draw the figure. Begin with the top square and describe each in succession, taking particular note of the relationship of each square to the preceding one. Answer all questions from participants and repeat your answers or instructions if necessary.

# 437. ACTIVE LISTENING

Here is a brief exercise that demonstrates the many uses of active listening in a group setting. Give copies of the sheet to people to fill out. Then use the answer sheet to lead a discussion.

---

## ACTIVE LISTENING

*Directions:* Read over each example and then indicate how you think each helps communication on a team. When you are finished, wait for your leader to give you the answers for discussion.

| Active Listening Examples | How They Help |
|---|---|
| Yes, go on. | |
| Tell me more. | |
| Then the problem as you see it is . . . | |
| This is your decision and the reasons are . . . | |
| If I understand you correctly, you are saying that . . . | |
| Your major point is . . . | |
| You feel that we should . . . | |
| We seem to agree on. . ., but we still need to clarify (or decide that) . . . | |
| As a result of our discussion, our team seems to feel that . . . | |

---

## ACTIVE LISTENING ANSWERS

| Active Listening Examples | How They Help |
|---|---|
| Yes, go on.<br>Tell me more. | To encourage the person to expand further on his or her thinking. |
| Then the problem as you see it is . . . | To help the person clarify the problem in his or her own thinking. |
| This is your decision and the reasons are . . . | To encourage a person to hear what he or she has said in the way it sounded to others. |
| If I understand you correctly, you are saying that . . .<br>Your major point is . . .<br>You feel that we should . . . | To pull out the key ideas/feelings from a long statement or discussion. |
| We seem to agree on. . .,<br>but we still need to clarify | To summarize specific points of agreement and disagreement as a basis for further discussion. |
| As a result of our discussion, our team seems to feel that . . . | To express a possible consensus (a "trial balloon"). |

# 438. LISTENING TRIADS

A good exercise to help team members increase their active listening skills is Listening Triads.

## Preparation

In preparation for the activity, you will need to select at least four controversial topics (for example, gun control, capital punishment, abortion). Prepare a chart that lists the topics stated in both positive and negative terms. For example, "I favor (oppose) strong gun control laws."

## Process

- Create triads, subgroups of three people each.

- Explain that there will be three rounds of this activity. In each round, one person will be the Speaker, another the Listener, and the third the Observer. Roles will change each round so that each person will play each role once.

- Each round begins with the Speaker presenting a point of view on a controversial topic of his or her choice. The Listener's job is to paraphrase the Speaker's ideas before presenting his or her own point of view. The Observer's job is to take notes on anything—verbal or nonverbal—that helped or hindered effective communication between the Speaker and the Listener.

- The two-way conversations between the Speaker and the Listener should continue for two to three minutes, followed by feedback from the Observer. The Observer provides feedback to both the Speaker and the Listener.

- After three rounds, facilitate a discussion with the total group on learnings from the exercise, focusing on issues such as:

  - How did paraphrasing help the Listener?
  - How did paraphrasing help the Speaker?
  - How does active listening help teamwork?
  - When should active listening be used?

# 439. LISTENING QUIZ

Here is a quick little exercise that can be used as a discussion starter migrating to the development of team listening norms.

## Process

- Give copies of the Listening Quiz to all team members.
- After everyone has finished, lead a discussion on listening norms.

## Answers

1 = F; 2 = T; 3 = T; 4 = F; and 5 = T.

# LISTENING QUIZ

*Directions:* Indicate which of the following statements is true (T) or false (F) by placing the appropriate letter in the blank.

_____ 1. Technical information is more likely to be understood if you tell your teammate to listen carefully.

_____ 2. Key concepts are more easily understood and remembered if you use repetition to reinforce them.

_____ 3. You can determine whether a teammate understands what you have said by asking him or her to summarize what you have said.

_____ 4. Listening is more effective when you anticipate what your teammate is going to say.

_____ 5. When you are dealing with a long-winded person, it is OK to periodically interrupt him or her to paraphrase what has been said.

# 440. COMMUNICATION NORMS

Norms have a powerful effect on team communication. In many ways, norms have a bigger impact than communication skills. What norms have developed on your team? What are the understood rules regarding listening, interruptions, topics, openness, influence, tone, disagreements, and other key aspects of communication?

 **T I P** Spend thirty minutes discussing and recording the norms on your team. Then look over the list and identify the positive (helpful) and negative (counterproductive) norms. Finally, agree to change the negative norms and replace them with positive behaviors.

# 441. THE ECONOMICAL COMMUNICATOR

Consider this description.

> "Jack is economical in his communication. He speaks only four or five times in a two-hour meeting. He wastes few words, gets to the point, and does not repeat himself. Jack's participation usually has impact because he provides useful information the team needs at the time, summarizes the key points, conclusions, or tentative decisions, or simply points out how the group has been wasting time and needs to move on." (Parker, 1996, p. 36)

 **QUESTIONS**

- Who are the economical communicators on your team?
- What is their impact?

# 442. FACILITATING OPEN COMMUNICATION

If your team does not practice open communication, you may want to try this simple exercise. It's an exercise in brainstorming that puts the negative phrases that block open communication out on the table. The belief is that, once out in the open, they are less likely to be used in the future.

## Process

- Remind the team about the rules of brainstorming, such as "no evaluation," "quantity is the goal," and "hitchhiking is encouraged."

- Print in large letters at the top of a flip chart or computer screen, "Phrases That Block Brainstorming."

- Explain that they will now brainstorm as many "blocking" phrases as possible.

- You may want to get things rolling by giving some examples such as:

  - "We tried that last year."

  - "Management will never go for it."

  - "When you've been around as long as I have, you know nothing ever changes."

- Record the responses just as they are presented. As appropriate, reinforce the rules.

- After all ideas are out, discuss the responses using some of the following questions:

  - Which phrases have you heard used on our team?

  - Which phrases have the most negative impact on open communication?

  - Why is it important to minimize the use of these phrases in our team communication?

  - What is the best way to minimize the use of these phrases in the future?

# 443. COMMUNICATING INFORMATION EXERCISE

Here's a classic communication exercise you can use to make many points.

## Process

- Divide the team into two subgroups of at least five people each.

- Have each subgroup sit in an area where they cannot overhear the other group.

- Give one person in each group a copy of a story to read silently.

- After a few minutes, ask that person to pass the story on to the person next to them verbally, but to whisper so the other people in that subgroup cannot hear.

- The person listening cannot ask questions or in any other way clarify the message.

- The second person passes the story on in the same way until it reaches the last person in the subgroup.

- Then ask the last person to tell the story to the total subgroup.

## Story

John Sizemore, director of sales, tells Jenny Chang, manager of software development, that Betty Cheaves, a key customer with Omnisoft, needs an enhancement of our enterprise software, COMMPORT. Betty needs the work completed by the end of the second quarter (2Q) for deployment by the end of 3Q. Chang says this is just not possible, given the major project her group is engaged in for a new customer, Gamesareus.com.

### QUESTIONS

- How close was the final version to the original story?

- What caused the changes in the story?

- How is this different from or similar to how information is communicated on our team?

- What can be done to improve the communication of information on our team?

**T I P** If you have several subgroups doing this exercise, allow the members of one of the subgroups to ask questions to clarify the story as it is being passed on. See how two-way communication changes the results.

# 444. COMMUNICATING TECHNICAL INSTRUCTIONS

Here's a simple exercise for improving communication in a technical team.

## Process

- Give each person a sheet of paper. A typical 8 1/2 x 11 size will do.

- Ask everyone to close their eyes and listen to your instructions.

- Present the following instructions:

  Fold the sheet I gave you in half. Then fold it in half again. Tear the right-hand corner off. Then turn the sheet over and tear the left-hand corner off.

- Ask all team members to hold up their sheets of paper. Many of the sheets of paper will look different. You can then hold up a sheet of paper that you prepared prior to the exercise based on the instructions as you understood them.

- Facilitate a discussion based on some or all of these questions:

  - Why were the results different?

  - Would the results have been different if you had been able to see your paper (but not the paper of your teammates)?

  - Would the results have been different if you had been allowed to ask questions?

  - Would the results have been different if this had been a team effort?

  - How is this different from or similar to the way we communicate technical information on a daily basis?

# 445. STAKEHOLDER COMMUNICATION

While your internal communication may be satisfactory, your communication with external stakeholders such as customers, suppliers, and support groups may be the cause of a derailment. The best way to start the improvement process is to find out how those others feel about your communication efforts.

## Process

- Communicate the purpose of the assessment to the stakeholders.

- Send a copy of the survey to the stakeholders. Provide a date for returning the survey to you.

- Compile the results from all the surveys. At a minimum, the summary should include frequencies of the responses and the mean (average) for each statement on the survey.

- Present the summary at a team meeting.

- Facilitate a discussion of the responses to develop an understanding and agreement on the main messages you are receiving from your stakeholders.

- Conclude with a discussion of ways the team can communicate more effectively with the stakeholders.

# CUSTOMER FEEDBACK

*Directions:* Please provide us with your honest perceptions of how we are communicating with you.

Read each of the following statements and indicate to what extent you agree with them according to the following scale:

1 = Strongly Disagree    2 = Disagree    3 = Neither Disagree nor Agree    4 = Agree    5 =Strongly Agree

Place your response in the space to the left of each statement.

_____ 1. Our team responds to your requests in a timely manner.

_____ 2. Our team regularly asks for ways that we can improve our communication with you.

_____ 3. Our team's communications with you are always clear.

_____ 4. Our team meetings with you are helpful.

_____ 5. Our team seems intent on having a successful relationship with you.

_____ 6. Our team responds to your complaints effectively.

_____ 7. Members of our team are effective communicators.

_____ 8. Members of our team seem to share information with each other about your operation.

_____ 9. Our team is easy to do business with.

_____ 10. Given complete freedom of choice, you would choose to work with our team.

11. One way our team can improve its communication with you is:

## 446. WORK TEAM LISTENING

In this interesting and useful article, Michael Bruner discusses and provides tools for focusing such team listening issues as culture, facilities, electronic communication, nonverbal listening, and problem solving. You can find the article in the Team Tool Shed.

## 447. COMMUNICATIONS SKILLS VIDEOS

CRM has a number of excellent videos designed to facilitate the learning of communication skills. These videos include:

- *Communicating Non-Defensively.* This twenty-minute video focuses on how to provide instructions, feedback, and even criticism in such a way as to avoid defensiveness. There is a leader's guide and a participant's workbook.

- *The Power of Future Conversation.* In this eighteen-minute video, Kim Krisco tells how to identify communication that is stuck in the past and explore solutions through future-focused conversation. A leader's guide is included.

- *Communication: The Nonverbal Agenda.* The focus here, as you might guess, is on the impact of nonverbal language and how to interpret facial expressions, voice tones, and postures to improve communication. A leader's guide comes with this twenty-minute video.

- *Power of Listening.* Using dramatized scenes, animation, and advice from a communications expert, this twenty-three-minute video will help your team understand and use active listening tools. A leader's guide is included.

For more information, including the ability to preview some of the videos online, go to www.crmlearning.com.

# 448. CRISIS COMMUNICATION

An excellent video focuses on how a team deals with a crisis situation. One of the most important areas is communication. The video, *Teamwork in Crisis: The Miracle of Flight 232,* shows in dramatic detail what can happen when team members communicate effectively to achieve an important goal: saving 296 lives. While your team may never (we hope) face anything as life-threatening as a plane crash, you may come up against a business crisis that requires effective internal and external communication. The twenty-eight-minute video includes excellent support materials, with a participant workbook and a leader's guide.

Obtain more information, including a preview copy, from CRM Learning at www.crmlearning.com.

**IN THIS AISLE YOU HAVE LOCATED A VARIETY** of assessments, concepts, exercises, and other tools to get your team's communications back on track. The tools included communication among team members as well as with management and other stakeholders. But you should not limit yourself to this aisle. Spend some time in the aisles that include tools that deal with external relations (Aisle 12), meetings (Aisle 11), conflict (Aisle 13), and trust (Aisle 14), among others.

# AISLE 16

# REGAIN MEMBER COMMITMENT

## OVERVIEW

**WHEN A TEAM BREAKS DOWN,** people very often complain about the lack of commitment. It's often unclear what people mean by this. But it is clear, however, that commitment, once lost, is difficult to regain.

Lack of commitment comes in a variety of forms. Do you sense a lack of commitment on your team? Is this why you think your team has lost its way? What form of commitment are you talking about?

- Members are no longer committed to the goals of the team. Is this a problem with the members or with the goals?

- Members are no longer committed to each other. Is this a problem with the members or with the culture of the team?

- Members are no longer committed to the leader. Is this a problem with the members or with the leader?

**327**

- Members are no longer committed to the customer. Is this a problem with the members or with the customer?

- Management is no longer committed to the team. Is this a problem with the team or with management?

- Support groups are no longer committed to the team. Is this a problem with the team or with the support groups?

Let's be clear about commitment. A commitment is a promise or pledge to do something. Our view is that team commitment is a promise to "do whatever it takes to help the team succeed."

- For team members this means delivering on promises to get the work done, complete action items, speak positively about the team, and pitch in and help teammates.

- For team leaders it means ensuring that their actions match their words, delivering on promises, and doing whatever it takes to help the team get the needed resources.

- For management, commitment takes the form of providing the necessary resources, being realistic in expectations of the team, and demonstrating interest and support for the team's goals.

- For support groups, being committed to a team involves timely responses to their requests for help, providing the resources really needed by the team, and demonstrating support for their goals.

Can you say, without equivocation, that the members of your team will "do whatever it takes to help the team succeed"? If not, read on. Here you will find tools to assess the level of commitment on your team, concepts that explain the importance of commitment, and ideas for increasing member commitment to the goals of the team and to one another.

## 449. THE ROAD TO COMMITMENT

The road to commitment is paved with involvement. It is as simple as that. You get team members, management, support groups, stakeholders, and others committed by involving them in a variety of ways. You don't obtain commitment by ordering it, demanding it, begging for it, praying for it, or paying for it. People will be committed to other people, ideas, and decisions if they have been involved in some way that has meaning for them.

**QUESTION**  Are you comfortable with the degree and nature of involvement on your team?

## 450. COMMITMENT AND GOALS

Goals provide perhaps the best vehicle for gaining member commitment. They provide the umbrella under which all members can come together. Goals provide the "glue" that binds people together and keeps them together. A member who believes in the goals will work had to implement those goals. *The key is involving members in the creation of the goals.*

**QUESTION**  Were members involved in a meaningful way in the creation of your team goals? If your answer is "no" you may have found the source of your commitment failure and the key to your team turnaround.

## 451. COMMITMENT AND DECISIONS

The decision-making process provides another means to create a committed group of team members.

### QUESTIONS

- Do you use the consensus method for key team decisions?
- Do members feel that team decisions are "their decisions"?

 **T I P**  When members are involved in team decisions, they will support those decisions and work hard to implement them. It's that simple.

# 452. PUBLIC COMMITMENT

A technique recommended by Zenger et al. (1994) is asking each member of the team directly whether he or she agrees with the decision. It gives each person an opportunity to discuss any lingering doubts and helps ensure a real consensus. If a member expresses some concerns about the decision, ask the person to indicate what modifications will make this decision acceptable. As a team leader or meeting facilitator, you must remain open to altering the decision based on this feedback. In the end, while this process will take longer, it will result in member commitment to the decision.

# 453. COMMITMENT AND NORMS

Norms are the behavioral guidelines that tell team members what's expected of them as a member of the team. Norms are guidelines for making decisions, participating in meetings, communicating with teammates, resolving conflicts, and so forth. You can establish norms by fiat by simply issuing a list for all to follow. However, the way to gain commitment to those norms, and thereby persuade members to follow them, is to involve members in a participatory exercise designed to create a set of norms. Norms are powerful drivers of member behavior. You can enhance that power by gaining commitment to them via involvement.

 **T I P** When members are involved in shaping team norms, they will support those norms and willingly live by them. It's that simple.

# 454. COMMITMENT AND ALIGNMENT

For a team leader, consistency in words and actions is critical to the attainment of commitment from team members. Members look to you to see whether you "walk the talk." It comes down to credibility. Are you creditable? One reason your team may be off track is that members are suspicious of the leadership. When there is no alignment between your promises and your deliverables, commitment suffers.

And this concept applies to members as well as leaders. When team members cannot have faith in their teammates, commitment to the goals of the team suffers.

 **T I P**  It is better to say "no" than to tell people what they want to hear and then not deliver on your promise.

## 455. COMMITMENT TO THE WORK PLAN

In some organizations, teams are not involved in the goal-setting process. For a variety of reasons, involvement at this level is just not feasible. However, in those situations, it is essential that team members be involved in the implementation work plan. Team members can understand and accept their lack of involvement in the strategic planning process, but they may be unwilling to accept lack of participation in the development of the work plan. Since team members are closer to the action, they will often have practical ideas for successfully implementing goals. In fact, Locke and Latham (1984, p. 45), in their study of goal setting in organizations, found that "participation, while not usually necessary in setting goals, may be very useful when it comes to implementing them."

 **T I P**  Get your team back on track by revisiting your work plan to hear the input of team members in suggesting better ways to reach the goals.

# 456. COMMITMENT AND HONESTY

What happens when your team cannot deliver on an obligation to a stakeholder? What happens when a member of your team fails to deliver on a promise to a teammate? These are critical situations in the creation of a team commitment. The development of a culture of commitment on your team demands that members simply tell the truth. They must be honest in their statements about their obligations; they should not "sugar coat" or tell half-truths when confronted with such a situation. If a deadline was not met, a team member should make note of it and then indicate when it will happen.

**QUESTION** Take a hard look at your team over the past three months: Have you been open and honest about your promises?

# 457. COMMITMENT AND RECOGNITION

Another way to erode member commitment and the commitment of key support groups is failing to appropriately credit and recognize the performance of others. The trust of members—and thereby their commitment to the team—is diminished when they do not receive recognition for their efforts and, worse, when others take credit for their work! Similarly, when support groups help your team reach its goals, they expect to be acknowledged for their efforts. Once again, if you do not recognize them, these support groups come to believe that you are either taking them for granted or simply taking credit for their work. In either case, you will not obtain their commitment next time.

**TIP** Take some time to think about how your team recognizes and acknowledges the contributions of members and others who help the team succeed. Then develop some guidelines for getting back on track.

## 458. FOCUS ON PERFORMANCE

Katzenbach and Smith (1993) put the spotlight on building member commitment through specific performance objectives. Performance objectives result from a process that starts with senior management providing an overarching goal or team assignment, which the team, in turn, translates into a shared goal or purpose. Finally, the team's purpose is further refined (and this is the critical step) into a series of performance targets or objectives, such as increase customer satisfaction by 10 percent. These objectives emphasize what each team member has to do jointly with his or her teammates to accomplish the team's objectives. This is the glue that binds members together and sustains commitment.

**QUESTION**  Does your team have performance objectives developed by and supported by team members?

## 459. COMMITMENT AND ACCOUNTABILITY

Once clear team performance objectives have been set, the next step is to figure out how to accomplish them and who should be responsible for various tasks. Team members should discuss who should do what and, equally important, who is the best person to take on a specific task. Teams should also consider dividing up the work in such a way that there is a reasonable and fair distribution of the assignments. At that point members agree to do their part. With such a participatory process, members are more likely to feel accountable to their teammates . . . to do the work in such a way that it helps the team succeed. When members feel accountable, a team of committed members follows.

**QUESTION**  Does your team process foster accountability among members?

# 460. EXHORTATION AND COMMITMENT

Too often team leaders, managers, and others believe that a good motivational speech that exhorts members to be "committed" is all that is needed. Our advice: Unless you are a great motivational speaker like Jesse Jackson, forget about it. You may pump a few people up for a few minutes, but the long-term lasting effect will be minimal.

 **T I P** Save the money you would spend on a motivational speaker and invest in a solid team facilitator who can help your team develop a set of performance objectives and a participative work plan that divides up the tasks in a way that holds everyone accountable.

# 461. A COMMITMENT STORY

Here's a scenario from one of my past assignments:

> A senior management steering committee set up an employee action team to figure out ways to reduce cycle time (the time it takes to produce the product and ship it to the customer). The team consisted of employees from various functions involved with the product. A senior manager came to the first team meeting and said that the steering committee had decided that cycle time for this product could be reduced from eighty-two to twenty-eight days. The manager said, "Your charge is to come up with ways to accomplish this goal." When asked if they had any questions, one member (who clearly was speaking for the team) responded, "What do you need us for?"

 **QUESTIONS**

- What's the problem here?
- Why is the team unhappy?
- How do you think the senior management team should have handled the situation, assuming they wanted team members to be committed to the goal?

# 462. A SIGN OF COMMITMENT

At a client company, I designed an employee action team to address work environment issues that emerged from an organizational survey. Management asked the team to deal with issues such as morale, communications, meetings, and recognition. Since the team was to be composed solely of volunteers, a notice went out asking for people to indicate if they were willing to serve on the team. We expected fewer than ten people to volunteer. In fact, we would have been happy with ten, as that makes a good size for a work team. However, eighteen people volunteered! Later, when we asked these people why they wanted to be on the team, they all said the goals were issues they cared about and wanted to see addressed.

**QUESTIONS**

- What does this story tell you about commitment?

- Given complete freedom of choice, would members of your team volunteer to serve on your team?

# 463. MAKING A DECISION AND MAKING A COMMITMENT

In their decision cycle, O'Neill and O'Neill (1974) distinguish between making a decision and making a commitment. Taking action to indicate genuine commitment to a change can facilitate the processing of that change. Making a decision is an *internal* process, while commitment is an *external* process. We take that to mean decision making is a cognitive activity, while commitment requires some action on our part. It is a variation of "walking the talk," where talking is the decision and walking is the commitment.

**QUESTION**  Is your team composed of "talkers" or "walkers"?

# 464. COMMITMENT TO CUSTOMERS

Another area you may need to look at as a source for team derailment is your team's commitment to your customers. And here, of course, we are talking about both internal and external customers . . . all teams have customers. How would you characterize your commitment to customers and clients?

## Process

- Give each member of the team a copy of the survey.
- Ask them to complete it individually.
- Pull the group together and discuss the results.
- Facilitate a discussion focused on ways to increase team commitment to your customers.

 **T I P** As part of your discussion, pick a key customer and ask yourself: Would this customer check the same quotes?

# COMMITMENT TO CUSTOMERS

*Directions:* Take a look at the following quotes. If the quote describes your team, place a check in the box to the left of the quote.

☐ We do whatever it takes to satisfy the customer.

☐ We are available to the customer 24/7.

☐ Quality is whatever the customer says it is.

☐ Our number one performance goal is customer satisfaction.

☐ Our first priority is to deliver on our promises to our customers.

☐ Employee satisfaction ranks second to customer satisfaction.

☐ Each day we ask ourselves, "What have we done to help our customers today?"

# 465. THE CONTRAINDICATIONS OF COMMITMENT IN A TEAM-BASED ORGANIZATION

Mohrman, Cohen, and Mohrman (1995) point out that "The team-based organization demands high commitment to both work and co-workers." Commitment means working hard to solve complex business problems and to achieve performance objectives that span traditional functional lines. It also means working closely and effectively with co-workers. However, the new organization emphasizes temporary relationships, ad hoc teams, and virtual teaming. These trends, coupled with the new employment contract that has redefined the organization's commitment to the employee, have strained both the concept and the reality of commitment among team members. We have paraphrased the following questions posed by Mohrman, Cohen, and Mohrman for you to consider with your teammates.

### QUESTIONS

- Can we be expected to be committed to our team's goals, work plans, norms, and so forth, given the temporary nature of work and relationships?

- Can we expect commitment from team members when the organization cannot promise job security?

- Given these trends, will team members be willing to fully invest themselves in the work and in the team?

## 466. EMPOWERMENT AND COMMITMENT

A pathway to commitment is through empowerment. When you place your trust in a team member by empowering him or her, you are on your way to gaining a committed person—a person committed to the team's goals and to his or her teammates. This is critical because a committed team member will readily contribute his or her expertise, facilitate the work of the team, and support the goals of the organization.

## 467. SIGNPOSTS OF COMMITMENT OR LACK THEREOF

Here are some warning signs that you may be experiencing a lack of commitment.

### Process

- Use copies of the checklist on the next page to highlight signs of trouble.
- Hand out copies to team members and ask them to fill it out.
- Afterward, facilitate a discussion of any items checked "yes," including an analysis of why it occurs and its impact on commitment.

# COMMITMENT SIGNPOSTS

*Directions:* Please review the following list of actions. Circle either "yes" or "no" for each one. If any of these actions occur, to any extent, on your team, you must answer "yes."

Yes    No    1. Key team members are consistently absent from meetings.

Yes    No    2. Members consistently arrive late and/or leave early.

Yes    No    3. Substitutes, who are neither briefed nor empowered, attend in place of members.

Yes    No    4. Key members are not mentally "there" during team meetings.

Yes    No    5. Members do not deliver on their action items, and no one seems upset.

Yes    No    6. Members seem to be more interested in discussing topics unrelated to the team's mission.

Yes    No    7. Meetings are formal and stuffy, and members do not seem to enjoy being around their teammates.

Yes    No    8. Outside of meetings, small groups of members complain about their team assignments as being a "waste of time."

 **T I P** If you sense a loss of commitment among team members, look first to the level and degree of empowerment among team members. You may find that members are not committed to the team because they sense a lack of trust in them.

# 468. THE BEAUTY OF COMMITMENT

How do you react to this quote from Murray Kempton?

**"The beauty of strong, lasting commitment is often best understood by a man incapable of it."**
*—Murray Kempton*

 ### QUESTIONS

- What does Kempton mean?
- Why is commitment best understood by someone who is incapable of it?
- Is it realistic to talk about the "beauty" of commitment?
- How do you build "strong, lasting commitment" in a team environment?

# 469. AS A RULE OF THUMB

Management guru Tom Peters once said:

**"As a rule of thumb, involve everyone in everything."**
*—Quoted in Karvelas (1998).*

 ### QUESTIONS

- What do you think Peters really means by this?
- Is it realistic to "involve everyone in everything"?
- What are some things you have not involved team members in?
- How would you change that in the future?
- What are some areas that members must absolutely be involved in?

# 470. COMMITMENT AND PASSION

With great commitment to a goal, you get passion. And with passion you can do most anything. So spending time involving people in a way that leads to commitment is worth the investment. As Emerson once said:

**"Nothing great was ever accomplished without enthusiasm."**
*—Ralph Waldo Emerson*

# 471. IF YOU DON'T KNOW WHERE YOU'RE GOING . . .

We have taken some liberties with a famous quote from Lewis Carroll's Cheshire Cat:

**"If you don't know where you're going, any degree of commitment is sufficient."**

**THIS AISLE INCLUDES A NUMBER OF CONCEPTS** that stress the importance of member commitment to a variety of factors that determine team success. It is just not possible to be successful without commitment. However, you should also check out the tools in aisles that focus on accountability (Aisle 10), goals (Aisle 1), and performance (Aisle 18), as well as others that may provide just the right help for your team at this time.

# RESTORE CONSENSUS DECISION MAKING

## OVERVIEW

**THE MANNER IN WHICH YOUR TEAM MAKES A DECISION** says a great deal about the culture of the team. It is also a predictor of the effectiveness of the team. Research studies indicate that group decision making produces results that are superior to individual decision making. There are several methods of group decision making, but it is generally agreed that the consensus method is the best approach for most team decisions.

The consensus approach, however, is neither the most efficient nor the least stressful for a team. A consensus assumes that the decisions cannot be made without the "approval" of every member, but it does not mean that everyone on the team must agree totally with the outcome. It simply means that each team member is willing to go along with the decision or, in the classic consensus phrase, "can live with it."

Because the process demands full participation and openness to different points of view, it is usually not used by new and/or immature teams that lack solid norms and embedded teamwork skills. Therefore, if your team is not using the consensus method, it may be an indicator of problems in your team process.

Unlike tension-reducing techniques such as majority vote or decision by one person, the consensus method looks at a variety of options as a way of finding the "best" solution to the problem. While this process can be time-consuming at first, it tends to result in a decision that is supported by all and that has a better chance of being successfully implemented. On the other hand, once a team has positive interpersonal norms, successful working relationships, openness and trust, and teamwork skills, a consensus can be achieved rather quickly. In the long run, a consensus decision saves time because a team is less likely to revisit a decision made by the consensus method.

If your team is not using the consensus method for key decisions, ask "Why?" Then take a look at the decision-making process in your team as a way of assessing its effectiveness. The tools in this section provide help in understanding the consensus method and techniques for introducing the process into your team. Here you will find tools for

- Understanding various decision methods;

- Establishing the conditions for an effective decision;

- Creating the guidelines for making a decision using the consensus method; and

- Exercises and activities to embed the consensus method on your team.

## 472. CONSENSUS CONDITIONS

A consensus decision ought to involve the following conditions:

- All members have had a chance to express their opinion on the decision;

- All members can say they understand the decision;

- All members are able to articulate or rephrase the decision in their own words;

- All members are prepared to support the decision;

- All members will work to see that the decision is implemented; and
- All members will express support for the decision publicly without reservation.

# 473. GUIDELINES FOR REACHING A CONSENSUS

Here are some guidelines to help your team restore consensus decision making as the norm on your team.

- Present your point of view clearly with as many facts as possible.
- Listen to the reactions of your teammates to your position.
- Listen actively to the points of view of others on your team.
- Avoid changing your mind just to avoid conflict.
- Resist attempts to vote or average.
- Facilitate the involvement of all team members.
- Do not play "win-lose," but rather look for the "best" solution or decision.
- Do not "horse trade" by giving in on one issue because someone else supported your point of view on another issue.

# 474. WHEN TO USE THE CONSENSUS METHOD

If your team decides (by consensus, of course) that you should return to or make greater use of the consensus method, there are some situations where it works best.

- When there is no expert in the group or readily available to the group;
- When sufficient time is available;
- When there is no clear-cut answer available; and
- Most importantly, when commitment on the part of team members to the decision is essential.

# 475. WHEN NOT TO USE THE CONSENSUS METHOD

At the same time, you should be aware of the situations for which the consensus method is inappropriate.

- When there is an available factual, legal, or policy solution;
- When there is someone on the team who knows or can find the answer;
- When a quick decision is essential; and/or
- When the decision is not of major consequence.

# 476. DO WE HAVE A CONSENSUS?

After your team has spent some time discussing the various aspects of a particular issue, ask each team member how he or she feels about the proposed decision that is on the table by selecting one of these five options:

1. I can give an unqualified "yes" to the decision.
2. I find the decision acceptable.
3. I can live with it, although I'm not especially enthusiastic about it; but I will support its implementation.
4. I do not fully agree with the decision, but I do not choose to block it. I will support its implementation.
5. I do not agree with the decision and I feel we should explore other options.

 **T I P**  If all the responses from team members are either 1, 2, 3 or 4, you have a consensus and are ready to move on.

 **QUESTION**  Would you be comfortable if all of the members responded with a "4"?

# 477. CONSENSUS WITH QUALIFICATION

In a useful study of senior management decision making, Eisenstadt, Kahwaju, and Bourgeois (1997) developed the concept of "consensus with qualification." What they found was that effective teams try to reach a consensus, but if they cannot, the member with the most knowledge makes the decision with input from the rest of the team. In this way, the team can move on rather than be paralyzed by its inability to reach a consensus on a key decision.

### QUESTIONS

- How do you feel about adopting this variation on the consensus method?
- Would it work for your team?

# 478. QUALITY OR ACCEPTANCE

A useful way to look at your team's decisions was developed by Rick Roskin (1975). Roskin said there are two dimensions that are important in assessing your team's decisions:

1. The objective *quality* or effectiveness of the decision.
2. The subjective *acceptance* of the decision by those who must execute it.

A team will typically give more attention to either the quality or the acceptance of the decision. In other words, your team will either care more about the effectiveness of the decision or about how well it is accepted by the people who are responsible for implementing that decision. The interaction of these two dimensions creates four decision styles:

- *Command.* The leader makes the decision without involving the people will be responsible for implementing it. This style is sometimes called autocratic.
- *Consensus.* The decision results from input provided by all the parties affected by the decision and is, to some degree, acceptable to all of them. This is our standard definition of a consensus.

- *Consultation.* The leader makes the decision after gathering input from the people concerned with the decision. The decision may be, but is not necessarily, acceptable to them.

- *Convenience.* The leader uses whatever method is easiest at the time, with no consideration given to finding the best method.

Roskin pictured the four styles as follows:

| | | |
|---|---|---|
| Q | Quality is more important than acceptance | COMMAND |
| QA | Quality and acceptance are both important | CONSULTATION |
| A | Acceptance is more important than quality | CONSENSUS |
| N | Neither quality nor acceptance is important | CONVENIENCE |

As a matter of note, I do not agree that a consensus implies that acceptance is more important than quality. I would argue that you are more likely to have a quality decision that has a better chance of being accepted when you use the consensus method correctly.

**QUESTIONS**

- What is your team's primary decision style?

- Are you more concerned with the quality or the acceptance of the decision?

- Do you consider both?

- Do you give equal weight to both?

# 479. FALSE-POSITIVE CONSENSUS

One of the dangers of working toward a consensus decision is *groupthink.* Groupthink is a phenomenon whereby team members suppress their personal views, values, and sometimes even data in order to allow the team to reach a decision. Members suppress their views because of "peer pressure" and out of a desire to maintain group harmony and achieve a consensus. When groupthink takes over a team's decision-making process, the outcome is something we call a "false-positive consensus." Members fail to identify issues that need to be considered, do not bring up questions that should be asked, and override information that needs to be examined. Symptoms of groupthink include:

- Reaching a decision without sufficient discussion or study;
- Believing the team is invulnerable;
- Rationalizing away undesirable information; and
- Developing and promoting stereotypes of outsiders, especially critics.

**QUESTION** Do you see any evidence of groupthink or false-positive consensus on your team?

 **T I P** If you suspect groupthink, develop targeted norms around open communication and challenging assumptions.

 **T I P** Use the excellent video, *Groupthink,* to stimulate a discussion of these issues. You will find a description of the video at www.crmlearning.com.

# 480. CONSENSUS AND FACILITATION SKILLS

One of the disadvantages of trying to use the consensus method is the need for high level facilitation skills. Because a consensus requires that all members have an opportunity to express their points of view, minority views are not suppressed, both sides of an issue are examined, and compromises are fashioned, solid facilitation skills are necessary. Facilitation skills can come from one person (the facilitator or leader) or may be embedded in the team and shared by various members. Mature teams tend to have the embedded skills and norms to facilitate a consensus.

 **T I P** One way to test for the maturity level of your team is to determine whether sufficient facilitation skills exist on the team.

# 481. GETTING TO CONSENSUS

Zenger, Musselwhite, Hurson, and Perrin (1994, p. 62) point out:

> "A consensus is general agreement by every member of the team to support a decision and actively participate in the related course of action. The decision may not be the first choice of every team member. . . . At the same time, each person understands why the group hasn't adopted his or her first choice and can live with the decision of the group as a whole. You know you've got consensus when every team member can leave the meeting saying:
> - 'I've heard their positions.'
> - 'I believe they've heard mine.'
> - 'The decision doesn't compromise my values.'
> - 'I can support the decision.'"

# 482. CONSENSUS SIGNS

Zenger et al. (1994) offer this helpful list of clues that it is time for you to reach a consensus with your team:

- Does the team have little experience with consensus?

- Do some team members express their real views only outside of team meetings?

- Does the team often make hasty decisions or fail to identify the requirements for a sound decision?

**QUESTION**  Would you answer "yes" to any of these questions?

# 483. TIPS FOR REACHING A CONSENSUS

Here is an outline of a process for reaching a consensus:

1. Describe the decision to be made or problem to be solved: "By the end of this meeting, we need to agree to either continue or drop the Zansibar Project."

2. Review the definition of a consensus: "A consensus is. . . ."

3. Explain the importance of reaching a consensus: "It's important to reach a true consensus on the future of the project because we need your total commitment to. . . ."

4. Remind the team of its decision-making norms: "As you recall, our norms for reaching a consensus include allowing everyone an opportunity to express his or her point of view."

5. Review the advantages and disadvantages of all options: "Let's review all the reasons why we should continue the project and the reasons why we should terminate the project."

6. Test for a possible consensus: "It seems that most of us can support the idea of stopping the project in thirty days, provided that. . . ."

7. Check for everyone's commitment to the decision: "Before we move ahead, let's be certain everyone is onboard with the decision. Raja, are you OK with this? Jennifer, can you live with the decision?"

8. Develop an implementation plan: "Let's review the steps necessary to put this decision into practice and identify team member responsibilities for each step."

# 484. DECISION-MAKING METHODS

Use the following assessment to see how your team is doing with its decision-making methods.

## Process

You can simply ask everyone to complete the survey and then facilitate an open discussion of the results or you can collect the surveys, tally the responses, and create a mean for both usage and effectiveness for each method. You can then analyze the results by looking at methods that are

- *High Usage and High Effectiveness*—We use this method a great deal and members find it useful. That's positive.

- *High Usage and Low Effectiveness*—We use this method a lot, but it is not effective. This suggests a need to change to another method or improve the implementation of this method.

- *Low Usage and High Effectiveness*—We do not use this method much, but when we do members believe it is effective. This suggests a need to increase the usage of this method.

- *Low Usage and Low Effectiveness*—We do not use it much, and when we do it is not effective. No change is suggested.

# TEAM DECISION MAKING ASSESSMENT

*Instructions:* Take a look at the following list of decision methods and indicate in the first column to what extent your team uses each method, according to the following scale:

1 = Not at All    2 = To Some Extent    3 = To a Moderate Extent    4 = To a Great Extent    5 = To a Very Great Extent

    Next, indicate the degree of effectiveness the team achieves with that method, according to the following scale:

1 = Very Ineffective    2 = Ineffective    3 = Neither Effective nor Ineffective    4 = Effective    5 = Very Effective

| Usage | Method | Effectiveness |
|---|---|---|
| _____ | 1. Decision by leader or manager without member input | _____ |
| _____ | 2. Decision by leader with member input | _____ |
| _____ | 3. Decision by expert in/out of team | _____ |
| _____ | 4. Decision by majority vote | _____ |
| _____ | 5. Decision by averaging member opinions | _____ |
| _____ | 6. Decision by minority | _____ |
| _____ | 7. Decision by consensus | _____ |

# 485. AUTOCRATIC: LEADER DECIDES WITH NO INPUT FROM MEMBERS

What's so bad about this approach? Well, in some situations, it works just fine. For example, the autocratic method can be useful when there is no value in obtaining input from members because they have little experience in the matter, when a quick decision is necessary (as in an emergency), and when there is only one correct solution, such as a decision required by law or company policy.

 **T I P** There is a danger in defining all decisions in such a way that they meet the criteria for using this method. For example, some leaders feel that there can be no input on an unpopular issue such as a layoff, and yet team members can provide valuable insight into a sensible plan for implementing a layoff and dealing with the post-layoff environment.

# 486. THE "PLOP"

Some teams make a decision by taking no action, a method sometimes called the "plop." Have you seen this method employed on your team? Here's the scenario: An issue or problem is presented and there is some discussion. However, the discussion just sort of ends and the team moves on to another agenda item. Members leave the room not knowing what, if anything, was decided and, therefore, what they should do.

# 487. MAJORITY VOTE

The voting method is pretty straightforward. An issue or proposed decision is presented. Members vote for or against the proposal. If it receives a majority of the votes, it becomes a decision of the team.

 **QUESTIONS**

- What are the advantages of this method?
- What are the disadvantages?

- What are some typical team decisions for which this method would work best?
- What are some situations in which you would not recommend using it?

# 488. UNANIMOUS VOTE

This is a little like consensus and a little like majority vote. However, the standard is higher. In this case, every member of the team must agree with and support the decision. This goes beyond: "I can live with it." All teams would love to have unanimous support for all decisions, but it is a very high standard and, in the case of some decisions, not necessary. Unanimous means the team cannot move on unless each team member favors the decision.

# 489. INDIVIDUAL VERSUS TEAM DECISION METHOD

Here's a quick exercise to look at the value of each method.

## Process

- Divide the team into two subgroups.
- Ask one group to come up with a list of the advantages of individual decision making.
- Ask the other group to prepare a list of the advantages of team decision making.
- Ask each subgroup in turn to present its list.
- Facilitate a discussion of the situations in which your team might ask one person to make the decision and situations in which you should use a team decision approach.
- Conclude by agreeing on some norms for team decisions in the future.

# 490. "SOCIALIZE IT"

Some teams use an informal method to take a "reading" of the members' feelings about a proposed decision before it is presented at a team meeting. The operative phrase is "Let's socialize it with the members before our meeting next week." The goal is to identify the level of support for the decision, address concerns that members have about the decision, and shape the presentation of the proposal at the meeting. In some case, the "socializing" may result in the decision being pulled back.

### QUESTIONS

- Do you use socializing?

- Do you find it helpful?

- If you do not use it, do you think it would help your team decision-making process?

# 491. WHAT IS AN EFFECTIVE DECISION?

Here is a checklist to help you review some recent team decisions.

- ☐ All members had an opportunity to participate.
- ☐ Many sides of the issue were considered.
- ☐ Members were open to opposing points of view.
- ☐ The decision was consistent with the team's goals.
- ☐ Members supported the decision and indicated a willingness to implement it.

 **TIP** As a team, select a recent key decision. Review the decision in light of this checklist. The decision was not effective unless it meets *all* of the above criteria.

## 492. USING SURVIVAL GAMES TO LEARN THE CONSENSUS METHOD

There are many so-called survival exercises that are designed to teach teams how to arrive at a consensus. These games range from the classic "Lost on the Moon" to "Arctic Survival." Sources for these games include:

- Pfeiffer: www.pfeiffer.com
- HRD Press: www.hrdpress.com.
- Human Synergistics International: www.humansyn.com
- Organizational Design & Development: www.hrdq.com
- Teleometrics International: www.teleometrics.com

## 493. ESCAPE FROM GILLIGAN'S ISLAND: A PLAYFUL ALTERNATIVE

We developed a "spoof" on all those serious survival games called Escape from Gilligan's Island (Thiagarajan & Parker, 1999). You can find it in the Team Tool Shed.

# 494. A GOOD PLACE TO START

So you've decided as a team to make more use of the consensus method. We recommend that you go back to the goals of the team. Perhaps you've also decided that a good way to get your team back on track is to revisit your existing goals or start afresh with a whole new set of team goals. Since commitment to team goals is critical, it will be important to go for a genuine consensus on your new goals. As a result, you will have a fresh, current set of goals, real-time practice in using the consensus method, and a commitment to support those goals by the people who will be responsible for implementing them.

**IN THIS AISLE YOU HAVE FOUND TOOLS THAT FOCUS SPECIFICALLY** on what a consensus decision is and on how to reach an effective consensus. In addition, you will find related tools in the goals, empowerment, norms, and meetings aisles (Aisles 1, 4, 7, and 11, respectively).

 **AISLE 18**

# REASSESS TEAM PERFORMANCE

## OVERVIEW

**PERIODICALLY, A TEAM SHOULD STOP TO EXAMINE** how well it is doing and what may be interfering with its effectiveness. Even if it turns out that you are doing well, it's good to know that too.

Teams, much like individuals, should take an annual physical—a checkup that examines their vital signs. Research tells us that a concern about one's progress is a sign of a healthy person and of a healthy team.

When is the last time your team did an assessment of its performance?

An assessment is the first step toward getting well and getting back on track. This self-assessment can be formal or informal.

Informal checkups can take the form of a team leader or facilitator asking, "How are we doing?" A solid group discussion, based on this and other simple questions, can be an effective exercise. There are several quick and easy team assessments in this aisle that can be completed in a brief period of time.

A formal assessment can take more time and involve more effort. It may involve a survey instrument, interviews, or focus groups. However, there are also brief, written surveys that do not take long to complete and score. Examples of such instruments are also found in this section.

Mature high-performing teams are self-conscious. They are like the former mayor of New York, Ed Koch, who was always asking city residents, "How am I doing?" Similarly, effective teams want to know how they are doing and how they can get better at what they are doing. In addition, if your team seems to be off track, a team assessment is the place to start. The results can help pinpoint your strengths and weaknesses and suggest areas for improvement. These data can form the basis for a team development action plan.

## 495. REGULAR ASSESSMENTS: A SIGN OF A HEALTHY TEAM

Assessments are also a sign of a mature, high-performing team. Team building is a cyclical, regenerative process. Successful teams regularly assess their strengths and weaknesses, develop plans to reinforce and build on their strengths, and look for ways to eliminate or reduce their weaknesses.

**QUESTION**  Does your team engage in a regular assessment process?

## 496. TEAM ASSESSMENT AS AN ANNUAL PHYSICAL

We are encouraged to visit our doctor on a regular basis for medical checkups. Depending on your situation the examination may involve a variety of different tests. Once the data are received, the doctor reviews the results with you and, if necessary, a treatment plan is developed by you and your doctor. The goal of this process is continued health. In much the same way, we encourage teams to engage in an annual assessment of their vital signs, such as goal clarity, positive interpersonal relationships, open communication, and effective decision making. As in the case of your personal health checkup, a team assessment will vary depending on the condition and stage of the team.

**T I P**  Schedule an appointment with your team for an assessment much as you would schedule an appointment with your doctor for a checkup.

## 497. CATEGORIES OF TEAM PERFORMANCE

Here's a useful guide to help you decide what aspect of team performance you want to evaluate.

| Category | What to Measure |
| --- | --- |
| Team | Plan vs. Actual |
| | Performance vs. Objectives |
| | Member Satisfaction |
| | Customer Satisfaction |
| Leader | Member Perceptions |
| | Management Perceptions |
| | Customer Perceptions |
| | Self-Assessment |
| Members | Peer Perceptions |
| | Leader Perceptions |
| | Self-Assessment |

## 498. MYTHS THAT INTERFERE WITH TEAM ASSESSMENTS

As you look at this list or myths about teams, think about whether any of them apply to your team (Harrington-Mackin, 1996).

- People are causing all the problems on the team, and there is nothing we can do about people.

- More training will solve the team's problems.

- All systems have flaws that cause them not to work well and so do teams. Examination will make little difference.

- Teams are the right way to structure the modern organization, and we'll just have to bear with the problems.

- If the teams aren't working, we must be doing something wrong. They're working at other places.

- Control and accountability are not compatible with empowerment and teams.

- Disbanding a team represents a failure.

## 499. ASSESSING TEAM PERFORMANCE: A PROCESS

Here's a protocol for a team assessment process.

| What | Who | When |
|------|-----|------|
| Decide What to Assess | | |
| Select Tool or Method | | |
| Prepare Tool or Method | | |
| Complete Data Collection | | |
| Summarize Results | | |
| Present Results | | |
| Facilitate Action Planning | | |
| Communicate Plan | | |
| Implement Plan | | |
| Evaluate Results | | |

## 500. TIPS FOR CONDUCTING A TEAM SELF-EVALUATION

Rees (1997) has developed a list of suggestions for conducting a team assessment that we have adapted below:

- Only members of the team and other invited people should be present for the evaluation discussion. The team leader should participate in the evaluation as a team member with equal input.

- Set aside plenty of time for discussion and minimize outside distractions.

- Allow team members several minutes of quiet time to complete the assessment form or to review the survey data.

- When team members are reviewing the survey results, ask them to write down their main reactions. Reactions could be surprises, questions, strengths, areas for improvement, and others that are relevant to your team.

- Appoint a facilitator, who will remain neutral during the discussion, move the discussion along, and help the team reach a consensus on action plans.

- Appoint a scribe to record the key agreements and action items.

- Record the team's ideas for improvement on a flip chart or LCD projector so everyone can see the items.

- Review and prioritize the list of ideas for team improvements before the end of the meeting.

- Arrange to have the list distributed to the members shortly after the meeting.

- Decide what follow-up actions are necessary.

- Thank the members for their participation in this important exercise.

- Conduct an informal assessment of the meeting.

# 501. INFORMAL ASSESSMENT

An informal assessment can begin with a basic, open-ended question such as: "How are we doing?"

As members respond to that question, you can probe for more information and opinions with such comments and questions as:

- "Tell us more about that."

- "How do the rest of you feel about that?"

- "How often has that happened?"

- "What's the impact of that?"

- "What can we do about that?"

# 502. SIMPLE ASSESSMENT

We sometimes use two questions to guide a team assessment discussion at a team meeting:

1. "What's going well that we should preserve and continue?"
2. "In what ways does the team need to improve?"

# 503. QUICK TEAM CHECK

Here's a written survey that takes about five minutes to complete. You can use it as a kickoff to a discussion at a team meeting or you can collect and score the survey.

## Process

- Collect the surveys.
- Summarize the results.
- Create a distribution of responses (number of people who circled "1," number of people who circled "2," and so on) and a mean for each success factor.
- Share these data with the team.
- Use the results to develop an action plan for team improvement.

# QUICK TEAM CHECK

*Directions:* Please review each of the team success factors listed below. Then indicate the extent to which you agree that it is true about this team by circling one number on the scale as follows:

1 = Strongly Disagree    2 = Disagree Somewhat    3 = Neither Disagree nor Agree    4 = Agree Somewhat    5 = Strongly Agree

| Success Factors | Circle One Number |
|---|---|
| 1. We have clear goals. | 1  2  3  4  5 |
| 2. The climate is relaxed. | 1  2  3  4  5 |
| 3. Team member roles are clear. | 1  2  3  4  5 |
| 4. Everyone participates. | 1  2  3  4  5 |
| 5. We have sufficient resources. | 1  2  3  4  5 |
| 6. Communication flows freely. | 1  2  3  4  5 |
| 7. Management supports the team. | 1  2  3  4  5 |
| 8. Meetings are useful. | 1  2  3  4  5 |
| 9. Conflicts are resolved smoothly. | 1  2  3  4  5 |
| 10. External relationships are effective. | 1  2  3  4  5 |

**Total Score:**

## 504. CREATING A HOME-GROWN SURVEY

One of our clients wanted to improve overall morale in the organization and decided to start with a survey to identify the issues of concern to all employees. We began by forming a small team of five people who represented each of the five business units. At the first meeting we brainstormed "issues of concern to employees" and came up with concerns about new employee orientation, business meetings, conflict resolution, and management style, among others. We then used those issues to draft a survey instrument that addressed those issues. The team made changes, and the final version was ready for administration. The team was responsible for holding brief meetings with people in their areas, where they explained and administered the survey. Employees completed the survey during the meeting, ensuring a high return rate. Completed surveys were mailed to a computing service that summarized the results and prepared a report. At an offsite meeting, the results were presented and action teams were formed to address each of the major issues. The teams analyzed the data, developed problem statements, collected additional information, looked at alternative solutions, and proposed solutions. All of the recommendations were implemented, and one year later the survey was repeated to check for progress over time. And, yes, the survey results were significantly more positive!

## 505. TEAM DEVELOPMENT SURVEY (TDS)

For teams looking for a more formal assessment instrument, the TDS makes sense. This survey, based on the twelve characteristics of an effective team that originally appeared in *Team Players and Teamwork* (1990, 1996), is available from Consulting Psychologists Press at www.cpp-dp.com. The survey yields scores on the twelve characteristics along two dimensions: (1) description—to what extent does it describe our team?—and (2) importance—how important is this characteristic to our success?

## 506. THE TEAM PERFORMANCE MODEL

The Team Performance Model, developed by Allan Drexler, David Sibbet, and Russell Forrester (1988), is another formal assessment tool that is widely used. The instrument includes seventy statements that you are asked to agree or disagree with and three general questions. The seventy statements describe the operations, interactions, or effectiveness of teams at various stages of development. The results yield a team score for each of seven stages of team performance—from orientation and trust building to high performance and renewal. You can find information on the model, including how to purchase it, from Sibbet's website: www.grove.com.

## 507. ZOOMERANG: A GREAT WEB SOURCE

At this site you can create your own survey, distribute it to a list of people, have the responses scored, and create a summary report. You begin by selecting a question type (yes/no, multiple choice) from a long list of templates, select a title for your survey, write the questions, address the respondents, prepare an introduction, and analyze the results. There are lots of helpful tips and a variety of options. You can find them at www.zoomerang.com.

## 508. FOCUS GROUP FORMAT

Another approach is to think of your team as a focus group. The focus group format uses a few well-designed questions (coupled with follow-up probes) to collect data about likes, dislikes, and recommendations. A focus group requires (1) a facilitator, (2) a scribe, (3) several key questions, and (4) a way of capturing the responses. Some good team assessment questions are:

- What are our strengths?

- What's going well and should be continued?

- What things should we stop doing because they are reducing our effectiveness?

- What things should we begin doing because they will increase our effectiveness?

- What outside help do we need that will increase our effectiveness?

- How can we improve our team?

## 509. I DON'T LIKE THE RESULTS!

One of our clients saw the results of an assessment survey that indicated a low level of satisfaction, especially with the leader. In fact, there were a number of narrative comments that were quite critical of her performance as team leader. When she saw these data at a preview session, she promptly decided not to give the report to the team. We argued, but she was insistent. It was our position that this decision was both unprofessional and unethical for a number of reasons, not the least of which was that a commitment had been made to provide the results to the team.

 **TIP** When you decide to engage in a team assessment, be prepared to go all the way. In other words, be prepared to share the results with the members of the team regardless of the outcome. If not, you are likely to make a bad situation worse because you will have lowered the trust level—among other things.

# 510. USE YOUR CORPORATE EMPLOYEE ATTITUDE SURVEY

A number of our clients use the annual employee attitude survey to collect data specific to their teams. There are a number of ways to go:

- Ask the corporate survey administrators to create a subgrouping that includes the members of your team so you obtain team-specific data.

- Ask the administrators to add a few questions that apply specifically to your team.

- Use the corporate survey questions and results to initiate a discussion that focuses on your team, specifically how team members would answer these same questions for your team.

- Select a number of questions from the corporate survey and create your own team-specific survey.

# 511. ASSESSING THE TEAM CHARTER

Some teams go back to basics and evaluate the essential team functions such as goals, strategy, roles, and process—all the elements in the start-up charter of a team (Harrington-Mackin, 1996). The typical team charter categories include:

1. The original problem
2. Goals
3. Key team activities
4. Key expected results
5. Available resources
6. Communication expectations
7. The nonnegotiable boundaries of the team
8. Member selection
9. Team authority or empowerment
10. Team roles
11. Time frames and major milestones

## 512. HOW TO MEASURE THE RESULTS OF WORK TEAMS WORKSHOP

This is the title of a highly regarded two-day workshop by our colleague, Jack Zigon. Jack is the "master of measurement." You can get more information about the program at Jack's incredibly useful website, www.zigonperf.com.

## 513. HOW TO MEASURE THE RESULTS OF WORK TEAMS HANDBOOK

This 300+ page looseleaf binder is a rich resource on the team measurement process. It includes practical advice and examples on how to identify team accomplishments, create measures, develop performance standards, and create a feedback system and a number of sample team measures from some of Jack's projects. You can find more information at www.zigonperf.com.

## 514. TEAM PERFORMANCE MEASURES

Jack Zigon's website is an incredible resource for locating measures for a wide variety of teams. Bookmark www.zigonperf.com

## 515. TEAM PERFORMANCE JOURNAL

Yes, there is a professional journal devoted to team performance that includes articles you will find useful as you explore this topic. It's published in England. You can find information at their website, www.mcb.uk/tpm.htm.

## 516. TEAM DEVELOPMENT: A GRID PERSPECTIVE

This simple but powerful assessment tool can help your team look at two aspects of team effectiveness: (1) *self-direction:* the level of team empowerment, and (2) *self-renewal:* the willingness to learn and grow (Parker & Kropp, 2000). In this participatory activity, members plot the team on a grid that has these two dimensions. It is a powerful exercise because you can post the grid on the wall and ask each member to place a mark on the grid that indicates his or her perceptions of the team. You can find this activity in the Team Tool Shed.

## 517. GOT CULTURE? A TEAM ASSESSMENT TOOL

Another assessment tool from Parker and Kropp (2000) is Got Culture? A Team Assessment Tool. This instrument measures team effectiveness in four aspects of culture: (1) *role clarity,* (2) *respect,* (3) *communication,* and (4) *rewards.* The process is interactive. Members complete the survey, interpret the results, and develop action plans all in the same meeting. You can find the survey in the Team Tool Shed.

## 518. TEAM LEADER ASSESSMENT

A brief leader assessment tool is called simply Team Leader Assessment (TLA) and is found in Parker (1998). The instrument focuses on interpersonal behaviors, such as communication, openness, support, and encouragement. This assessment is also found in the Team Tool Shed.

# 519. OBSERVATION

What do you think about this quote from the "wisdom" of Yogi Berra?

**"You can observe a lot just by watching."**
*—Yogi Berra*

## QUESTIONS

- What can be learned about your team from observation?
- What activities, events, and so forth should be observed to obtain a "flavor" of the team?
- Who should do the observing?
- What types of things should the observer be looking for?

**THIS AISLE INCLUDES A VARIETY OF DIFFERENT APPROACHES** to the assessment of team performance—from the simple to the more complex. Other aisles include related tools in the areas of goal setting (Aisle 1), role clarification (Aisle 3), and gaining commitment (Aisle 16).

 **AISLE 19**

# REVAMP YOUR TEAM REWARDS

## OVERVIEW

**MATURE TEAMS TEND TO HAVE A VARIETY OF WAYS** of recognizing team members and rewarding overall team performance. It is important to understand that individual team member recognition should continue in spite the existence of overall team rewards that foster collaboration. I prefer a smorgasbord of team rewards that provide options for dealing with a variety of different situations. In other words, one size does not fit all.

If your team is relying on one type of team reward, you are limiting the ways you can use incentives to foster more effective teamwork and motivate team players. In most cases, rewards and recognition are designed and administered by the organization's human resources department. However, some organizations have decentralized the process to an employee steering team or to individual teams. In my view, the more teams can be empowered to develop and implement their own rewards and recognition programs, the stronger the impact.

The message is: If you believe that team rewards and recognition will help get your team back on track by providing appropriate incentives, empower yourself to make it happen. The resources in this aisle will help lead the way. Here you will find tools to enhance your existing recognition efforts, establish a team reward program, and add some variety to the type of awards that are currently used by your team.

## 520. RECOGNITION: THE MORE THE MERRIER

We refer to recognition as after the fact acknowledgement of good work by the team or a team player. The situation goes something like this: You or your team does something beyond the norm and we thank you for it. As *The One-Minute Manager* (Blanchard, 2000) might say, "We catch you doing something right!" Our belief is: Don't be stingy with the recognition . . . spread it around as much as possible. Recognition usually is a low-cost or no-cost item, so be generous.

## 521. THE GOALS OF RECOGNITION

When you recognize a person or team, your goals are (1) to get the person to continue the same behavior or performance, (2) to encourage others to engage in the same or similar behavior, and (3) to tell the person that his or her performance is appreciated.

 **T I P** Be specific about what the person or team is being recognized for.

## 522. CRITERIA FOR A SUCCESSFUL RECOGNITION AND REWARD SYSTEM

Consider this checklist for either looking at your current program or as guidelines for establishing a new program.

- ☑ The awards are appropriate for the effort involved.
- ☑ The program is equitable for all employees (all team members have a "shot" at being rewarded).
- ☑ The awards are competitive with awards offered by your competitors.
- ☑ Team members are involved in the design and administration of the program.
- ☑ Team members understand the program, especially how rewards are distributed.

## 523. TEAM REWARD

Reward programs are payments made to teams based on a *pre-announced formula.* In other words, in advance, team members know that if they do *this,* they will get *that.* For example, if a systems design team meets the requirements by a certain date and stays within budget, each team member will receive a bonus of $200. The concept of the reward is that everyone will work hard to meet the requirements in order to receive the reward. It should also foster collaboration among team members.

**QUESTION** What are some of the ways your team could devise a team reward program?

## 524. PROJECT TEAM AWARD

Great Plains Software makes heavy use of project teams for the development of new software products. They use a two-part team bonus program. Half of the bonus is received when the team hits the targeted release date of the product, while the second half is received ninety days following release, based on performance of the product. Payout of this bonus requires a near-zero level of detectable bugs as determined by a combination of measures that include customer satisfaction scores, feedback from specific users, and problem calls to the help desk. Since projects can last nine months, project team leaders celebrate milestones along the way with dinners, picnics, and other forms of informal recognition. At the conclusion of the project, the team also creates a "Friends List" to recognize non-team members who supported the project along the way. Friends receive gift certificates and thank you letters. For more on this program and twenty-six other case studies of team rewards and recognition, see Parker, McAdams, & Zielinski (2000).

## 525. CASH VERSUS NON-CASH AWARDS

Which is better? Do team members want money or merchandise? Obviously, it depends on the person. However, generally speaking, non-cash incentives work best because they carry a "trophy value" that has great staying power over time. While a cash bonus is great at the time it is received, it is soon spent and disappears. However, each time you look at that television set or plaque, you are reminded of what your team did to earn it . . . and you might just be motivated to do it again.

## 526. NON-CASH AWARDS

Examples of non-cash awards are limited only by your imagination. Some non-cash awards are non-cost, but most cost the organization some money to administer. Examples include such things as:

- A thank you—delivered in person or via a note or both
- A letter of congratulations
- A trophy
- Company merchandise
- Gift certificate
- Dinner for two
- A free lunch or breakfast
- A credit to a card issued by the company for purchases at local stores
- Merchandise from a catalogue
- Travel for business or vacation with the family
- Stock options

## 527. CHOICE

Recognition experts agree that the element of choice increases the value of an award. In other words, giving team members the option of choosing a gift from a catalogue increases its value because one member may want a fishing rod, while another would prefer a new briefcase. One team member enjoys fine dining at a gourmet cafe, while another prefers the informal atmosphere of a seafood restaurant down at the local wharf. Both awards may cost the same, but both people receive something they value.

## 528. INTRINSIC REWARDS

An intrinsic reward is anything that is satisfying and motivating in and of itself. It appeals to the inner self of the team member. Intrinsic rewards are of value to the person and often enhance self-worth. The value comes from within the person. As in all rewards, it should involve choice. In the following sections we provide examples of intrinsic rewards for team members.

## 529. CHALLENGE

Ask the team to take on a tough problem, a difficult customer, or to fix a troublesome product. They'll feel proud to have been asked.

## 530. CONSTRUCTIVE FEEDBACK

Provide timely, specific, handwritten comments on documents prepared by the team. Be sure to sign them.

## 531. EMPOWERMENT

Give the team the freedom to develop a plan, manage their budget, and make key decisions with minimal interference.

## 532. FLEXIBILITY

Give the team the opportunity to work flexible hours, work at home, or have periodic offsite meetings at company expense.

## 533. RESOURCES

Provide the team with new tools, equipment, software, or other resources and the authority to make decisions about their use.

## 534. ASK FOR HELP

Ask the team for its opinion on a tough problem or new business opportunity.

## 535. USE THEIR EXPERTISE

Ask the team to help another team get started or solve a problem.

## 536. REPRESENTATION

Ask the team to represent the organization at a conference, business meeting, or other special event. Introduce members to an important customer or stakeholder.

## 537. OPPORTUNITIES TO LEARN

Give the team the opportunity to learn a new system, operate some new equipment, or in other ways increase their skills and knowledge, perhaps through classes online.

## 538. EXTRINSIC REWARDS

Extrinsic rewards come from the external environment in which team members work or live. Many psychologists think of extrinsic rewards as "satisfiers" rather than as motivators because they do not appeal to the inner self of the team member.

**QUESTIONS**

- Do extrinsic rewards such as money motivate people?
- What motivates you?

## 539. NON-CASH EXTRINSIC REWARDS

Most people think of extrinsic rewards as direct cash payments such as a bonus, incentive pay, or commission. However, there can be low cost or no cost rewards provided by an external person. The following sections give some examples.

**QUESTION**  Which types of extrinsic rewards appeal to you?

## 540. VERBAL RECOGNITION

The manager of the department or team leader makes positive comments about the work of the team at a company meeting.

## 541. PUBLIC PRESENTATION

Ask the team to give a presentation on their work at a staff meeting or company conference.

## 542. PUBLIC RECOGNITION

In a prominent location in the building or on the company's website, display examples of the team's work, pictures of the members, and letters of commendation from customers or stakeholders.

## 543. ORGANIZATIONAL RECOGNITION

Place a story and picture about the team in the company or community newspaper or on the website.

## 544. FUN EVENT

Send the team on an outing to a ball game, boat ride, or show.

## 545. PROFESSIONAL RECOGNITION

Encourage the team to speak about their work at a professional conference or trade show.

## 546. PERSONAL RECOGNITION

Invite the team to your home for a barbecue or other party or just treat them to lunch.

## 547. MANAGEMENT RECOGNITION

Ask a senior manager or the team's sponsor to attend a team meeting to personally praise the team for its work.

## 548. TEAM RECOGNITION

Give each team member a shirt, hat, or other merchandise with the team's name and/or logo on it.

## 549. CLARIFY THE REASONS TO CELEBRATE

Whenever you recognize a team or person, be clear about the reasons for the acknowledgement. Communicate the reasons both to the team and to the rest of the organization. It is important that everyone know why a team was selected for recognition because (a) we want the team to continue the positive behavior and (b) we want other teams to do the same or similar things.

## 550. MERCK'S REASONS TO CELEBRATE

At Merck and Company's Wilson, North Carolina, plant, there is a wonderful recognition program called "Reasons to Celebrate" and an organizational unit incentive program called "Pay for Performance." Both programs are described in an article called "Reasons to Celebrate" in the September 2000 issue of *Incentive* magazine. The article is also available on Glenn Parker's website at www.glennparker.com/Freebees/. Teams are free to nominate any other team or team member for a gift certificate worth up to $300 for individuals and $500 for teams. Each team receives a recognition budget, which they are encouraged to spend.

## 551. CREATE MANY WINNERS, FEW LOSERS

First, don't even think about another "employee of the month" or "team of the month" award. These winner-take-all awards create one winner and many losers, just the opposite of what we want. The rule of thumb in recognition is: The more the merrier! Your goal should be to give out lots of small forms of recognition (see above examples), rather than one large one. And even when you feel it is necessary to recognize one person for extraordinary effort as a team player, include a number of other "winners" who also contributed to the total team results. As is so frequently said during the time of entertainment awards ceremonies, "It's an honor just to nominated."

## 552. INVOLVE EMPLOYEES IN THE SELECTION PROCESS

Many organizations have found that including team members in the selection process increases the value of the award because the process is seen as fair to everyone. One of our clients has a recognition committee that includes a few managers but is heavily weighted toward non-management employees. In addition, committee membership rotates on a regular basis to allow everyone an opportunity to participate in the process.

## 553. PARTICIPATION SIGNALS TRUST

Giving team members an opportunity to participate in the recognition process by developing the criteria and process, nominating teammates, selecting recipients, and designing the presentation is a sign that they can be trusted to handle something this important.

## 554. MAKE IT FUN

One team gave out "academy awards" to team members and made it fun. Here's what they did:

- *Best Supporting Player:* To the manager who was most supportive of the team during the past year.

- *Ralph Nader Award:* To the member who challenged the system (and everything else) . . . and lived to tell about it.

- *Dominos Delivers Citation:* To the team member who could be counted on to deliver work and anything else asked for on time, every time.

- *Continental Air On Time Every Time Award:* To the team member who showed up on time and prepared for every team meeting.

- *Parker Process Award:* To the team member who was most supportive of the team process.

- *Betty Crocker Award:* To the member who brought in the best snacks to team meetings.

# 555. MAKE IT SMART

Here's a quick little recognition job aid using the old familiar SMART format. You can use it as a checklist to assess your current recognition efforts.

- ☑ *Sincere.* The award as well the presentation of the award should come across to both the recipient and others as genuine.
- ☑ *Meaningful.* The form of recognition and the presentation should be aligned with the organization's goals, values, and strategy.
- ☑ *Adaptable.* The award and the presentation should reflect the organization's interest in keeping the recognition program flexible and fresh.
- ☑ *Relevant.* The award should be personal in the sense of tailored to the needs of the recipient rather than a "one size fits all."
- ☑ *Timely.* The award should be given closely following the time of the performance or behavior that is being recognized.

*Note:* Our thanks to Jim Brintnall of Successories, Inc., for this tip.

# 556. DINNER FOR TWO PLEASE

One of our clients recognized his team for contributing to the overall success of the organization by purchasing gift certificates for dinner at a number of different local restaurants. At a team meeting, the certificates were distributed to team members based on preferences. Members who were not completely satisfied with their choice traded with their teammates. In the end, the team leader made sure everyone received a certificate to a restaurant of his or her choice by offering to take back and replace any certificate with one that matched the preference of the person. The certificates were for family-style restaurants as well as gourmet restaurants, in an effort to accommodate the diverse preferences of team members. We like the idea because it clearly stated what the recognition was designed to reward, and it could be shared with family members.

## 557. WHEN A TEAM DINNER IS NOT A REWARD

Keep in mind that many team members do not value a business dinner with teammates as a reward. In fact, for some people it is an inconvenience, while for others it may be a punishment because it is more time away from home. On the other hand, an occasional team dinner or lunch can be a good time to get to know each other better and build some espirit de corps.

## 558. REWARDING TEAMS

The recent book, *Rewarding Teams: Lessons from the Trenches,* contains twenty-seven cases of team rewards from large companies such as Merck and Chase to small, privately held businesses and nonprofit organizations.

 **T I P** Ask each team member to read the book and come with two ideas from the cases that can be adapted for use with your team.

## 559. HOW DO YOU LIKE YOUR RECOGNITION?

 This is a self-assessment exercise that helps team members look at what types of recognition motivates them (Thiagarajan & Parker, 1999). A list includes twenty items (similar to many of the examples cited above) and asks the person to select the ones he or she would like to receive. Ten of the items are intrinsic and ten are extrinsic motivators. As a result, each person receives an intrinsic and extrinsic score that reflects which category of reward he or she most appreciates. You can find the exercise in the Team Tool Shed.

## 560. INCENTIVE MAGAZINE

A good source for articles about motivation, incentive programs, and merchandise as well as tips and tools from vendors and consultants is the monthly magazine, *Incentive,* published by Bill Publications in New York. Their website is also helpful: www.incentivemag.com.

## 561. NATIONAL ASSOCIATION FOR EMPLOYEE RECOGNITION (NAER)

Check out this organization at their website, www.recogntion.org. You don't have to join the organization to gain some valuable information on recognition from the site.

## 562. MOTIVATION ONLINE

This useful website can be found at www.cultureworx.com. There is some solid information on motivation from a behavioral science point of view. They have a monthly newsletter that contains useful ideas about motivation and incentives. It's a good idea to sign up for this free service.

## 563. THE FUN OF RECOGNITION

Use this quote to stimulate a discussion of how recognition and rewards can help get your team back on track.

**"Recognition plans can add the fun, excitement, and satisfaction a company needs in these times of competitive market stress. They make everything work a bit better."**

*—Jerry McAdams, Co-Author,* **Rewarding Teams**

### QUESTIONS

- In what ways could a recognition program make your team work a bit better?
- Can you see any potential barriers to implementing a recognition program?
- What types of behaviors or performance could benefit from recognition by the team?
- How could you tell whether a recognition program is working?

## 564. REWARDING EMPLOYEES NEWSLETTER

This newsletter *(Bob Nelson's Rewarding Employees)* provides case studies, reviews, questions and answers, and short pieces on how companies reward and recognize employees, with no cost, cash, or non-cash incentives. It's available online at www.nelson-motivation.com.

## 565. EURIPIDES ON RECOGNITION

Even in ancient times, scholars were pondering the value of rewards.

**"In every work/a reward added makes the pleasure twice as great."**
   —*Euripides,* Rhesus

### QUESTIONS

- What do you think Euripides had in mind?
- Does a reward double your pleasure? How? Why?

## 566. 1001 WAYS TO REWARD EMPLOYEES

This book by Bob Nelson (1994), who is a well-known speaker on the topic of rewards and recognition, provides many case examples of recognition and reward programs in both profit and nonprofit organizations. It's a friendly, quick-read format and available from Nelson Motivation at 800-575-5521.

**THIS AISLE INCLUDES IDEAS, TOOLS, AND OTHER RESOURCES** for breathing some life back into your team reward and recognition program. You can find ancillary tools in aisles that deal with climate (Aisle 8), trust (Aisle 14), empowerment (Aisle 4), and goals (Aisle 1), as well as in the next aisle, Revive Team Celebrations.

 **AISLE 20**

# REVIVE TEAM CELEBRATIONS

## OVERVIEW

**ARE YOU HAVING FUN YET?** No? Why not? You can throw your own party, run your own picnic, or simply bring in a couple of pizzas. Teams need to celebrate all their accomplishments, both large and small. If your team is not taking some time out to recognize its successes, you are missing opportunities to build team spirit and commitment. One way to get your team back on track is to identify achievements and then commemorate them.

When I interview team members in connection with a diagnosis, people will often point to past events in the team's history that were memorable. All of these events were celebrations. The message: In the good old days of this team, we had fun because we regularly celebrated our accomplishments with some sort of event.

Many of my client teams work in support areas such as engineering, information technology, and human resources and, therefore, their work takes place behind the scenes. They do not receive the recognition that is more readily available to teams in sales, marketing, and operations. Some teams are just not on the front lines. They don't have regular contact with customers and, as a result, they don't have the "visibility" that generates kudos from others. These teams keep the organization afloat by making sure the bills are paid, payroll checks are cut, information systems are "up," machines are running smoothly, and the building is safe and clean. As the saying goes, "No one ever calls to say 'thanks for getting my expense check out on time.'" It's just expected.

It is very important for your team members to take the time and effort to reach around and pat themselves on the back. If you wait for others to plan a celebration for you, you may wait a long time. Too often people are quick to criticize but slow to praise. So when you've accomplished a goal, improved your processes, installed a new system, launched a new product, or put a new service on line, celebrate the event. Congratulate yourself, throw a party, have dinner together, distribute gifts, or bring in a party cake.

In this aisle we provide some ideas used by teams to celebrate accomplishments. Don't be limited by these ideas. Be creative. Involve team members in a brainstorming session devoted to "Ways to Celebrate Our Accomplishments."

## 567. WHY CELEBRATE?

Maybe it should be obvious, but if you are not celebrating very much at all, here are some reasons to start.

Celebrations:

- Build pride and commitment among team members;

- Encourage team members to continue the behaviors or performance that you are celebrating;

- Support the growth of a positive team climate;

- Help members get to know each other better;

- Send a message to members that their efforts are valued; and

- Are fun!

## 568. WHAT TO CELEBRATE

You can celebrate just about anything, but it should be something that members of the team care about. Some of the events teams typically celebrate include:

- Completion of the team's mission, charter, or goals;

- Acceptance and/or implementation of the team's proposed solution to a problem;

- Accomplishment of a major milestone of a project;

- Positive feedback from a customer or excellent results on a customer satisfaction survey;

- Solving a difficult problem or overcoming a major hurdle;

- Completing a project ahead of schedule and/or under budget;

- Landing a new customer/project or renewing an existing business relationship;

- No lost-time accidents for one year; and/or

- Error-free work for six consecutive months.

**QUESTION** What are some other reasons to celebrate based on your work area?

## 569. WHEN TO CELEBRATE?

The answer is simple: As close to the event as possible. When you obtain those positive customer satisfaction numbers, have a party next week. When management accepts your recommendations, go right out together after work. When you land that big contact, splurge on a great team dinner. As the time between the event and the celebration increases, the impact of the celebration decreases.

## 570. LOTS OF LITTLE EVENTS ARE BETTER THAN ONE BIG ONE

Don't wait for the annual awards dinner to celebrate your accomplishments. Rather, celebrate your successes year-round as they occur. It is better to have thirty small activities spread out through the year than one grand event.

 **T I P** At the end of your next team meeting, try to brainstorm thirty little celebrations.

## 571. PLAN YOUR OWN CELEBRATION

Most small events are low-cost activities that can be funded out of petty cash or out-of-pocket expenses. Some events are no cost. Therefore, don't wait for management approval to start. Consider yourself empowered to celebrate an accomplishment.

 **T I P** See whether you can come up at least ten no-cost events.

## 572. INVOLVE TEAM MEMBERS IN PLANNING THE CELEBRATION

Make the celebration a participatory exercise during which team members take responsibility for planning and implementing the activity. It's a great way to increase member involvement and build a positive climate. And the payoff is that team members receive the type of event they want.

## 573. MAKE IT A TEAM ACTIVITY

It is tempting to give everyone a hat or T-shirt as a way of celebrating a success. However, we recommend, whenever possible, making the celebration something the team does together, such as a boat ride or wine tasting. When the celebration is a team activity, it has the added bonus of being a team-building exercise.

## 574. DON'T FORGET YOUR SUPPORT SYSTEM

When you achieve a milestone or accomplish a goal, you probably did not do it alone. Therefore, when you plan your celebratory event, remember to include all the external network people who helped make you successful. Typical among a team's network are vendors, customers, suppliers, and support groups (IT, HR, research). Effective teams share the limelight because it is the right thing to do and because it builds support for collaboration in the future.

**QUESTION** Which support groups should be involved in your celebrations?

## 575. ONE TEAM'S WAY OF SAYING THANKS

An operations group in one of our client companies received great support from the software development team in the organization. The operations team received many accolades for the business results. While the operations folks had said "thanks" many times and even written letters to the division vice president commending the software team, they wanted to do more. One day the operations team invited the software developers over to their area for a surprise "thank you party." The party only consisted of cake and coffee, but to the software folks (who usually only heard from their clients when a system did not work), this celebration was memorable.

**QUESTION** When was the last time you shared a success with a support group?

# 576. ZENGER ON TEAM CELEBRATIONS

Here's what John Zenger and his colleagues (1994) have to say about when and how to plan a team celebration. The statement brings together many of the important ideas we've discussed:

> "Achieving team goals is clearly a cause for celebration, as is any positive event for the team. By giving team members a chance to enjoy both their success and one another, a celebration builds enthusiasm and teamwork. A celebration is also appropriate when the team finishes a project, seems to be losing enthusiasm, is working especially well together, or is having difficulty meeting its goals. To plan a celebration with your team, review any non-negotiables—budget, space, policies, etc.—and brainstorm a list of activities on a flip chart. . . . Then eliminate ideas that don't meet the non-negotiables, tally the team's top three, and reach consensus on one. Finally celebrate! And continue looking for ways to celebrate on a regular basis." (pp. 99–100)

# 577. MULTI-ETHNIC MEAL

One team, composed of members from a number of different cultures, decided to celebrate landing a new contract with a lunch. However, their lunch had a different flavor! A few members made up a menu composed of foods from different nations. Then each person was assigned to bring a specific dish to the lunch that reflected his or her culture. It was a great party, wonderful learning experience, and a positive team-building activity.

 **TIP** An alternative approach is asking different members of the team to host a dinner or lunch at an ethnic restaurant that serves food from his or her culture. The person selects the menu and then at the event explains something about each of the foods.

## 578. MAD MONEY

A colleague submitted this idea from her company. The company introduced a program called Make a Difference (MAD) in which team members earned MAD money for their accomplishments. They used play money for the awards, and team members saved their MAD money to use in an auction for merchandise. The MAD money concept promoted a higher level of performance and teamwork because the more successful team members were, the more money they earned. For more information about the MAD program, contact Penny Smith at psmith@tampabay.rr.com.

## 579. CELEBRATING HOSPITAL FOOD!

If you have had the misfortune to spend any time in a hospital, you know that most hospitals are not known for their cuisine. In fact, some people think the quality of the food is one of the reasons patients want to be discharged as soon as possible. One hospital that measures customer (patient) satisfaction with everything as part of their continuous improvement process actually received more than 90 percent satisfaction with their food service component for a recent one-month period. And that was a reason to celebrate! So, of course, the food service department prepared and served a special meal for a hospital board meeting. At the meeting, the food service director received a standing ovation.

## 580. PICNIC WITH A PURPOSE

Many companies have an annual picnic in the summer and holiday party in the winter. However, many teams have altered that tradition to turn the events into a celebration of a success. The old Fourth of July Picnic becomes the Customer Delight Picnic—same day, same food, same activities—but now we're celebrating achieving a "90 percent customer satisfaction rating!" The Annual Company Dinner reincarnates as the "Safety First Supper" to celebrate a significant decrease in lost-time accidents!

**T I P** Look for ways to turn your current employee focused activities into celebrations of success.

## 581. WHAT ABOUT BREAKFAST?

One team decided that a celebration at lunch had already been done and dinner was inconvenient for many people with families. So they opted for an upscale breakfast in a private room in the company cafeteria. The food service department came up with a wonderful menu and the manager distributed small gifts to everyone. The event was special because it was different, despite the fact that it took place on company premises.

## 582. TEAM CUISINE

Notice how many celebrations involve food? "Breaking bread" with people you care about is an old and valued tradition. Here's another celebration that involves a little team building as well. Under the direction of a chef, the team divides into subgroups, each with the task of preparing some portion of the meal, including setting the table and selecting the wine. Members have a good time while learning to collaborate with others. The celebration comes with eating the meal you just helped to prepare. I've found conference centers most willing to help design and implement this type of event.

## 583. PHOTO OPS

Most or all celebrations are great opportunities to take team photographs. Don't forget to bring your camera and take lots of pictures. After the celebration give each person a picture (enlarged and framed, if possible) to remember the event.

## 584. ALL TOGETHER NOW!

*All Together Now!* is the title of "a seriously fun collection of interactive games and activities" by my friend and colleague, Lorraine Ukens (1999). If you want to include some learning games in your celebration, this is a great resource.

## 585. SUCCESSORIES AS A SOURCE

A wonderful source for celebration ideas, including gifts, awards, cards, posters, books, and plaques is the motivation company, Successories. Visit their online store at www.successories.com.

**DON'T STOP HERE**. Check out the Resource Desk for more ideas or pop in the CD-ROM for a review of the reproducible tools there, and don't overlook the Guide to Team Depot Tools for help in locating just the right answer for your team.

# GUIDE TO TEAM DEPOT TOOLS

**HERE'S A LISTING OF THE TOOLS CATEGORIZED BY TYPE.** For example, if you are looking for a quick quote or longer assessment, check "Quotes" or "Assessments."

## Tool Type: Advice and Tips

## Tool Type: Books and Articles

## Tool Type: Examples and Samples

## Tool Type: Exercises, Activities, and Games

## Tool Type: Fundamentals

## Tool Type: Implements

## Tool Type: Quick Hits

# Tool Type: Quotes

| Number | Tool | Category | Aisle | Page |
|--------|------|----------|-------|------|
| 16 | A Clear, Elevating Goal | Goals | 1 | 23 |
| 52 | A Goal Is . . . | Goals | 1 | 46 |
| 3 | Are You a Visionary? | Goals | 1 | 16 |
| 49 | Team Wisdom | Goals | 1 | 45 |
| 47 | The Road to. . . ? | Goals | 1 | 44 |
| 48 | Wisdom for the Ages | Goals | 1 | 44 |
| 85 | "A Good Heart Is Better Than All the Heads in the World" | People | 2 | 72 |
| 86 | Players Who Play the Right Way | People | 2 | 73 |
| 89 | The Future Belongs to . . . | People | 2 | 74 |
| 88 | The Power of WE Is Stronger Than the Power of ME | People | 2 | 74 |
| 121 | The World Is Not Interested . . . | Roles | 3 | 96 |
| 151 | Forgiveness and Permission | Empowerment | 4 | 120 |
| 150 | I Believe . . . | Empowerment | 4 | 119 |
| 142 | "You're Empowered As Long As I Agree with Your Decisions!" | Empowerment | 4 | 115 |
| 174 | Take a Shot | Talent | 5 | 136 |
| 175 | "Talent Wins Games, but Teamwork Wins Championships" | Talent | 5 | 137 |
| 211 | Appreciation of Others | Style | 6 | 157 |
| 245 | "As a Rule of Thumb, Involve Everyone in Everything" | Norms | 7 | 177 |
| 244 | "If You Follow All the Rules, You Miss All the Fun" | Norms | 7 | 176 |
| 277 | Alice in Planning Land | Work Plan | 9 | 203 |

## Tool Type: Scenarios and Cases

# NUMERIC INDEX OF TEAM DEPOT TOOLS

# RESOURCE DESK

Ancona, D., & Caldwell, D. (1992, July). *Speeding product development: Making teamwork work.* Cambridge, MA: Sloan School of Management.

Asherman, I. (2000, December). Trust, relationships and the regulatory process. *Regulatory Affairs Focus.*

Belbin, M. (1981). *Team roles at work.* San Diego, CA: Pfeiffer & Company.

Blanchard, K. (2000). *The one-minute manager* (rev. ed.). New York: HarperCollins.

Block, P. (1987). *The empowered manager.* San Francisco, CA: Jossey-Bass.

Boyette, J., & Boyette, J. (1998). *The guru guide.* New York: John Wiley & Sons.

Bruner, M. (1998). Work team listening. In G. Parker (Ed.), *Best practices for teams.* Amherst, MA: HRD Press.

Carroll, L. (2000). *Alice's adventures in wonderland* (reissue ed.). New York: Signet Classics.

Cole, D. (1981). *Professional suicide: A survival kit for you and your job.* New York: McGraw-Hill.

Davis, M., McKay, M., & Robbins Eschelm, E. (2000). *The relaxation and stress reduction workbook* (5th ed.). New York: New Harbinger Press.

Deal, T., & Kennedy, A. (1982). *Corporate cultures.* Reading, MA: Addison-Wesley.

Drexler, A., Sibbet, D., & Forrester, R. (1988). The team performance model. In W.B. Reddy & K. Jamieson (Eds.), *Team building: Blueprints for productivity and satisfaction.* San Diego, CA: Pfeiffer & Company.

Duarte, D., & Snyder, N. (1999). *Mastering virtual teams.* San Francisco, CA: Jossey-Bass.

Dumaine, B. (1989, November 6). How managers can succeed through speed. *Fortune,* pp. 54–59.

Dyer, W. (1977). *Team building: Issues and alternatives.* Reading, MA: Addison-Wesley.

Eggleton, C.H., & Rice, J.C. (1996). *The fieldbook of team interventions.* Amherst, MA: HRD Press.

Eisenstadt, K., Kahwaju, J., & Bourgeois, L., III. (1997, July/August). How management teams can have a good fight. *Harvard Business Review,* pp. 77–85.

Elledge, R., & Phillips, S. (1994). *Team building for the future.* San Francisco, CA: Jossey-Bass/Pfeiffer.

Gibb, J. (1972). TORI theory and practice. In J.W. Pfeiffer & J.E. Jones, *The 1972 annual handbook for group facilitators.* San Francisco, CA: Jossey-Bass/Pfeiffer.

Gibb, J. (1978). *Trust.* Los Angeles: The Guild of Tutors Press.

Goleman, D. (1995). *Emotional intelligence.* New York: Bantam Books.

Hanson, M. (1998). *Golden ground rules.* Minneapolis, MN: Meeting Needs.

Harrison, R. (1973). Role negotiations: A tough-minded approach to team development. In W. Bennis et al. (Eds.), *Interpersonal dynamics.* Homewood, IL: Dorsey.

Harrington-Mackin, D. (1996). *Keeping the team going.* New York: AMACOM.

Hart, L. (1981). *Learning from conflict.* Reading, MA: Addison-Wesley.

Hastings, C., & Chaudhry-Lawton, R. (1987). *The superteam solution.* San Diego, CA: Pfeiffer & Company.

Herzberg, F. (1968, January/February). One more time: How do you motivate employees? *Harvard Business Review*, pp. 53–62.

Hitchcock, D.E., & Willard, M.L. (1995). *Why teams fail and what to do about it.* Homewood, IL: Irwin.

Human Synergistics. (1987). *Desert survival situation.* Plymouth, MI: Author.

Johnson, D., & Johnson, F. (1975). *Joining together: Group theory and group skills.* Boston, MA: Allyn and Bacon.

Johnson, D., & Johnson, F. (2000). *Joining together: Group theory and group skills* (7th ed.). Boston, MA: Allyn and Bacon.

Jung, C.G. (1923). *Psychological types.* New York: Pantheon.

Justice, T., & Jamieson, D. (1998). *The complete guide to facilitation.* Amherst, MA: HRD Press.

Kahn, R., Wolfe, E., Quinn, R., & Snock, J. (1964). *Organizational stress: Studies on role conflict and role ambiguity.* New York: John Wiley & Sons.

Karvelas, K. (1998). *Winning with teamwork.* Franklin Lake, NJ: Career Press.

Katzenbach, J.R., & Smith, D. (1993). *The wisdom of teams.* Boston, MA: Harvard Business School Press.

Kearny, L. (1995). *The facilitator's tool kit.* Amherst, MA: HRD Press.

Kline, T. (1999). *Remaking teams.* San Francisco, CA: Jossey-Bass.

Larson, C.E., & LaFasto, F.M.J. (1989). *Teamwork: What must go right/what can go wrong.* Thousand Oaks, CA: Sage.

Lawrence, P., & Lorsch, J. (1969). *Developing organizations.* Reading, MA: Addison-Wesley.

Lawrence-Lightfoot, S. (1999). *Respect: An exploration.* Reading, MA: Perseus Books.

Lipman-Blumen, J., & Leavitt, H.J. (1999, Spring). Hot groups "with attitude": A new organizational state of mind. *Organizational Dynamics,* pp. 63–73.

Locke, E.A., & Lathan, G.P. (1984). *Goal setting: A motivational strategy that works.* Englewood Cliffs, NJ: Prentice Hall.

Maani, K., & Benton, C. (1999, Spring). Rapid team learning: Lessons from team New Zealand America's cup campaign. *Organizational Dynamics,* pp. 48–64.

McAdams, J. (1996). *The reward plan advantage.* San Francisco, CA: Jossey-Bass.

McCallum, D. (1994). *Don't send your turkeys to eagle school.* Metairie, LA: Tool Thyme for Trainers.

McCallum, D. (1996). *The speed of the leader determines the rate of the pack.* Metairie, LA: Tool Thyme for Trainers.

McGee, E.C. (1998). Peer evaluation: Coaching for coaching. In G.M. Parker (Ed.), *Best practices for teams* (Vol. 2). Amherst, MA: HRD Press.

McGregor, D. (1960). *The human side of enterprise.* New York: McGraw-Hill.

Meeker, L. (1996). Trust: The great teamwork enabler. In G. Parker (Ed.), *The handbook of best practices for teams.* Amherst, MA: HRD Press.

Mohrman, S.A, Cohen, S., & Mohrman, A. (1995). *Designing team-based organizations.* San Francisco, CA: Jossey-Bass.

Moran, L., Musselwhite, E., & Zenger, J. (1996). *Keeping teams on track.* Burr Ridge, IL: Irwin.

Murray, M. (2001). *Beyond the myth and magic of mentoring.* San Francisco, CA: Jossey-Bass.

Navran, F. (1995). *Truth and trust.* Alberta, Canada: Athabasca University Educational Enterprises.

Nelson, B. (1994). *1001 ways to reward employees.* New York: Workman.

O'Neill, N., & O'Neill, G. (1974). *Shifting gears: Finding security in a changing world.* New York: M. Evans.

Parker, G.M. (1991). *Parker team player survey.* Palo Alto, CA: Xicom/Consulting Psychologists Press.

Parker, G.M. (1991). *Parker team player survey: Styles of another person.* Palo Alto, CA: Xicom/Consulting Psychologists Press.

Parker, G.M. (1992). *Team development survey.* Palo Alto, CA: Xicom/Consulting Psychologists Press.

Parker, G.M. (1994). *Cross-functional teams: Working with allies, enemies, and other strangers.* San Francisco, CA: Jossey-Bass.

Parker, G.M. (1996). *Team players and teamwork.* San Francisco, CA: Jossey-Bass.

Parker, G.M. (1997). *Cross-functional teams tool kit.* San Francisco, CA: Jossey-Bass/Pfeiffer.

Parker, G.M. (1997). *Team building workshop: Facilitator's guide.* Palo Alto, CA: Xicom/Consulting Psychologists Press.

Parker, G.M. (1998). *Teamwork: Action steps for building powerful teams.* Diehl, IL: Successories.

Parker, G.M. (1998). *25 instruments for team building.* Amherst, MA: HRD Press.

Parker, G.M., & Kropp, R. (1992). *50 activities for team building* (Vol. 1). Amherst, MA: HRD Press.

Parker, G.M., & Kropp, R. (1994). *50 activities for self-directed teams.* Amherst, MA: HRD Press.

Parker, G.M., & Kropp, R. (2000). *Team workout: 50 interactive activities.* Amherst, MA: HRD Press.

Parker, G.M., McAdams, J., & Zielinski, D. (2000). *Rewarding teams: Lessons from the trenches.* San Francisco, CA: Jossey-Bass.

Parker, G.M., McAdams, J., & Zielinski, D. (2000, September). Reasons to celebrate. *Incentive,* pp. 96–97.

Parker, G.M., & Thiagarajan, S. (2000). *Team players: Games to explore team player styles* (Version 2.0). Bloomington, IN: Workshops by Thiagi.

Pfeiffer, J.W., & Jones, J.E. (1969). *The handbook of structured experiences for human relations training* (Vol. 1). San Francisco, CA: Jossey-Bass/Pfeiffer.

Rees, F. (1997). *Teamwork from start to finish.* San Francisco, CA: Jossey-Bass/Pfeiffer.

Roskin, R. (1975). Decision style inventory. In J.E. Jones & J.W. Pfeiffer (Eds.), *The 1975 annual handbook for group facilitators.* San Francisco, CA: Jossey-Bass/Pfeiffer.

Rubin, I., Plovich, M., & Fry, R. (1978). *Task-oriented team development.* New York: McGraw-Hill.

Ryan, K., & Oestreich, D. (1991). *Driving fear out of the workplace.* San Francisco, CA: Jossey-Bass.

Senge, P. (1990). *The fifth discipline.* New York: Doubleday.

Shaw, R. (1997). *Trust in the balance.* San Francisco, CA: Jossey-Bass.

Silberman, M. (1999). *101 ways to make meetings active.* San Francisco, CA: Jossey-Bass/Pfeiffer.

Thiagarajan, S., & Parker, G.M. (1999). *Teamwork and teamplay.* San Francisco, CA: Jossey-Bass/Pfeiffer.

Thomas, K., & Kilmann, R. (1974). *Thomas-Kilmann conflict mode.* Palo Alto, CA: Xicom/Consulting Psychologists Press.

Thomas, K., & Tymon, W. (1993). *The empowerment inventory.* Palo Alto, CA: Xicom/Consulting Psychologists Press.

Thomas, K., & Tymon, W. (1994). The elements of empowerment. In G.M. Parker (Ed.), *The handbook of best practices for teams* (Vol. 1). Amherst, MA: HRD Press.

Tuckman, B.W. (1965). Developmental sequence in small groups. *Psychological Bulletin, 63*(6), 384–399.

Ury, W. (1993). *Getting past no: Negotiating your way from confrontation to cooperation.* New York: Bantam Doubleday.

Vogt, J., & Murrell, K. (1990). *Empowerment in organizations.* San Francisco, CA: Jossey-Bass/Pfeiffer.

Wellens, R., Byham, W., & Wilson, J. (1991). *Empowered teams.* San Francisco, CA: Jossey-Bass.

Wilson, J., George, J., & Wellins, R. (1994). *Leadership trapeze: Strategies for leadership in team-based organizations.* San Francisco, CA: Jossey-Bass.

Zenger, J., Musselwhite, E., Hurson, K., & Perrin, C. (1994). *Leading teams: Mastering the new role.* Burr Ridge, IL: Irwin, 1994.

# ABOUT THE AUTHOR

**AUTHOR AND CONSULTANT GLENN PARKER** works with organizations to create and sustain high performing teams, effective team players, and team-based systems. His best-selling book, *Team Players and Teamwork,* was selected as one of the ten best business books of 1990. Now in a paperback edition, *Team Players and Teamwork* (1996), has been published in several other languages and has been brought to the screen in the best-selling CRM video, *Team Building: What Makes a Good Team Player?* His training and team-building instrument, the *Parker Team Player Survey,* has become a standard in the field. Glenn recently created an innovative web-based course called *Being a Team Player* for distribution by Interactive Training, Inc. He is an adjunct faculty member at Rider University. Glenn is one of only seventy-five management thinkers recognized in the recent book, *The Guru Guide (1998).*

Glenn is co-author of *50 Activities for Team Building, Volume 1* (1998), which was selected by *Human Resource Executive* as one of 1992's Top Ten Training Tools. He is the author of three resources for cross-functional teams: (1) the book, *Cross-Functional Teams: Working with Allies, Enemies and Other Strangers* (1994), (2) a facilitator's manual: *Cross-Functional Teams Toolkit* (1997) and (3) *Cross-Functional Teams: The Simulation Game,* which he co-developed. Glenn is co-author of *50 Activities for Self-Directed Teams* (1994) and author of a collection of training resources and job aids, *The Team Kit (1995).* He is also editor of the HRD Press *Best Practices for Teams,* Vol. 1 (1996) and Vol. 2 (1998). His latest publications are *25 Instruments for Team Building* (1998), *Teamwork: 20 Steps for Building Powerful Teams* (1998), *Teamwork and*

*Teamplay: Games and Activities for Training and Building Teams* (1999), *Rewarding Teams: Lessons from the Trenches* (2000), and *Team Workout: 50 Interactive Activities* (2000).

Glenn does not just write about teamwork. He is a hands-on consultant and trainer who works with start-up and ongoing teams of all types in a variety of industries. He facilitates team building, conducts training workshops, consults with management, and gives presentations for organizations across a wide variety of industries. His clients have included pharmaceutical companies, a variety of industrial organizations, companies in telecommunications, service businesses, health care providers, retailers, and government agencies.

Glenn holds a B.A. from City College of New York, an M.A. from the University of Illinois, and has studied for a doctorate at Cornell University. He is much in demand as a speaker at corporate meetings and at national conferences sponsored by the American Society for Training and Development (ASTD), Lakewood Conferences, and Center for the Study of Work Teams. He keynoted a recent BEST OF TEAMS Conference. He is past president of the ASTD Mid-New Jersey Chapter and has served as chairperson of the ASTD Publishing Review Committee.

In his spare time, Glenn is an active volunteer with The American Cancer Society, plays with his grandchildren, rides his bike, roots for the Philadephia 76ers, and plans his next vacation.

# HOW TO USE THE CD-ROM

## System Requirements

### Windows PC

* 486 or Pentium processor-based personal computer

* Microsoft Windows 95 or Windows NT 3.51 or later

* Minimum RAM: 8 MB for Windows 95 and NT

* Available space on hard disk: 8 MB Windows 95 and NT

* 2X speed CD-ROM drive or faster

Netscape 3.0 or higher browser or MS Internet Explorer 3.0 or higher

### Macintosh

* Macintosh with a 68020 or higher processor or Power Macintosh

* Apple OS version 7.0 or later

* Minimum RAM: 12 MB for Macintosh

* Available space on hard disk: 6MB Macintosh

* 2X speed CD-ROM drive or faster

Netscape 3.0 or higher browser or MS Internet Explorer 3.0 or higher

*NOTE: This CD requires Netscape 3.0 or MS Internet Explorer 3.0 or higher.* You can download these products using the links on the CD-ROM Help Page.

## Getting Started

Insert the CD-ROM into your drive. The CD-ROM will usually launch automatically. If it does not, click on the CD-ROM drive on your computer to launch. You will see an opening page. You can click on this page or wait for it to fade to the Copyright Page. After you click to agree to the terms of the Copyright Page, the Home Page will appear.

## Moving Around

Use the buttons at the left of each screen or the underlined text at the bottom of each screen to move among the menu pages. To view a document listed on one of the menu pages, simply click on the name of the document. To quit a document at any time, click the box at the upper right-hand corner of the screen.

Use the scrollbar at the right of the screen to scroll up and down each page.

To quit the CD-ROM, you can click the Quit option at the bottom of each menu page, hit Control-Q, or click the box at the upper right-hand corner of the screen.

## To Download Documents

Open the document you wish to download. Under the File pulldown menu, choose Save As. Save the document onto your hard drive with a different name. It is important to use a different name; otherwise the document may remain a read-only file.

You can also click on your CD drive in Windows Explorer and select a document to copy it to your hard drive and rename it.

# In Case of Trouble

If you experience difficulty using the *Team Depot* CD-ROM, please follow these steps:

1. Make sure your hardware and systems configurations conform to the systems requirements noted under "Systems Requirements" above.

2. Review the installation procedure for your type of hardware and operating system. It is possible to reinstall the software if necessary.

3. You may call Jossey-Bass/Pfeiffer Customer Service at (800) 956-7739 between the hours of 8 A.M. and 5 P.M. Pacific Time, and ask for Technical Support. It is also possible to contact Technical Support by e-mail at *techsupport@JosseyBass.com.*

Please have the following information available:

* Type of computer and operating system

* Version of Windows or Mac OS being used

* Any error messages displayed

* Complete description of the problem

(It is best if you are sitting at your computer when making the call.)